THE STORY OF THE NEWS AGENCY EPOCH

BARRIERS DOWN

THE STORY OF THE NEWS AGENCY EPOCH

BARRIERS DOWN

By KENT COOPER

KENNIKAT PRESS
Port Washington, N. Y./London

BARRIERS DOWN

True and Unbiased News—the highest original moral concept ever developed in America and given the world.

—K. C.

Dedicated
TO THE EMPLOYEES OF THE ASSOCIATED PRESS
whose work through the years has given it a
consummate personality,
and
TO THE MEMBERS OF THE ASSOCIATED PRESS
without whose support that personality
could not have been developed.

Contents

CHAPTER   PAGE

I   A CRUSADE IS BORN   3

II   AS VICTORIA REIGNED   10

III   A GREAT MORAL CONCEPT   15

IV   REUTERS REX   23

V   "WE ARE FRENCH"   34

VI   PROPAGANDA ASPIRATIONS   45

VII   INTRODUCING DON JORGE MITRE   54

VIII   TOWARD A NEW CONTRACT   61

IX   THE FIRST CONCESSION   70

X   REWARD OF MERIT   81

XI   PEACE DEPENDS UPON A FREE PRESS . . .   87

XII   ISOLATING THE VANQUISHED   96

XIII   A KNIGHT CONVINCED   109

XIV   IN THE WESTERN PACIFIC   119

XV   WITHOUT GOVERNMENT INFLUENCE . . .   126

XVI   A GREAT PRESIDENT   133

XVII   NIPPON SHIMBUN RENGO   144

XVIII   "CONFERENCE OF PRESS EXPERTS" . . .   154

XIX   A STEP TOWARD FREEDOM   168

CHAPTER		PAGE
XX	REUTERS HEARS FROM JAPAN	175
XXI	VOLCANIC MATERIAL	182
XXII	CROSSING THE RUBICON	189
XXIII	REUTERS GETS A SHOCK	201
XXIV	AROUND THE WORLD TO LONDON	209
XXV	REUTERS IN WRATH	221
XXVI	AN ANSWER IS GIVEN	231
XXVII	MELODRAMA BY THE THAMES	242
XXVIII	A STROKE AGAINST MONOPOLY	251
XXIX	EMANCIPATION!	261
XXX	RUSSIA OPENS ITS DOORS	269
XXXI	REUTERS TAKES NEW FORM	278
XXXII	TRUTH—THE BEST PROPAGANDA	291
XXXIII	A DIFFERENT APPROACH	300
XXXIV	RETROSPECT	315

BARRIERS DOWN

I

A Crusade Is Born

THE hero of this story is a composite personality made up of generations of American newspapermen—The Associated Press. It is a co-operative news-gathering association that collects the news of the world for its member newspapers, large and small. It has had the loyalty of its members and employees longer than any other co-operative of its size and kind the world has known. Remarkable differences, rare likenesses, mediocre and keen mentalities have been a part of it. Every newspaperman who has lived in this country in the last hundred years has in some form or another, and at some time or another, in some way felt its influence upon the newspaper with which he has been connected. And the life of every American is affected by the news it records. It is supported by newspaper interests as widely diversified as the *Christian Science Monitor,* the Hearst newspapers, the Scripps-Howard newspapers, the Frank E. Gannett newspapers, and by other chain newspapers, as well as by more than twelve hundred singly owned newspapers.

The Associated Press is the only co-operative press association in this country, but there are scores of news agencies in the world. In the United States, besides The Associated Press, there are the United Press and the International News Service. They differ from The Associated Press in that they are privately owned and operated for profit.

From prehistoric times to the era of electric communication news was transmitted through couriers who were the first news carriers. In the middle of the nineteenth century the telegraph took the place of the courier. Later came the cable.

Utilizing these rapid means of communication, the news agencies were created. They became collectors and distributors of national and international information in all countries. The Associated Press is the oldest of them all. Its force has been felt throughout the entire world. Its news service tells of the actions and accomplishments of individuals and of nations. But over a period of one hundred years there are stories of its own accomplishments that have never been told. For instance, there is the story of its effort to liberalize the methods of international news exchange and its effort to make news at the source equally available to all who seek it there.

This particular story begins with the date of September 8, 1914. As World War I was unleashing its fury on Europe, Melville E. Stone, then general manager of The Associated Press, received a cablegram which set in motion a chain of circumstances that made epochal history. It was from *La Nación,* of Buenos Aires, one of the great newspapers of South America. The message asked for the text of the German communiqués and all official news concerning the war.

There certainly was nothing sensational about that. Still, this inconsequential little cable was to turn the whole force of The Associated Press against the great monopoly of European proprietary news agencies which had, as early as the last century, restricted The Associated Press activities to North America. The contract that thus limited The Associated Press was a part of the great barrier erected against the international freedom of news exchange so that the three members of the monopoly might control these channels.

Not only did The Associated Press move to free itself but what happened to this message in the general office of The Associated Press may have resulted in the United Press Associations getting its first idea of foreign news dissemination even ahead of The Associated Press. The dispatch never having been answered, *La Nación* later applied to the United Press Associations which, being a young agency then seven years old, without any international commitments that prevented, was free to serve anyone anywhere who could pay the price. There *La Nación* got service.

But the development of most importance was that out of this short message there grew in America the greatest crusade of newspaperdom. The Associated Press, barred from acting promptly in the foreign field because its contract with the European monopoly forbade, went through two decades in which it waged a struggle not only for its freedom but for the principle of freedom of international news exchange by all those who were under any restrictions in any country.

With the United Press, which had no restrictive contracts, it was a case of enlarging its market in the sale of news and extending its reputation abroad. With The Associated Press it was a case of breaking down the barriers that hindered the exchange of news between the press of all nations—the kind of news exchange that brings peoples of all nations to understand each other and thus reduces to a minimum the causes of wars.

The climax for The Associated Press in its relations with the European monopoly came in 1934. And at that time, in conformity with a proposal made by me, The Associated Press and the United Press signed a contract establishing between themselves the principle of non-exclusive access to foreign news at its source. That contract was one of the most remarkable documents in history, even though it does refer only to a matter of international news dissemination and not to international politics. But that is getting ahead of the story.

Prior to the first World War there were in Europe three great news agencies. They were Reuters of England, Havas of France, and Wolff of Berlin. Each bore the name of its founder. Each began activities in the days before the telegraph.

Unlike today, when the prime business of news agencies is to collect and distribute news to newspapers, the customers of these three pioneers originally were banking and commercial houses interested in market prices and developments affecting trade. The three news agencies were in no sense press associations; that is, they were in no sense servants of the press. Indeed, they did not let newspapers have their services at all until the telegraph came into being. This for the reason that they felt that newspaper publication of their prices and news would lose them the patronage of all the banks and merchants who, seeing in the newspapers what interested them in their business, would have no need of direct information from the news agencies at high subscription rates.

Of the three, Havas claimed to be the first who engaged in collecting and disseminating market prices and intelligence in an organized manner. Havas dated his beginning to 1835. Wolff claimed a beginning practically contemporaneously with Havas. Reuter began operations in Germany in the forties but his real beginning was when he transferred his activities to London in 1851.

As dispatchers of market prices their business was profitable but they reached no standing of public importance until they began serving news to newspapers. Then their power and prestige developed. Each got the idea of serving newspapers from an enterprise that had its inception in New York City in 1848, namely, The Associated Press which, being exactly what the name implies, is an association of newspapers. It was organized by newspapers to save duplication of expenses in collecting the same news. It did save its sponsors money.

In the next decade Reuter sold the same idea to the London newspapers by giving them a part of the economy of the plan and keeping the rest as profit for himself. Havas and Wolff soon followed Reuter in exploiting the newspaper field profitably.

From these beginnings there arose the first, the greatest and the most powerful international monopoly of the nineteenth century. Its potentialities and its activities, viewed in the liberal spirit of 1942, were astounding. When Reuter, Havas and Wolff pooled their resources, established complete news agency control of international news and allotted to themselves the news agency exploitation in all the countries of the world, they brought under their control the power to decide what the people of each nation would be allowed to know of the peoples of other nations and in what shade of meaning the news was to be presented.

Moreover, to perfect this monopoly they either established news agencies of their own in the smaller countries or accepted the patronage of agencies which in some countries were actually branches of the government. The latter always responded to the requirement of their governments that they influence and deceive readers at home as well as abroad. Some of this was done and is still being done on a grand scale. International attitudes have developed from the impressions and prejudices aroused by what the news agencies reported. Monopoly made the system of deception work. The mighty foreign propaganda carried on through these channels in the last hundred years has been one of the causes of wars that never has been uncovered. Based on the American conception of ethical standards, the situations that confronted newspapers in some countries prior to the second World War were simply immoral; such as these:

Reuters for many years dominated the news agencies of other countries; so did Havas; so did Wolff;

Havas, of France, an agency of a country in Europe, for years had autocratic control of what the newspapers in the whole of South America could obtain from the monopoly in the way of foreign news;

Over the critical period of a great era, one individual, Reuter, had the final word on international news exchange throughout the entire world—a domination the like of which for international ramifications, complications and regimenting of world opinion has never been equaled.

This control of international news exchange seemed to me to cry out for correction through the application of a practical idealism in international news relationships. Though I tried to advance the idea of the Versailles Treaty providing both for a free press and for freedom of international news exchange, my effort, backed only by my own voice, was unsuccessful.

In the next postwar era a free press and freedom of international news exchange everywhere must be guaranteed. There can be no permanent peace unless men of all lands can have truthful, unbiased news of each other which shall be freely available at the source to all who seek it there, wherever that may be. The flow of news must not be impeded. Those whose business it is to get the news at the source must be under no restraint or dictation by governments. This can come to pass only when, as to news collection, all the barriers are down.

II

As Victoria Reigned

WHAT happens to the news channels of the world is of importance because international news directly and indirectly affects the life of every human being in the world.

There was a time when this was not so. Electricity brought the change. Did Divine Providence acquaint mankind with electricity because Divine Providence wanted to bring men into closer comradeship? For actually the first commercial application of electricity was to bring people closer together. International electric telegraphs, international electric cables, international electric wireless, and finally the international electric telephone annihilated the distance between nations and between continents.

Before the electric era British shipping alone, protected by the British navy, first built up and then kept the British Empire together. With the advent of the cable the British quickened the pace of empire and bulwarked its strength with strands of submarine wire. What went through these wires? Information on business trades and trends, individual and mass fortunes and misfortunes, births, accomplishments, deaths—in other words, NEWS.

The cable brought Australia, South Africa, India, China, Japan, Canada and all the British world instantaneously to London on the Thames. Though Cyrus Field, an American, laid the first cable, Britain, far ahead of any other nation, concentrated upon the cable business. First it tied its Empire together. Then it stretched out and tied other nations to it. The cables carried the news. And in harmony with Victorian practices, the news that went through this vast network of cables gave luster to the British cause! News of Britain! More and more news of Britain! What happened in Britain was known throughout the empire the day it occurred!

Out of this activity there emerged a great figure. Oddly enough he was a German, and he galvanized into success the opportunity that such a system of news communication afforded Britain. That German was Paul Julius Reuter, founder of Reuters, the British news agency.

Long after Britain had tied the world together with strands of cables and had given preference rates for news dissemination that gave world domination to the British Reuters News Agency, the French, the Germans and the Americans went at the business of laying cables for themselves. Only the American-owned cable companies refused to follow the others in making practical rates for news transmission; rates attractive enough to encourage the export of news from the United States.

Moreover, The Associated Press, which in the last century included all American newspapers and had all the news sources in the United States, elected to bar

itself from any news dissemination outside of this country. It did this by agreeing that only Reuters could send
the news of The Associated Press to foreign countries.

So Reuters decided what news was to be sent from
America. It told the world about the Indians on the war
path in the West, lynchings in the South and bizarre
crimes in the North. The charge for decades was that
nothing creditable to America ever was sent. American
businessmen criticized The Associated Press for permitting Reuters to belittle America abroad.

With Julius Reuter at the head of its world news dissemination, England strove for world trade. It is not
difficult to see that, holding control of world news communications and with the genius of a Reuter, it had the
means for success. France and Germany, after a late start,
tried to emulate, but never were able to overtake the
English methods which awakened them to the fact that
men seek news. Other nations learned that prejudice
could be aroused through the taint that the news con-
tains.

The United States, completely isolationist through the
nineteenth century, did not visualize the importance of
international news. The American people lacked interest. Broadly, the only foreign news they read was furnished by The Associated Press, the organization of that
era that was the forerunner of The Associated Press of
today. And the only foreign news that The Associated
Press of that era had, came from the great monopolistic
European agencies headed by Reuters.

There was a reason for that lack of interest on the part
of the people of the United States respecting foreign

news. While in the Victorian era Britain was laying cables and cementing the British Empire with an adequate news exchange, in the United States a domestic empire of states was being built by the people of this nation.

Our country was not broken up by intervening oceans. It was busy in its own affairs. What the cables did for Britain, the domestic telegraphs did for the United States. News reports knitted the nation closely together.

In 1898 came our war with Spain. For nearly one hundred years the United States had not been at war with a European nation. We were momentarily awakened from our isolation. We got out our maps and found where the Philippines were, and how near they were to Japan even in those days!

When the government sent the battleship *Oregon* from California to the West Indies around Cape Horn to join the Atlantic fleet's attack on Cervera's Spanish armada we fretted and worried that this one battleship at some place on its lonely voyage would be met and overwhelmed by Cervera.

As we worried we looked at our maps to see the length of that voyage, and we saw how big a continent there was south of us—and how many countries it had—all of which we had discarded from memory, if we ever learned it in our school days. And on our maps we found islands in the West Indies of which we had never heard. War is like that. It made us study geography then as it did in 1914, and as it is doing in 1942!

With the end of the Spanish-American War we settled back once more content with our isolation. It was not until the first World War came—indeed, not until we were drawn into it—that the people of the United States really became aware of the magnitude of the world. The awakening of interest in foreign affairs quickened to intensity. It was at that time that the message from Buenos Aires reached The Associated Press general headquarters in New York.

III

A Great Moral Concept

THE cablegram from *La Nación* requesting service from The Associated Press lay in a basket among unanswered communications for several days until I happened to run across it. At the time I was chief of the Traffic Department. My finding it was quite accidental. I was looking for something else. However, I immediately became interested, for while the Traffic Department theoretically was mainly concerned with communications, it actually had a great diversity of activities.

The war had quickened the interest of newspapers for membership in The Associated Press, so we were getting many requests from the United States. What claimed my attention about this cable was that it came from a country—from a continent, for that matter—in which The Associated Press never had served any newspaper, and it was asking for service. Here was a call from a new territory, and I guess the pioneering spirit was in my blood. I wondered why nobody had done anything about the message. It was several days old. If it was an oversight there was some excuse for it because the office was being flooded with details on the world-rocking news of the first battle of the Marne, to say nothing of all the other news of the war.

I decided that the quickest way to get action was for me to go direct to the general manager. I showed him the message.

"I'd be glad to handle this," I said.

The general manager read it. He leaned back in his chair and looked thoughtfully at the ceiling.

"Well, Cooper," he said, "I'll tell you why this message hasn't been answered. I have a theory that inquiries that can't be favorably answered, such as this one, automatically answer themselves. If the sender doesn't get a reply, he can be pretty sure that what he proposed is either uninteresting or impossible of accomplishment."

This idea was new to me.

"You mean . . ."

"What I mean " he smiled, "is this: We can't serve *La Nación*."

"But why?"

His explanation shocked me.

Little as I then knew about the news agency system around the world, I realized that I had known even less than I imagined. But what I learned only made me more interested and more determined. There had been crusades before—there could be another one. Briefly told, Mr. Stone unfolded this story:

From the incorporation of The Associated Press in its present form in 1900, and back to 1893, there was a quadrilateral contract with the three greatest European news agencies—Reuters of London, Havas of Paris, and Wolff of Berlin. Through this trio The Associated Press also had indirect relations with a large number of small news organizations throughout the world. These organizations in 1920 were: Amtliche Nachrichtenstelle, Austria; Agence Télégraphique Belge, Belgium; Agence Télégraphique Bulgars, Bulgaria; Bureau de Presse Czechoslovakia, Czechoslovakia; Ritzaus Bureau, Denmark; Agence Télégraphique Esthonienne, Esthonia; Finska Notisbyran, Finland; Athena, Greece; Nederlandsch Telegraaf Agentschap, Holland; Agence Télégraphique Hongroise, Hungary; Stefani, Italy; Kokusai, Japan; Avola, Yugoslavia; Agence Télégraphique Lettone, Latvia; Agence Télégraphique Lithuanienne, Lithuania; Norsk Telegram-bureau, Norway; Agence Télégraphique Polonaise, Poland; Rador, Rumania; Rosta, Russia; Fabra, Spain; Tidningarnas Telegrambyra, Sweden; Agence Télégraphique Suisse, Switzerland; Anotolie, Turkey.

For long years Reuters, acceptably to Havas and Wolff, had divided the globe among the three according to Reuters' idea of proper spheres of influence for each. The list gives some little idea of the units involved.

Reuters received English-speaking North America, in which since 1893 The Associated Press had bought exclusive territorial rights for the United States and its possessions. The Associated Press also was granted a free hand in Canada. Later this free hand was extended to include Mexico, Central America and the West Indies where Reuters and Havas held the sovereign rights. The two, however, admitted no control whatever to Wolff, the German agency, in the Western Hemisphere. Reuters had Great Britain, including all the colonies and dominions, and Egypt, Turkey, Japan, China and what might be called the suzerain states, or those in which England had exerted a sphere of influence.

Havas (in 1942 succeeded by Téléradio) controlled

the French Empire, Switzerland and all the Latin countries, including Italy, Spain, Portugal and those in South
America.

To Wolff (in 1942 known as Deutsches Nachrichtenbüro or simply DNB) fell the Scandinavian states, with
Russia and all the Slav nations. Austria also came under
jurisdiction of the German agency.

So the big three—with their innumerable little de-
pendencies, not one of which could make an arrangement with any outsider, save by permission of its chief—
practically controlled the news channels of the world at
the time Mr. Stone explained matters to me in 1914.

All except The Associated Press were responsive to,
subservient to, or actual bureaus of their respective governments. All except The Associated Press were proprietary, that is, they were privately owned and were conducted for the purpose of making money, or they were
owned by governments. On the other hand, The Associated Press, which in its early years had, for lack of
funds, to depend largely upon the facilities of the older
European agencies for foreign news, stood unique as a
co-operative, nonprofit-making concern. It is a membership organization composed of the newspapers it serves.
It engages in no propaganda and would not accept government subsidy if it were forced upon it. It is indeed,
a servant of a free press.

To The Associated Press I give credit for the creation
of what has turned out to be the finest moral concept
ever developed in America and given the world. That
concept is that news must be truthful and unbiased. I
cannot, however, say that this great moral concept was

born as the result of philosophic study or as the result of prayer. It came about this way:

In the journalism of the middle and the second half of the nineteenth century, newspapers were biased politically. Their news columns reeked with prejudice on anything in which the editors had taken a stand. Opinions were not confined to the editorial page. Local news often was perverted to uphold the policies of the newspaper. It was a violent journalism and the thunder of it did not die out until the great editors of its era had gone.

Newspapers throughout the land distrusted the news of each other. The news of each was presented with bias. This was particularly true of political news. Supporters of any one candidate differed in the nature of their support. So it was that when news was exchanged between cities by partisan newspapers each recipient, to some degree, distrusted the sender.

With the invention of the telegraph in America, financial limitations drove the newspapers to the necessity of co-operatively meeting the expense of transmission of a certain class of news: deaths, fires, market prices, textual matter, etc. The Associated Press was born. As it enlarged its activities and began transmitting news of a more general character and finally political news, the members of the co-operative, all with differing opinions, found they could agree upon but one thing: that The Associated Press, which they established, should send nothing but truthful, unbiased news. If, therefore, The Associated Press favored this or that cause, or this or that political candidate, there was always an opposition critic who with fiery emphasis demanded that the error not be

repeated. Thus there emerged from distrust what has become a hallowed moral concept of The Associated Press:
that its news must be true and unbiased.

While this principle had become the policy of The Associated Press, it took a really great character, who believed in independent, honest journalism, to turn that
idea into a practical ideal. Honest, true and unbiased
news was bible to him. Mr. Stone, my predecessor, put
into forceful and lasting effect the moral concept that
necessity had invented. During his long administration
he made the organization strong because he never permitted it to stray from the principles of accuracy and impartiality.

While many of the European agencies endeavored to
maintain accuracy, they were subject to outside influence
in the matter of bias. Moreover, they were really not
press associations of the type of The Associated Press,
which served only newspapers. They had commercial
interests, including banking; news was more or less sec-
ondary. Some of the smaller of them paid no attention to
news whatever, excepting the "handouts" that came
from government offices or the major agencies. Many of
these proprietary agencies were under government control and were used for the distribution of propaganda at
home and abroad. Some found this line of endeavor
much more profitable than the collection and dissemination of ordinary news.

If Havas was indeed the first to begin the compilation
of market prices for private customers, he was also the
least imaginative of the three, Wolff and Reuter being
the other two. Havas never dreamed of world activities,
being entirely content to confine his operations to

France, with limited ambitions in other Latin countries. Transitions in the French Government during the nineteenth century may have required Havas to confine himself to the domestic field. The actual management of the Havas Agency in its early days fell upon Henri Houssaye, its managing director. Credited with being much more imaginative than the founder, Henri Houssaye was quick to embrace the idea of a world alliance when Reuter proposed it.

The first approach by Reuter, however, was to Wolff, not to Havas. This is understandable because German influences in England were strong in the early days of Queen Victoria's reign. The approach, therefore, to the German news agency was a natural one, even had Reuter himself not been born in that country.

Wolff embraced the idea of an alliance which later took the form of a monopoly. When the first contract was made between Reuters, Wolff and Havas, Wolff may have wielded as much influence as Reuter. But as time went on German influence in England waned. Toward the close of the nineteenth century, with the ascendancy of Emperor Wilhelm II, Reuter's son, Herbert, who had relieved his father of the burdens of directing Reuters News Agency, turned more and more to Henri Houssaye, of Havas. Because of French antipathy toward Germany, Houssaye was willing enough to furnish to Reuters the balance of power in the triumvirate. Actually, the story is that, after the turn of the century, international bankers headed by the Rothschilds became interested in the ownership of all three agencies. Certainly they were important customers. Whether or not they were owners, they were credited with having influence with the three agencies second only to the influence of their respective governments.

Of all the agencies that were in the alliance just prior to the first World War, Reuters, with headquarters in London, was undoubtedly the most powerful. Dignified, conservative, omniscient, it had during the long years of its service become a household word throughout the empire. Also it had become a part of the tradition of Britain. It carried on its operations and drank tea daily at 4 P.M. in its rambling offices, which lay in ancient Old Jewry near the Bank of England. These offices were so dingy with age that practically none of its employees knew when the occupancy of the building began, much less the history of Reuters itself.

IV

Reuters Rex

THE origin and position of Reuters in empire news affairs have become a legend. Literature about the agency is scattered. But Hollywood, overlooking nothing, dramatized Paul Julius Reuter's beginning in a motion picture entitled *A Message from Reuters*. The story of the picture, however, dealt only with the early days of the news agency.

Reuter, born in Kassel, Germany, used carrier pigeons to exchange market quotations and important governmental messages between capitals. Others were doing it. When telegraphs and cables supplanted carrier pigeons, others quit the field. Reuter did not. He saw an unusual opportunity in the laying of the cable across the English Channel from Dover to Calais. Transferring his headquarters to London and becoming a naturalized British subject he immediately began exchanging quotations by cable for brokers on the London Stock Exchange and the Paris Bourse.

In a little two-room office on the first floor of No. 1 Royal Exchange, long-since rebuilt, he began the business. Later he moved to the comparatively new quarters in Old Jewry.

Ten years and five months after May, 1848, when The Associated Press was organized in New York City, Reuter called upon Mr. Walter, editor of the London *Times*, and proposed to bring a budget of news from the continent for the *Times* and other London newspapers. The basis of the proposal was exactly the same upon which The Associated Press had been formed in New York ten years before, namely, to divide among several newspapers the telegraphic costs of the transmission of news.

In New York it was a matter of The Associated Press dividing among newspapers the expense of bringing the news from London. In London it was the matter of Mr. Reuter dividing among newspapers the expense of bringing the news from the continent of Europe. The only generic difference between the two enterprises was that the New York publishers themselves organized The Associated Press on a mutual basis and without profit to avoid duplication of costs, whereas Reuter, who was not a newspaperman, organized his agency as an enterprise solely owned by him and entirely for his private profit.

He felt that the plan should be attractive to the *Times* and the other London papers because it would reduce their costs through avoiding duplication even though at the same time it gave him a financial reward. The editor of the *Times* felt that the *Times* had no need of such a service because of its own staff of correspondents and its ability to pay the expenses their work incurred.

Mr. Reuter then went to the editor of the *Morning Advertiser*, who noticed that he spoke with an accent which, though his English was good, at once indicated his German nationality.

"My name," he said, "is Reuter. Most probably you

have never heard of me before." The editor of the *Advertiser* said he had not.

"I am," he resumed, "a Prussian and have been employed for many years as a courier to several courts of Europe from the government of Berlin, and in that capacity I have formed personal intimacies with most of the European governments. It has occurred to me that I might, therefore, be able to supply, by telegraph, the daily press of London with earlier and more accurate intelligence of importance, and, at the same time, at a cheaper rate than the morning journals are now paying for their telegraphic communications from the continent. But," Mr. Reuter added, "before bringing under your consideration my proposals and plans it is right I should mention that previous to coming to you I called on the manager of the *Times* as the leading journal to submit my views to him."

The editor of the *Advertiser* told Reuter that his action was perfectly proper because, he said, "the *Times* is not only the leading journal of Great Britain but of Europe and the world." Then he asked Reuter if the manager of the *Times* entertained his proposals. "He listened to them," said Mr. Reuter, "and to my exposition on the ground on which I felt I could carry them out, and said he had no doubt I felt confident I could accomplish all I was willing to undertake, but, he added, that they generally found they could do their own business better than any one else.

"That, of course, I regarded as a negative to the proposals I had made to the *Times*. Therefore, I have come next to you as editor of the *Morning Advertiser*, to lay my plans before you and to submit my proposals for your consideration."

Reuter then entered into full particulars in so convincing a manner that the editor of the *Advertiser* said he would be very much interested except that he had his own staff of correspondents on the continent. The sum the *Advertiser* was paying monthly for its telegrams was £40 or approximately $200, meager compared to the $100,000 a month The Associated Press is paying in 1942 to bring the news from Europe. While pledging himself to transmit "earlier, more ample, more accurate and more important information from the Continent," Reuter offered to charge only £30 per month for it all. The editor of the *Advertiser* expressed doubt of a service he had not even tested. Reuter then offered to deliver it free for two weeks on the assurances of the *Advertiser* that if the service was satisfactory the terms would be agreed to.

"In this way," Reuter said, "you will be able to institute a comparison between the value and the number, as well as the relative cheapness of my telegraphic messages from the continent, and those you receive from your correspondents under your existing arrangement."

The liberality of the offer pleased the editor of the *Advertiser*. Reuter added: "As I am going to make the same proposals to all the other morning papers—the *Telegraph,* the *Morning Herald,* the *Standard,* the *Chronicle,* the *Star* and the *Post,* will you permit me to say to the respective managers of these journals that you have accepted my proposals? Because," he continued, "that may have the effect of inducing them also to accept my offer."

The editor of the *Advertiser* consented, whereupon Reuter told him: "If you had declined to accept my proposals as the *Times* has done, I would not have called upon the managers of any of the other papers, but would have abandoned the idea altogether of organizing a system of telegraphic communication from abroad."

But all the other morning papers accepted and found Reuter's service superior. From that day is dated the beginning of Reuters Agency. Later the *Times* also subscribed to Reuters just as some ninety years afterward the *Times* subscribed to The Associated Press service, long after all the other London papers were receiving it!

Reuters Agency, which theretofore had collected and disseminated intelligence for governments, bankers and brokers only, began a service for newspapers which grew as the cable and telegraphic communications of the Victorian empire were extended.

One idea that Reuter conceived made his name famous. That was that all newspapers which printed his telegrams had to agree to carry his name at the end of each published message. This accomplished two things: it made the name famous and it let the public know who was responsible for the information in the message. In other words, Reuter was the first individual to let the public know "who said so" as respects the origin of news dispatches. Englishmen saw the name in their newspapers, wondered "who is Mr. Reuter?"; also they wondered how to pronounce the name.

This resulted in the publication of the following lines in the *St. James Gazette* in the early sixties:

IN PRAISE OF REUTER

I sing of one no Pow'r has trounced,
Whose place in every strife is neuter,
Whose name is sometimes mispronounced
            As Reuter.

How oft, as through the news we go,
When breakfast leaves an hour to loiter,
We quite forget the thanks we owe
            To Reuter.

His web around the globe is spun,
He is, indeed, the world's exploiter:
'Neath ocean, e'en, the whispers run
            Of Reuter.

Who half so well resolves a doubt?
When tact is needed, who adroiter?
I trow Earth could not spin without
            Its Reuter.

Let praise arise in every land
To thee, the student's guide and tutor:
I bless thee here as Reuter and
            As "Rooter!"

Regardless of the quibbling as to the pronunciation of
the name, historians of the year 1873 were already talking of the enormous influence of the Reuters Agency
throughout the world only fifteen years after it began,
just as Sir Roderick Jones, in 1925, the third head of
the agency which Reuter established, said:

"Recognized in foreign countries everywhere as a
typical British institution conducted upon honest and
responsible lines, the agency, in the ordinary pursuit of
its activities, probably has done more than any other sin-

gle institution abroad to create British atmosphere and to spread British ideas."

There is not much extant that can be quoted from either of the Reuters, father or son, as to the British influence and British domination that was engendered by Reuters news as transmitted throughout the world. They simply brought it about without calling attention to it.

Moreover, there is nothing publicly known as to what had happened in Reuters prior to the suicide of Baron Herbert de Reuter, son of the founder, in 1915. But if any one of the stories that have been told as to how matters stood in Reuters at that time is true, that one story is sufficient confirmation of the dangers inherent in private ownership for profit of such an extraordinary world-wide news agency as Reuters. Those who were in Reuters and know what really caused the tragedy are taciturn about it, but they have referred ominously to the great dangers that confronted Reuters in the matter of stock control prior to the time that Sir Roderick took over. As a result of his activities all the outstanding shares were got hold of and held in his control until 1925.

Sir Roderick, a gentleman of business capabilities, became as head of Reuters a figure in the British newspaper world. He also stood high in the esteem of his government during the first World War when he was in charge of Cable and Wireless War Propaganda until the Ministry of Information was established, at which time he was appointed director of propaganda.

Speaking before the Institute of Journalists in London in October of 1930, as reported by the *Journal* of the institute, Sir Roderick painted a colorful picture of the ramifications and importance of Reuters.

"Many of you well know," he said, "how an old gentleman from Germany about eighty years ago laid the foundation stone of Reuters' Agency in this country. Germany and German influences were very popular in this country in those days, the days of Baron Stockmar, the early days of the Victorian era.

"Having created this agency, Baron de Reuter brought the principal agency in each country on the Continent of Europe into alliance with Reuters, and so Reuters became the head of a great league of agencies. That league not only exists to this day, but year by year and decade by decade it grows stronger.

"Apart from the services coming into this country, we have very heavy services going out to every part of the world. The result is that Reuters' news, in some form or another, finds its way, without a single exception, into every country in the world—literally from China to Peru.

"In no spirit of boasting, I think I can say without fear of contradiction that Reuters has a pre-eminent claim in this respect.

"For the most part, of course, the news does not go under Reuter's name. It goes in the case of agencies on the Continent under the name of those agencies, passes through their crucible, and is dealt with by them according to the requirements of their newspapers and, no doubt, according to their national ideas.

"It is transmitted to every Dominion—to Canada, Australia, New Zealand, and South Africa, and, of course, to India, the Crown colonies, the Protectorates, and to all manner of isolated places, outposts of Empire. So long as a place is part of the Empire, it gets Reuters' reports, whether it be Malta or Hongkong or some spot in the heart of Africa.

"In some parts of Africa messages are proclaimed by beat of drum, in striking contrast with our more modern ways of disseminating news by wireless. No doubt, in time, the beat of the drum will pass into oblivion, but at this moment it is interesting to know that there are places in the world where that primitive method of broadcasting news still exists.

"I have touched on Reuters' services on the Continent of Europe and in the Empire. I would like to say something of the Far East.

"In the Far East Reuters' services have existed for the last sixty years and there has been no other single factor which has contributed more in those sixty years to the maintenance of British prestige. There have been other great factors and, for periods, greater factors, but I do not think there is any other factor that has been consistently working directly and indirectly throughout that period with such effect for the advancement of British influence."

Speaking, then, in 1930, sixteen years after I began my efforts to free The Associated Press from the monopolistic control of foreign agencies, the managing director of Reuters, which at the time had exclusive exploitation rights, for example in Japan, proclaimed that Reuters dominated all else in the advancement of British influence in that country. In a news way he could do this as against The Associated Press, for Reuter's contract with

The Associated Press blocked any Associated Press service in Japan. His efforts were to retain for Reuters that domination for all time in spite of the fact that as he spoke Japanese newspaper interests were chafing under the Reuters yoke, determined at all hazards to free themselves from it as early as could be, and appealing to me to open the doors of The Associated Press to them.

But Sir Roderick then had no idea of relinquishing any part of the activity which for sixty years had "contributed more than anything to the maintenance of British prestige in that part of the world." Aside from the pursuit of wealth, his policy was twofold: to maintain British prestige abroad and to prevent other agencies, such as The Associated Press, from getting a foothold in Reuters' domain so that they could tell the news of all countries in their own way. That is what I wanted The Associated Press to do everywhere: furnish the news in truthful, unbiased manner and without exalting any nation.

Sir Roderick strove for the next three years to retain Reuters' exclusive position, always serving his company as a knight of the empire. Less diplomatic than tradition paints either of his predecessors, the original Julius or his son Herbert, the time and his ability afforded Jones opportunity for success.

He succeeded. After ten years of untiring efforts to strengthen the business, then selling control to the Press Association, he remained as managing director. Thus he "ate his cake and had it too," remaining long enough to see some of the Reuters clients in rebellion over the income Reuters was able to obtain in opportune times. And rebellion against the determination that Reuters' domain never would see successful inroads of other news agencies.

In 1914 when Mr. Stone told me the story of foreign news monopoly, Reuters sat at the crossroads of the world of news and controlled traffic.

V

"We Are French"

THE reason for *La Nación's* appeal to The Associated Press for the German communiqués became clear when that newspaper's cablegram was turned over to Havas, which was then to France what Reuters was to England. Havas had declined to make available to South America the German war reports on the ground that they came from an enemy nation. As Mr. Stone explained it to his Board of Directors later:

"When the war began and while it proceeded, for some length of time the Havas Agency, as a French agency, refused to send the German communiqué to the South American states; they could not send it from France. They could have sent it from New York. I said to them one day: 'Why on earth don't you send from Paris the German official statement?'

"They said: 'We are French; we cannot do it.' "

The point, of course, was that the French Government wished to prevent so far as possible the dissemination of Germany's war claims abroad. Likewise the French Government refused to permit newspapers in France to print them. The French people were not permitted to know what was going on except what France and its allies were doing. As the French Havas Agency owned the news rights to South America, the whole continent was treated as a French vassal state in a news way. And as it kept an enemy communiqué from being read in South America, it could instill French flavor in all the Havas news that was read in that great continent. All South America could be blanked out on anything not pro-French—the only entire continent that could be treated thus by any single news agency.

When I learned of this extraordinary situation I felt that The Associated Press by its contract was a party to this suppression of legitimate news in many countries. The natural corollary to this was that it was not defensible for The Associated Press to continue a contract whereby it guaranteed any agency a monopoly of a nation outside its own national territory, or even in its home territory if by so doing it kept the people of that nation in the dark.

Out of this conviction came my idea that The Associated Press news standards should prevail everywhere. As the European agencies had exclusive access to most government information I realized this would be impossible unless access at the source to the news of all nations should be denied no one.

Before I advocated the principle I sought people who could tell me more about the complications of the foreign news situation. Among these was the late Elmer Roberts, then chief of The Associated Press in Paris but doing a spell of duty in New York. He was a man of wide experience in many countries and had an intimate knowledge of the conditions that made it possible for three European agencies to control virtually the whole news world.

It was a discouraging story as Roberts told it. In its essence it meant, as I had suspected, that the agencies drew their vast influence from the support—and in some instances the control—of their governments. Because of this strength, some observers were wont to regard the monopoly as unbreakable. In any event, there was no gainsaying that the big three, collectively and individually exercised a dictatorship over their weaker colleagues in the smaller countries. Doubtless it was at times a benevolent hegemony, but it still was domination under a firm hand.

Roberts's account left me gloomy. While unassigned to the task, I set about to find ways and means of rectifying this situation. One with whom I discussed it was the late V. S. McClatchy, publisher of the Sacramento (California) *Bee* and a director of The Associated Press. This great publisher, easy of approach, promptly became a convert to my idealistic quest.

Mr. McClatchy, as a Californian, always looked westward because of Japan, which he distrusted. Even then he visioned and talked about the day when Japan would attack Hawaii and California. He was certain that the relations of the United States and the countries of the Western Pacific were being poisoned because of foreign propaganda which was being distributed in the Western Pacific. He was particularly concerned with the attitude of the Japanese.

Mr. McClatchy seized eagerly on what I had to say, for it presented to him an opening whereby America could move to meet this menace. If a free exchange of news could be secured, it would mean that Japan and China could be served with the unbiased, uncolored facts which would represent this country in its true light. And by the same token, the United States would learn the truth about the Western Pacific.

While Mr. McClatchy's chief concern was Japan, he quickly recognized that the place to begin operations was in Europe, because of Reuters, which had a monopoly in Japan. It was from Europe, too, that freedom of action in South America must spring. So it came about that within a few weeks Mr. McClatchy was fostering in the Board of Directors a program calculated to unlock South America to The Associated Press. He also sought the help of the late Adolph S. Ochs, publisher of the New York *Times*. So convincing was the Californian that he gained Mr. Ochs's interest.

For me in these early days, however, the high-water mark came when I got acquainted with Frank B. Noyes, then president of The Associated Press and one of the most distinguished figures in world journalism. Throughout the ensuing years he held The Associated Press firmly on the course toward the idealism that I pictured, albeit with extreme conservatism.

Perhaps I should explain that the entire news service and personnel of The Associated Press are exclusively under the direction of, not the president, but the general manager by resolution of the Board of Directors. President Noyes, therefore, actually came in contact with a very limited number of employees. When I called upon him at his office at the Washington *Star* I had never before discussed Associated Press matters with him.

"How is the work of your department coming along?" he asked me.

So eager was I to get him interested in this international news exchange matter that I gave him a poor answer to his question. Having been with The Associated Press for four years and having had no business contact with him, since Mr. Stone and not Mr. Noyes was my chief, I did not want this chance of intriguing his interest in the South American matter to slip away. I was afraid my call upon him would end before I could present what was then of greatest interest to me.

"While the establishment of the Traffic Department was my idea, and while I head it, my greatest present interest is to break down the news exchange barriers of the world" came out as my reply in just so many words.

The veteran publisher was patient and tolerant, yet I suppose he would have been no more surprised had I started to take up the carpet from the floor of his office. Although he knew of the foreign agency contracts and what they provided, he had not negotiated them, and there had been nothing in many years to bring their existence to his attention. If he thought of them at all he thought of them as an asset that had been acquired by The Associated Press twenty years earlier at a time when it was in a fight for existence against a competitor that succumbed in the late nineties.

"What do you consider to be news exchange barriers?" asked Mr. Noyes.

"The contracts with the foreign news agencies," I replied.

"Well, what is wrong with them, and what would you

do about this matter you call the news exchange barriers?" continued Mr. Noyes.

"The first thing I would do," I said, "would be to comply with the request in that *La Nación* cablegram, at least as a courtesy."

Mr. Noyes had not heard about the cablegram and seemed willing enough to listen to what there was about it and what I had in mind respecting the news agency situation. He then reiterated what Mr. Stone had said: that South America could not be served because of the contractual relationship with Havas and the other two European news agencies, a four-party contract which controlled this situation; The Associated Press being the fourth party. Mr. Noyes did not go into detail. I thought his reticence was that he did not want to disclose his reactions to one of Mr. Stone's subordinates.

The subject, however, continued to interest me and wherever I could I got additional information on how the European agencies did their work, what cable rates they had, and the cost of putting their services out, I gained some information through the representatives of the agencies who worked in the New York office of The Associated Press. All of it I disclosed to Mr. Stone and any director who asked me, including Mr. Noyes.

I have personally known all the directors who have served since 1900 except five who were on the board before 1910. In conformity with the By-Laws, each director is a member of The Associated Press and each member of The Associated Press is the owner or representative of a newspaper. So all directors must be newspapermen. Being a cross section of American publishers, there have

been those representing large and small papers. Several
of them represented or owned unusually successful newspapers. Some have either established or built up their
properties into great American institutions.

There were Victor Lawson, of the Chicago *Daily
News;* W. R. Nelson, of the Kansas City *Star;* Herman
Ridder, of the New York *Staats-Zeitung;* W. L. McLean,
of the Philadelphia *Bulletin,* and Charles H. Taylor, of
the Boston *Globe.* All these, including Mr. McClatchy,
have died. Others, of equal renown, are still serving on
the board in 1942.

But one who interested himself in all the branches of
the work I was doing for The Associated Press and who,
like Mr. Noyes, on more than one occasion gave evidence
of personal regard for me was Adolph Ochs. Moreover,
Mr. Ochs had a profound interest in the welfare of The
Associated Press. He often said, and I think he sincerely
felt, that The Associated Press was the greatest institution in the world, far more admired by him than his own
great property, the New York *Times.* He often said that
had it not been for The Associated Press, the New York
Times might have failed to reach the goal he set and
attained for it. Mr. Ochs was one of two directors I have
known whose feeling for The Associated Press reached
the point of affection. Mr. Noyes is the other one.

Many members of the board felt that serving on the
board was the highest honor that could come to a newspaperman. Some of them took a great deal of interest;
others, less. It was that way about this matter of the foreign news agencies. Many directors took great interest in
how The Associated Press could help to meet local pub-

lication problems but European affairs and the matter of the news agencies over there did not interest them much. Those matters, they felt, were in good hands with Mr. Noyes and Mr. Stone. After Mr. Stone retired they were in good hands with Mr. Noyes.

In the winter of 1914 the board was debating whether The Associated Press should not make an effort to break through the Havas control of the vast South American territory. The matter arose during consideration of an application by a Mexico City newspaper for membership in The Associated Press. In the course of the session President Noyes remarked:

"I think we would be a little better off if we made the news available to Mexico, for example, rather than to have somebody else supply it."

"I think," said Mr. Stone, "it would be very desirable if we could do it—if we could have our service rendered all over Central and South America, instead of handing it over to the Havas Agency which is an agency very markedly hostile to the United States. But in the quadrilateral arrangement with the Havas Agency, Reuters and Wolff, the Latin countries of South America are in the territory of the Havas Agency."

"I submit," said Mr. McClatchy, "when the opportunity offers, we remove that condition, so that we shall be free to go into South America and assist the organization of a news agency there."

"Now wait a minute!" cautioned Mr. Stone. "I know them all, and I have talked with them over and over again. I know exactly what that situation is. There are several things about it. Until we want to break with the Havas people I cannot go in and tear this thing out of their hands or make any overtures."

The point was raised that there were obstacles in the way because of cable communications. The only direct line between the United States and Central and South America at that time ran down the west coast of South America and crossed over to Buenos Aires, but did not come up the east coast.

London, on the other hand, was connected directly with Rio by cable and the line ran south from there to Buenos Aires and then across to Chile and the west coast. Havas sent its report to its South American zone from the Reuters London office.

On further insistence by Mr. McClatchy, Mr. Stone declared that there was no hope of accomplishing anything until the monopoly of cable transmission could be broken down, and then with that conservatism which marked his management, he added:

"Now it is all very easy to say, cut off the Havas people in South America, and it is even easier to say that you had better get rid of the Havas and Wolff agencies and the Reuter Agency, because these are not ideal agencies —that they are government agencies and all that sort of thing—but I pledge you my word that when you get rid of those agencies, the expenses of The Associated Press for foreign news will bound up to double at least.

"We are tied up with the Havas Agency not alone in South America, but if a railroad accident occurs anywhere in France we get it through them. Our competitors would be glad to supplant us in that relationship."

This might have been true. I did not believe it would happen because if it had, the competition would have suffered under the very restraint that The Associated Press then suffered while The Associated Press would have been as free as its competition has always been. But as it did not happen, it is useless to speculate on where the competing American news agencies would stand today if it had happened. As it was, it took The Associated Press some twenty years to get freedom of action, to extend American news agency standards as first developed by The Associated Press and ever since adhered to by its competitors in the United States.

In precluding The Associated Press from disseminating news abroad, Reuters and Havas served three purposes: (1) they kept out Associated Press competition; (2) they were free to present American news disparagingly to the United States if they presented it at all; (3) they could present news of their own countries most favorably and without it being contradicted. Their own countries were always glorified. This was done by reporting great advances at home in English and French civilizations, the benefits of which would, of course, be bestowed on the world. Figuratively speaking, in the United States, according to Reuters and Havas, it wasn't safe to travel on account of the Indians.

The tenacious hold that a nineteenth century territorial allotment for news dissemination had upon the world was evidenced by each year's discussion of the subject by The Associated Press Board of Directors, continuing until 1934.

From September, 1914, until the spring of 1918 I did not enter the board's discussions; not being an officer or director, I was not often in the board room during meetings. But weekly, if not daily, I brought the South American matter to Mr. Stone's attention because of some things my investigations had developed.

I was permitted to read the stenographic reports of the board meetings. When I noticed that a bar to action was reported to the board as being due to the cable situation I called upon the management of the All America Cables, which had lines to all South American coastal countries except Brazil. I found that their facilities were adequate for press reports, that the toll rate was excessive, but that on a contract for quantity the rate would be lowered.

This and other matters I reported to Mr. Stone, who seemed nettled that I was exciting so much interest in trying to invade Havas's territory. He said that if this effort to disrupt the agency relationship did not stop there would be a break and that the result would be disastrous for The Associated Press.

Members of the board who were interesting themselves in the proposals continued to ask me questions and I tried to supply the answers. I often talked to Mr. Noyes. That fact alone was the basis of my greatest hopes. Then when the United Press began service to *La Nación,* of Buenos Aires, I was often invited to be present at the board's discussions. On one occasion I ventured to express the hope that, *La Nación* having the United Press, *La Prensa,* of the same city, should have The Associated Press. I was sure that a way could be found to bring this about.

VI

Propaganda Aspirations

THE hurdle by The Associated Press of the great international news barriers really falls into three phases: the efforts to secure a free hand (1) in South America, (2) in Europe and (3) in the Far East. Consideration of the South American matter wasn't slow in getting under way, but it was close to four years before The Associated Press permitted an effort to be made to breach the stubbornly defended position of Havas. During that period the engagements were many and diverse. The United Press in 1916 opportunely began a service to *La Nación* of Buenos Aires which, though it did not last long, gave impetus to more determined action on the part of The Associated Press with Havas.

When America entered the first World War in April, 1917, the government put some pressure upon The Associated Press as respects American propaganda activities. The word "propaganda" was not used in this connection because it had come to signify the aggressive publicity tactics of the French, English and Germans in the war that was already in its third year.

Nevertheless, the American Government wanted a

fairer presentation abroad of the altruistic motives of the United States in entering the war. As The Associated Press did not transmit news abroad it could not be of much service. Indeed, in seeking to break down the barrier and secure a free exchange of news the world over The Associated Press itself was trying to dredge out all propaganda from the news channels that tried to feed it to America.

It did not seem expedient, therefore, to propose reversing the flow to the rest of the world. So it had to refuse participation in a propaganda scheme of American origin.

A debate on the subject of propaganda had developed in a session of the Board of Directors of The Associated Press on October 14, 1917, during a discussion of the South American problems. This revolved about a project which some of our own Washington officials had for disseminating propaganda in South America.

Since this exposes a skeleton of sorts in the closet of our own American officialdom of the time, there may be some who will think that I might better leave that particular discussion alone. Still, recounting what was said at the time by some of the great figures in American journalism may serve a useful purpose in harmony with my hope that selfish propaganda be eradicated from news channels, leaving the stream of news purely objective.

The United States had gone to war then as it has now, and times were stressful then as they are now. Our French and English government allies had gone in heavily for propaganda and, having control of most of the world's cables, they did a thorough job of it. Sir Roderick

Jones was at the head of the British effort, and the Havas Agency was not lacking competent minds to carry on. The Wolff Agency of Berlin, however, having no cable communications anywhere, was at a distinct disadvantage. Wireless was in its infancy, and it was all that Germany had, which was all right with the Allied governments and the United States.

But Reuters and Havas, on the part of their governments, were doing such a voluminous job of telling the world how Britain and France were winning the war, with no credit given to the efforts of the United States, that every one in the American government from President Wilson down felt America was very much left out of it. President Wilson didn't like it at all but The Associated Press, being unwilling to play the propaganda game on behalf of the United States, as Reuters and Havas played it for Britain and France respectively, and being barred by its contracts from doing so, Wilson was left to his own devices in the spreading of American propaganda abroad. His "Committee on Public Information" under George Creel was created to do the job. Twenty-five years later, in the second World War, Elmer Davis was placed in charge of government press agents with the title of "Director of Office of War Information."

So the Board of Directors of The Associated Press in October, 1917, was having its discussions. Mr. Stone opened with a prefatory reference to the European agencies in general and to Havas in South America in particular. He called attention to the quadrilateral contract existing between The Associated Press and the big three

—Reuters of London, Havas of Paris, Wolff of Berlin—
and through them with the large number of small agencies.

"All of these are proprietary organizations," said Mr.
Stone. "Since the war, of course, the Wolff Agency and
the Austrian and Bulgarian and Turkish agencies have
been eliminated practically from the operation of that
contract.

"Now some of those agencies, being more or less governmental agencies, have been used for years to sow
propaganda throughout the world. Part of the territory
allotted to Havas was South America.

"The Havas Agency has not been altogether fair to the
United States. In its service of news, not only in France
but to South America, the United States has been pictured as a country engaged in race riots and suffering
through railway accidents, tornadoes, floods and crimi-
nals. The great spirit of the American nation never was
portrayed.

"We have avoided as best we could any effort on their
part to sow the seeds of propaganda in this country by
putting our own American representatives in almost all
of the important capitals of the world and excluding the
right of these agencies to give direct service to newspapers here."

This barring of foreign agencies from serving American newspapers always loomed of great importance in
Mr. Stone's mind. The Associated Press contract with
the agencies did indeed bar them from serving American
newspapers, which, therefore, could get the agency news
only through The Associated Press.

This bar, however, was not established through any

altruistic motive of protecting American newspapers against any evil intentions of the agencies. It was established solely because, if the foreign agencies served newspapers directly, The Associated Press could not compete with them on the same news.

That the contract did protect unsuspecting newspapers from being victimized with propaganda happened to be true. But realization of this and emphasis upon it came only after the agencies had been attacked. If the agencies were indeed as bad as they were charged, it was one justification for continuing the contract. For through the contract The Associated Press could stay the hand of the agencies and be the guardian of the newspapers—if they needed a guardian.

"After this world war came on," Mr. Stone continued, "there was a growing desire for more intimate relations with South America, and there was an imperative demand that we should do something. There was a demand on the part of some individuals in the government, because they felt—and felt with a good deal of justice—that through all these years, while there has been no intention of hostility, and no real hostility, on the part of the French agency [Havas] in serving South America, nevertheless it did not represent American life or American aspirations. The government felt that it was of very grave consequence that we should establish more intimate news relations with South America. There was also a very urgent demand on the part of the commercial interests of the United States for more intimate relations.

"Now this has developed an entirely new situation, and it becomes important for us to consider what we are going to do. Hitherto The Associated Press's activities in collecting and distributing news have been limited to service for its members. There is an earnest desire on the part of our government to portray America to these foreign countries.

"We have never undertaken propaganda, but there is a very earnest desire on the part of the authorities in Washington, and I conceive a not altogether unwise and unfair desire, that we shall not leave to a French agency the distribution of American news to South America, or to a British agency the distribution of news to China or Japan.

"I may say that I was asked to go to Washington some time ago. The United States was very anxious to soften the asperity toward us that was evident in South America, and the State Department asked me to employ the editors of almost every leading paper in South America on handsome salaries as correspondents of The Associated Press, and I was told that we could pay them handsome amounts whether they sent us any news or not and that the government would recoup us for anything that we paid. I said:

" 'Well, that means subsidy.'

" 'Well,' they said, 'The Associated Press would not be suspected of anything of the kind, because its reputation is such that it would not be.'

"And I very promptly replied that its reputation would not be such if we undertook a thing of that kind."

Mr. Stone said that the United States government also was interested in a better representation of the United States in China and Japan.

"The government is moved," he said, "by what they conceive to be a perfectly proper point of view—that they want something more than a mere news report to go back and forth between these countries. They want some sort of illuminating service from the United States to indicate that this country is not money-grabbing or territory-grabbing."

Mr. Stone's report of this unprecedented suggestion by the State Department evoked from Oswald Garrison Villard, then publisher of the New York *Evening Post,* a declaration which represented the consensus of the board. Said Mr. Villard:

"I don't think we ought to do that at all. That story you have told us of what someone in the government had in mind is certainly very shocking.

"If that is their idea of what The Associated Press can be induced to do, and the proper relation of the government to news service, it is very discouraging.

"Don't you think we are in position to break with the Havas Agency altogether?"

"No, I think this," Mr. Stone replied, "that after this war there probably will be an entire reorganization of the whole system. I think it is inevitable throughout the world. This would be an ideal:

"If the South American newspapers were capable of organizing a co-operative association similar to ours, and we made an exchange arrangement with them, that would be very desirable. But I do think that all news agencies after the war—I cannot see how it can be otherwise—are going to be democratized in large measure. I don't believe that this plan of having a government propaganda organization in every country is going to survive."

The trouble is that it did survive, as Mr. Stone himself later reported to the board in detail, and the aloofness of The Associated Press after the war helped it to survive. Indeed, Reuters, for one, became much more domineering than it had been in the Baron Herbert de Reuter days before the war. Its monopoly was used by the new, efficient and aggressive Reuters ownership to swell its own income and to effect this, and to hem Germany in, the strings of monopoly were drawn tighter by Reuters and Havas than ever before. That fact may have played an important part in bringing on the second World War.

At this session of the board it was recalled that Havas had made a slight concession to The Associated Press in respect to Latin America, back in 1902, when the four news organizations met in Paris to renew their contract. Under the original four-party treaty, The Associated Press was given exclusive rights to its own national territory by the three European agencies. As Mr. Stone explained to the board about the conference in 1902:

"I said on that occasion that I was not willing to renew the contract in that shape; that Havas had not been fair to us in South America; that it had poisoned the waters and that I personally could not see my way clear to renew it; that we must in any event declare the Caribbean Islands, including Cuba, and the Central American states as common ground. The Havas Agency, having had control of that territory theretofore, very strenuously objected.

"Baron Herbert de Reuter said to them frankly that he would stand by The Associated Press in any demand that we might make and that if they would break over this question, they would have to break with him also. Well, it was finally agreed that the Central American states and the Caribbean Islands should be common ground, as I asked, and that as to South America, this contract should go on from year to year. The contract is still existent."

The power and finality of Reuters in deciding which agency could operate in any land were exemplified in Mr. Stone's quotation of Baron de Reuter. Whatever side Reuters took in those days gained its point wherever the land was, or whatever its nationality. Reuters did indeed sit at the crossroads of the world of news and control traffic!

VII

Introducing Don Jorge Mitre

D ON JORGE MITRE, director of *La Nación* of
Buenos Aires, having discontinued the United
Press service, came to New York in 1918 to
obtain membership in The Associated Press. He at once
made it quite clear that one of the chief reasons why he
so earnestly sought membership was to escape what he
described as "the slow poison" of propaganda which was
poured into South America through the instrumentality
of Old World news agencies.

Now Don Jorge is the one who had sent that little
cablegram which served as a starting point of the chain
of circumstances that makes this story. He belongs to the
old and aristocratic Mitre family of Buenos Aires, being
a grandson of Bartolomé Mitre, and has a wholly charm-
ing personality of Chesterfieldian courtesy; but he is
persistent, nevertheless. Although he is no longer with
La Nación, in a letter to me in 1941 he recounted oc-
currences of that period and gave an illuminating presentation of what poison can go into international news.
I quote from it in part:

"The year 1914 caught *La Nación* and the majority of
newspapers in South America in the most absurd and

depressing conditions so far as foreign news was concerned. Far from being the masters of such services, we were merely their outlets.

"I wanted The Associated Press to extend its service to South America because I knew that its introduction would dignify and free our press from propaganda agencies whose services, in addition to being defective at the source, were neither economical nor efficient.

"The larger nations carry on their official relations with the smaller countries through protocol and other conventions. It is on the treatment accorded its press, however, that any given nation may see the true reflection of the respect it merits from any other nation.

"It almost goes without saying that both Brazil and Argentina were long considered conquered land so far as the Havas Agency propaganda purposes were concerned."

While Don Jorge's letter made it clear that the question of propaganda ran strongly in his mind, it was the inability of *La Nación* to get adequate coverage of the World War which forced him to take energetic action. Writing of this difficult situation, he pointed out by way of preface that the early military operations, prior to the battle of the Marne, "were not favorable to the French armies," and then:

"Havas told us it could not carry the German communiqués. In face of this extraordinary situation I was authorized to contract for a service over the cable from New York."

It was at this time that Don Jorge sent the cable.

"Meanwhile," he wrote, "as I was concentrating on

the improvement of our foreign news, I noticed a series of interviews by the United Press.

"We lacked these things. I wrote the United Press in an effort to get these interviews exclusively and in that way we got a service from that agency.

"Such deficiencies as existed were not insurmountable and as the United Press service had grown and began to interest other newspapers in South America, Mr. Roy W. Howard, whom I had met when the contract with *La Nación* was signed in Buenos Aires, decided to make a second trip here two years after his first journey. Soon after his arrival in Buenos Aires we had our first disagreement."

The details of the differences between Don Jorge and Mr. Howard, president of the United Press, are not an essential part of this story, but Mr. Mitre decided to break relations with the United Press. This was in the winter of 1917-18.

Don Jorge then proceeded to New York for the purpose of trying "to arrange for the service of The Associated Press and, failing that, to resume International News Service rather than go back to United Press." Recalling after twenty-two years the details of how he finally obtained The Associated Press service for *La Nación* in 1919, he concluded:

"Today [1941] the expansion of United States activities southward to our part of the Western Hemisphere seems natural. It was not so natural in 1914. Europe, practically the monopolist of our trade at that time, ably protected itself against a distant rival.

"I recall that it was hard to find a single American-made automobile on our streets. American cars, indeed, were considered to be dangerous because it was charged that they were made out of poor materials capable even of melting away.

"The same was claimed of American news services. The exaggerations of the so-called 'yellow press' of the United States were presented to us as the usual manner of news presentation in that country. European news agencies made the most of this and behind a mask of more serious, straight reporting, hid their intention to exploit our ignorance and establish in South America an organization for European propaganda at the expense of Argentine newspapers.

"The slow poison of that propaganda, carried on through many years, has contributed to extend misunderstanding and ill will among the nations of America. The hard facts we face today no doubt will aid our country to take its choice between those who are fighting for liberty and those who long for the triumph of the oppressors.

"In 1916, just a century after Argentina had won her political independence, the Argentine press became free of the shackles of cables and propaganda in which it had been bound. When recalling that good fight, so nobly won, I shall always remember the men whose vision most contributed to the final outcome."

Here is an Argentine who because of his wide observations knew exactly what Havas had for sixty years done in the matter of keeping his country in the dark—worse than that, selfishly making the Argentines dislike and distrust all other nations except France, and perhaps Britain since Britain owned the cables over which the propaganda was transmitted. England has always had good diplomatic representatives. If Havas were belittling the English in South America, the British government through Reuters or the cable company would correct the Havas trend, or else!

In this case France was not at war with the United States. But if it had been, it would not have been difficult to show how its control of South American news channels could then have turned all the countries of South America into enemies of the United States. How much of this sort of thing has been done to bring on wars cannot be definitely stated, but it has played a large part.

During Mr. Mitre's stay in New York I saw him often. He helped me a great deal in furnishing arguments as to why The Associated Press should enter South America. But the most effective thing that had yet happened to advance the board's interest in the cause I had made my own was Mr. Mitre's contact with individual members. He personally called upon several of them and, being proficient in speaking English, was equally convincing.

The help Mr. Mitre gave in promoting the entrance of The Associated Press into South America was not forgotten. When, at a later time, *La Prensa* of Buenos Aires tried to convince me that it would be better to exclude *La Nación,* I inwardly wondered whether I would have then been asking *La Prensa* to join The Associated Press had it not been for the diplomatic approach and convincing manner in which Mr. Mitre had advanced matters and more or less made possible my first visit to South America.

Other things had happened that made me feel that my efforts to make direct exchanges of news with the South American newspapers were going to bear fruit sooner or later, for that spring The Associated Press flatly demanded of Havas a free hand in South America. In order legally to be free to proceed, notice was served terminating the existing contract with Reuters, Havas and Wolff "for the purpose of negotiating a new treaty" which would give this liberty. This phrase, "for the purpose of negotiating a new treaty," was used later on two other occasions in connection with denouncing the news exchange contracts which had been made but did not work out.

Moreover, clearly indicating determination to get action, the Board of Directors upon the suggestion of President Noyes sent me to South America to survey the field, and they did this without even waiting to learn the reaction of the European agency directors to the daring threat to long-standing prerogatives.

Those were times when my associates of that period said that two threads ran prominently through the fabric which The Associated Press management was weaving: the insistence of myself, merely a departmental chief, on absolute freedom for the organization and the restraining influence of Mr. Stone. What Mr. Stone said in effect to me time and again was:

"Go ahead and advocate as much liberty as possible, but don't do anything to bring a break between The Associated Press and our European news agency allies."

Having no doubt myself but that The Associated Press would be better off without the entire combination of foreign news agencies unless it could have freedom of action, I may not have put as much restraint upon my activities to gain that freedom of action as Mr. Stone would have liked.

I had no way of gauging how much pressure could be applied without breaking the ties that bound The Associated Press to the combination, so I had to guess at it. I tried to be patient and discreet as Mr. Stone wanted me to be, but nevertheless I had an unalterable determination not to be delayed in the achievement of ultimately breaking down all international news barriers. That had not been entirely accomplished even a quarter of a century later, although the second World War again disrupted the agency relationship all over Europe and in the Western Pacific as the first World War did in Europe alone.

VIII

Toward A New Contract

DURING those days of the first World War it seemed to me very necessary that something be done in anticipation of the close of the war and the resumption of the agency relationship which was then disrupted with the Central Powers, on the one hand, and the Allies, on the other. It was disrupted then much as it is in 1942.

I very much wanted The Associated Press then to be the leader in building a new international news exchange that would take the place of a world partitioned up according to the selfish interests of a few as to news matters. Mr. Stone had told the Board of Directors that the old order of things with the agencies would change with the end of the war. I wanted to be sure of it. In the broad view I had taken of it, all South America was then incidental, but as it was not in the war zone it afforded an open field for action and a place to test the strength of my theory and the actual antagonism of the Havas Agency to our approaches.

The later negotiations for freedom of action in Japan and the Western Pacific were then in my mind for consideration in the dim future. The still greater matter which involved the union of all the European agencies seemed tremendously imposing but nothing could be done about it anyhow until the war ended.

Even in the early days of its consideration of South America, I wanted The Associated Press ultimately to shoot at the whole world, and did not refrain from saying so. Feeling as he did about the value to The Associated Press of the agency relationship, it was no wonder that Mr. Stone was content that no progress could be made.

As the then executive head of The Associated Press felt the organization could not function efficiently without the agencies, and as he would be the one to have to try to make it function without them, his heart was not in the task; for that reason it would have been bad business for a complete break to occur. I realized that fact.

My patience and the resulting delay were, therefore, not because of any conviction I had that the agencies were of value to The Associated Press, because that value actually was minimized in my mind by whatever discredit to The Associated Press the agency connection involved. But I recognized that it would be suicidal for The Associated Press not to have the agency connection unless the executive head was ready to make a spirited effort completely to displace the agencies by setting up Associated Press facilities that would get all the world's news at its source.

Mr. Stone was not convinced, as I was, that The Associated Press could furnish the funds to perform its duties to its members without the agency relationship. The idea of dependence upon the agencies had become so fixed with him as to overshadow the fact that The Associated Press had grown large and strong and was quite able to stand on its own feet.

However, as the board's discussions for a free hand abroad continued, I made a direct plea to Mr. Stone that something should be done. I had then been several years in the service of The Associated Press and had begun to feel very close to my general manager, having acquired a real affection for him that matched the admiration I had always held for him. I had begun to feel that this respect and affection were becoming mutual, and naturally I hoped it would increase as time went on. On one occasion I ventured to sound a very personal note in connection with my idea of international freedom of the press.

"Mr. Stone," I said, "it would be presumptuous on my part to offer you advice as to what you should or should not do in this matter. Still, I venture to suggest something which is close to my heart—that the attainment of this goal under your leadership would be a grand achievement with which to crown your already great career. I should like to see you do this and should be proud to work with you."

Mr. Stone seemed moved, and my enthusiasm got hold of me. We discussed at length the idea of liberating the European press and went over ways and means of carrying it out. Co-operative organizations like The Associated Press were suggested. I said I believed The Associated Press could insist to the agencies that the newspapers be given freedom of action. If it were made an Associated Press cause I hoped it could achieve its aims without a rupture with the relationship of Reuters, Havas and Wolff.

I said that I knew energetic methods would have to be employed, and that a break should not be feared. Nevertheless, I had no intention ultimately of stopping short of my complete objective, break or no break. I stressed the fact that I didn't believe a break would follow, which seemed to make a deep impression on Mr. Stone, who remained convinced until his death that a rupture would be disastrous to The Associated Press.

Melville Stone was then in his seventieth year, but he agreed to assume the leadership that I hoped he would, and he started out with real enthusiasm. But his interest waned when the Board of Directors decided to give notice of termination of the agency contract for the purpose of modifying it. Nevertheless, he went abroad to see what could be done.

In the early days of The Associated Press and in his younger years he had spent much time abroad. His acquaintance with influential people in Europe was wide. He met many of the crowned heads, including the czar of Russia, and the German Kaiser, but he now found that a couple of decades had brought about far-reaching changes by death and retirement of many important people he had known. Also trends of thought had changed.

Failure to find the old political friends who had influence with the news agencies dampened his ardor, and he accomplished nothing. And on his return home he did not keep as firm a hand as he had before on my advocacy of the cause. This change in his attitude was deliberate.

Thereafter various discussions with the Board of Directors brought out several fundamental points. One was that the main purpose of The Associated Press in getting a free hand in South America was to secure an exchange of news. Another was—and this was an echo of one of the cardinal principles of the organization—that The Associated Press was not going into South America to make money.

A further point that favored The Associated Press was the fact that while Havas, the French agency, had to pay twenty-five cents a word for having its news sent from London or Paris to Buenos Aires, at the behest of the State Department the American-owned cable from New York was beginning to give reduced rates from New York to Buenos Aires for American clients only. I had reported a year before that the company would do this on a basis of a large wordage. So the rate between these two cities had become sixteen cents a word and only two cents a word for each additional city at which messages were copied en route. These cities included Panama, Guayaquil, Lima, Valparaiso and Santiago. I reported that the United Press was sending news at these rates. Adolph Ochs seized upon my statement:

"The Havas Agency cannot meet American news competition in supplying news to South America," he said. "Havas should want it done by The Associated Press because the United Press is sending a service to South America at a much lower rate than the Havas Agency can supply it without the co-operation of The Associated Press. Isn't that true?"

"Absolutely true," I said.

"The problem before the Havas Agency," Mr. Ochs pointed out, "is that it will be driven out of South America by the United Press, which sends its foreign news from New York to South America. So the Havas Agency is losing its control of South America and can only maintain itself there through availability of The Associated Press service in New York. It is no ger possible for Havas to serve news to South America from Europe competitively owing to the lower rate now from here."

"If you will indulge me just a minute," said Mr. Stone, "I think I can say something that may be of definite value in this. Mr. Charles Houssaye, managing director of Havas, has said that if there is any discrimination in rates, so that it makes it impossible for the French agency to send its news all over South America as cheaply as we can send it, the government of France will reduce the rate to nothing in order to send it.

"Now, make no mistake about that. That is just his statement to me. Not that they want to do it, not that they have done it, but he is speaking about the rates offered by the American cable company.

"I said: 'You never can get the rates the United Press has.'

"He said: 'We will get the rates, and if it comes to a matter of competition, we will meet any rates given.' "

To this President Noyes replied that it seemed incredible the French government would do anything of the sort. The other members of the board apparently were not particularly concerned about it either. The important thing in this exchange, however, was the strong possibility that the United Press might oust Havas from the South American field altogether, and that if The Associated Press meantime hadn't secured an entree, it would be very much left out in the cold.

"Would it be possible," Mr. Stone was asked, "to

make a deal whereby we could furnish the service to South America, and we would pay the Havas Agency for the privilege of using their news down there but keep the thing in our hands? It would be our service."

"I don't believe the French government would tolerate it for a moment," said Mr. Stone.

"That would mean they would abandon South America. They would not do that," interposed Mr. McClatchy.

"The French government would not allow it," said Mr. Stone, "and in my judgment the Latin countries would not take the news."

"We have got to get rid of all of these government-owned, government-propaganda agencies abroad," declared Mr. Villard.

"Mr. Villard is entirely right," interposed Director John R. Rathom, publisher of the Providence (Rhode Island) *Journal.* "I think that The Associated Press cannot afford to contemplate a subordinate position in South America."

"I agree with you," Mr. Stone said. "We have said that."

"That is the whole point," added Mr. Noyes.

"The whole point," Mr. Villard resumed, "is that we are tied up with three government-owned, possibly government-subsidized, propaganda services. We, a non-money-making organization, are tied up with three money-making organizations, and it is an unholy alliance."

"I don't think that is at all fair," Mr. Stone declared.

"Why not?" asked Mr. Ochs.

"Havas is not government-owned in the slightest degree," Mr. Stone replied.

"It is government-controlled," Mr. Ochs declared.

"It is a money-making concern," added Mr. Villard.

"You have three money-making and two government-controlled organizations whose main object is to make money," Mr. Ochs continued, "and they are willing to take government money to advance the cause of their countries, and we cannot compete with them on fair terms because we are not that kind of an organization."

"When the news agency through which the news of Great Britain is collected is some other kind of agency," said Mr. Noyes, "then we can deal with it, and prefer it, but as long as the British people put up with that kind of an agency, and the French people put up with that kind of an agency, we have got to get the news from the agency that gets the news."

"I tell you one thing I have not suggested," said Mr. Stone, "I think we do have a card up our sleeve that will determine this. I do not believe that Reuters Agency will ever break with us on this question, and I believe that Havas must ultimately come to our terms."

Once again Mr. Stone's conception of the power of Reuters over all the other agencies and its monopoly of the news sources of the world was evidenced. He had not forgotten that the London representative of The Associated Press once luckily had acquired the entire European agency combination service through an approach solely to Baron de Reuter; that Reuter ruled the roost.

Nor had he forgotten in 1918 how Reuters's threat

to Havas in 1902 had brought Havas to terms in the matter of The Associated Press having a free hand in the West Indies. Actually, when it came to negotiating with Havas in 1918, Reuters was not even consulted.

IX

The First Concession

I SAILED from New York to South America in the summer of 1918 coincidentally with the start of the German submarine campaign on this side of the Atlantic. The long trek that I followed through the next fifteen years in pursuit of the establishment of The Associated Press's right to tell the news abroad in the American way had begun. During that time it took me to every continent and nearly every country in the world.

I went to South America firm in the conviction that The Associated Press Board of Directors really wanted the news service established in South America even though contractual matters with Havas had not been solved. I knew I had the benediction of Mr. Noyes. He had said to the board: "I would prefer that Mr. Cooper, who is enthusiastically advocating our entry into South America, should take the trip rather than Mr. Stone, who is unalterably opposed."

The long trip and the South American passengers aboard gave me further opportunity to practice the Spanish language. And dodging submarines, with ships

being sunk all around us, gave zest to the venture of a
news conquest.

The ever keen Roy Howard was in South America
on his second trip there when I arrived. We have been
friends since we were reporters on Indianapolis newspapers in the early days of this century. I was with the
Scripps-McRae Press Association, one of the news agencies absorbed by the United Press Associations in 1907.
Howard, who had been a New York correspondent
for the Scripps-McRae League, predecessor of Scripps-
Howard, became the New York bureau manager of the
newly incorporated United Press, so we both found
ourselves with the same employer. When I left the
United Press to go with The Associated Press I jocu-
larly told Howard that two Indianapolis boys, who were
friends, couldn't profitably aspire to get to the top in
the same organization. With further jocularity I said I
had better go to The Associated Press and try to get to
the top. All this by way of stating that through forty
years, part of the time with the same employer and part
of the time in a competitive relationship, we have never
permitted anything to mar our friendship. Today, as
the surviving partner in Scripps-Howard and chairman
of the Executive Committee of the United Press, Roy is
also a member of The Associated Press on behalf of the
Scripps-Howard New York newspaper, the *World-Telegram*.

Back in 1918 he had gone to South America in connection with the United Press break with *La Nación,* as
referred to previously, and had already been in that
continent several months when he heard I was coming.

As I learned when I got there, he had every intention of remaining until I came and to stay as long as I did. Actually my leisurely trip kept him there so long that he could not get steamship accommodations to return directly to America after he made sure of my departure, with the result that he had to return to New York via Spain, Paris and Brest. From Brest on November 7, 1918, he sent the well-remembered message "URGENT ARMISTICE ALLIES SIGNED ELEVEN SMORNING. HOSTILITIES CEASED TWO SAFTERNOON. SEDAN TAKEN SMORNING BY AMERICANS."

It was my South American trip, I fear, that actually was the cause of Howard's being at Brest where Admiral Wilson told him of the Paris armistice report on November 7. When our paths crossed a year later I told him I regretted I unintentionally played a contributing part in the premature United Press armistice report that "ended" the first world war four days before hostilities ceased.

On the day I arrived in Buenos Aires on my exploratory mission the first to welcome me was the president of the opposition, and because we liked each other, and because the fortunes of the United Press were wrapped up in the actions that The Associated Press took in the southern continent and vice versa, Howard and I traveled together visiting many countries, each not disclosing to the other what he was actually doing. Having lost La Nación, Howard's keen ambition at the moment was to make a contract with La Prensa of Buenos Aires, one of the wealthiest newspapers in the world. Howard knew enough of the temperament of the proprietor of

La Prensa to be sure that if The Associated Press served *La Nación, La Prensa* would not be happy with the same service. He also felt that if The Associated Press accepted *La Prensa's* plea for exclusivity, *La Nación* could do no better than to return to the United Press.

Negotiations, however, resulted in The Associated Press getting both *La Prensa* and *La Nación,* and the United Press getting neither. But *La Prensa,* during the years that it shared The Associated Press with *La Nación,* was never happy. Ultimately the United Press did get *La Prensa.*

I saw Don Ezequel Paz, proprietor of *La Prensa,* in July, 1918, and told him I was quite certain he would be a member of The Associated Press. He said I could consider that he had already conformed in the matter of qualifying for membership. He then told me that Mr. Howard and Mr. Miller, who later became a vice-president of the United Press for South America, were waiting in another room for his answer to their proposals. When I saw Howard that night he laughingly told me it was then he got his congé. He said that Don Ezequel came into the room, squared his shoulders and, speaking delicious Castilian, announced: "I am now a member of The Associated Press."

During this time Mr. Mitre, of *La Nación,* was in New York endeavoring to arrange for Associated Press membership, and the final decision for him was to come, he expected, at the October meeting of the Board of Directors. At that meeting I made a report in which I said:

"The situation was considered with two things in mind:

" (1) The best method of securing the news of South America.

" (2) The best method of making The Associated Press general news report available for established South American newspapers.

"As to the first, I am convinced there is but one proper way and that is by reciprocal arrangement, either membership or contract, with the best class of South American newspapers. Under present conditions we rely on Havas which, as a South American news source, is just a little better than nothing. As to the details in making the news available to us, we can act in one of two ways: either arrange this for ourselves or explain modern news-collecting methods to Havas."

I said there were newspapers in South America that wanted The Associated Press news report and they did not want the report of any other agency. They were willing to give The Associated Press their news, become members and share the expenses of the organization with the membership in North America.

The board was interested in the confirmation I gave them of the report of the State Department that a news organization was in operation in South America with the name of Prensa Asociada, which is the Spanish equivalent for "Associated Press." A representative of this concern, which was backed by the German government, undertook to negotiate with me for the South American rights to The Associated Press service. His proposals opened my eyes to the unlimited efforts that the German government would make in the matter of propaganda.

"I should like to purchase the exclusive rights of The

Associated Press service for all parts of South America," he said.

As I was interested in knowing the extent of his backing I asked him what amount he would offer.

"I would prefer that you would fix the amount," he answered.

When I declined, he named a figure which only caused me to smile. Quickly he trebled it. I smiled again. Then he offered ten times the original amount. I saw that he was serious.

"Not if you offered me ten thousand times the highest amount you can name could you purchase The Associated Press rights in South America," I said. "Moreover, I should hope that the reputable newspapers on this continent will accept the real Associated Press and that its presence here will discredit your La Prensa Asociada."

Even then he insisted upon continuing the discussion, so I put an end to it.

Many South American papers were laboring under the impression that Prensa Asociada was in reality The Associated Press of New York. The United States was at war with Germany at the time and the South American Prensa Asociada was giving a pro-German slant in its news about the United States war effort—propaganda in its vilest form. Havas had not even exposed this fraud.

I told the board that, aside from securing South American news from original sources, I felt that we must without delay and in order to protect our name and our standing, proceed on our own account to elect members in South America . . . "Any plan," I said, "that means that we are to hold off and let the Havas Agency perfect

arrangements to sell our news in South America will
never protect our name or satisfy the best of the South
American newspapers that prefer to be allied directly
with us, or give us prompt access to news in South America that we can have by making arrangements for membership with papers themselves.

"My suggestion," I continued, "is that if possible we
get *La Nación* and *La Prensa* to agree on the service as
the first step. Then we should serve *La Razón,* the evening paper. It is the strongest evening paper in South
America. We should have those three papers if we are
to have any service. They have the news of South
America.

"When we have those three papers, it is a very simple
matter to arrange an exchange of news on the west
coast of South America at Valparaiso and Santiago and
Antofagasta in Chile, and at Lima in Peru, and at Guayaquil in Ecuador, and Panama in the Zone."

This actually is the way the thing worked out a little
later when the board proceeded to act on my recommendations. In spite of the strong rivalry between *La
Prensa* and *La Nación,* which at times verged on hostility, these two morning papers became members of
The Associated Press. *La Razón,* then the great afternoon paper of Buenos Aires, also joined.

I said that "by starting with these three papers the
others must come." And when asked how many papers
I thought The Associated Press could get in South
America if Havas permitted it to have any service there,
I answered I thought The Associated Press could get
twelve or fifteen memberships. Actually when I went

back to South America to begin the service a month later, twenty-five newspapers became members.

At that session of the board, after making my report, Don Jorge Mitre appeared in pursuit of his ambition to secure a membership in The Associated Press for *La Nación*. Don Jorge, be it said, had been camping on The Associated Press premises for some months, with a persistence which, as I have said, won the admiration of the directors. His final appearance before the board brought his quest for membership to a successful termination. He was then asked his view as to what would happen after the war in respect to the desire of South American newspapers for extended news service.

"I personally think," he replied, "that the attention and interest for news without propaganda will have been so developed that it will continue permanently."

In the long run this proved to be true, although the South American field provided many tough jumps for The Associated Press as well as the United Press.

After Don Jorge Mitre left the Board room, the directors immediately decided on speedy action for what was characterized one of the most important matters that had been under the consideration of the board for a long time.

President Noyes was authorized to take such steps as were necessary to constitute a news service to South America and for election of South American newspapers to membership in The Associated Press. The board also signified its desire that I return to South America to carry out this mission and President Noyes delegated full authority to me to elect members, make contracts and establish the service.

But no new contract with Havas had been negotiated. The director of Havas, who had charge of the South American field, was Charles Houssaye, whose death in Paris in 1942 has just been reported by The Associated Press as I write these lines. He was the son of Henri Houssaye, who was one of the first managing directors of the Havas Agency.

Charles Houssaye was a man of unusually attractive manners, friendly disposed and intensely devoted not only to Havas but to the entente that had so long existed between The Associated Press, Reuters, Wolff and Havas. In an association that began with my first negotiation with him in the fall of 1918 and which continued until the disappearance of Havas in 1940 due to the fall of France, I had never met a man so exclusively concerned with the welfare of the business in which he was engaged.

He believed Havas to be a pillar upon which the fate of the French Republic rested. But he was receptive to consideration of new proposals, although intensely jealous of the prerogatives and territorial rights of Havas.

In 1918 Houssaye had been invited to New York by Mr. Stone to discuss matters. He spent many weeks here without reaching the point of negotiations. Finally, one day after the board had definitely determined matters, Mr. Stone asked me to negotiate with Houssaye. I was delighted to do so, and Houssaye, who had been kept in waiting and in ignorance of what The Associated Press wanted of him, said he felt relieved that at last he was going to find out.

The fact that I had learned Spanish and that Mr. Houssaye was proficient in that language, having spent ten years in Buenos Aires in one period of his career, resulted in our use of that language in the negotiations. This was necessary since he did not speak English and I did not then speak French. Moreover, this was sentimentally proper, I suppose, considering it is the language of all of the countries of South America except Brazil.

Both of us eager for action, it did not take a half hour to conclude matters completely. The contract provided that Havas give to The Associated Press "a free hand in respect to service in the cities and republics of South America"—but with reservations. One of these stipulated that The Associated Press must reimburse Havas if the latter lost any income through newspapers in Brazil, Uruguay, Paraguay and Argentine being taken into The Associated Press membership. All were fields for development. Another provided that Havas could continue to use The Associated Press report for South America, that is to say, the French agency could utilize The Associated Press's own news service in competition with The Associated Press itself!

Naturally these restrictions were onerous from the standpoint of The Associated Press and provided a bone of increasingly vigorous contention. However, this treaty was the best that could be had for the moment because I was still enjoined not to break with Havas. It did open the door to South America, to which continent I was eager to return.

I was willing to accept the onerous conditions because, in the first place, I did not believe that the cost

of the Havas service to the larger South American newspapers with which I expected to negotiate would be an
item of any importance in their consideration of adding
The Associated Press service. Second, I never believed
Havas could compete with The Associated Press even
though it had all our own service to use in addition to
its own. Havas editors did not have the zest for news that
is peculiar to American newsmen. The Associated Press
service at that time totaled over 100,000 words daily,
and it took editorial competence to select the few thousand words which were the capacity of the American-
owned cable to South America for news wordage.

I had long had an intimate friendship with John L.
Merrill, then president of that American-owned cable.
I knew very well that Mr. Merrill's company, being an
American company and at that time co-operating with
the State Department to enlarge cable traffic with South
America, would welcome the entrance of The Associated
Press into the South American field. Indeed, I was sure
that his company, which had been serving news to South
American newspapers on its own account, would let The
Associated Press take over that function if the papers
that the cable company served were agreeable to The
Associated Press proposals.

And so three days before the Armistice of November
11, 1918, the contracts with Havas and the cable company were signed. Three days after the Armistice I
sailed away hopefully on a news conquest of South
America on behalf of The Associated Press.

X

Reward of Merit

THE annual luncheon of The Associated Press for 1919—always an affair of country-wide interest—was held on April 22 at the Waldorf-Astoria in New York City. President Noyes presided, and his introductory remarks disclosed that the luncheon had been given a Pan-American character and was by way of being a harvest festival in celebration of the first fruits of the new policy of The Associated Press.

"On January 1st of this year," he began, "The Associated Press received into membership a number of important newspapers of South America and Panama and began a news service to its new members.

"They were: *La Nación, La Prensa, Herald, Standard, La Razón, Patria degli Italiano,* of Buenos Aires, Argentina; *Correio de Manha, Jornal do Brazil, O Imparcial,* of Rio de Janeiro, Brazil; *El Mercurio* of Antofagasta, Chile; *El Mercurio, La Nación, Ultimas Noticias,* of Santiago, Chile; *El Mercurio* (Morning), *El Mercurio* (Evening), of Valparaiso, Chile; *El Telegrafo, Ilustrado,* of Guayaquil, Ecuador; *El Diario, Star & Herald,* of Panama; *El Comercio* (Morning), *El Comercio* (Evening), *La Cronica, La Prensa* (Morning), *La Prensa* (Evening), *El Tiempo,* of Lima, Peru.

"At the same time," Mr. Noyes continued, "we greatly increased our facilities for gathering the news of South America.

"I believe myself that this new relation of North and South American newspapers will do more to strengthen the ties of friendship and commerce than any possible propaganda might accomplish, for we are getting to know each other and to understand each other more sympathetically."

Mr. Noyes referred to the Pan-American aspect of the luncheon and, by way of preface for another announcement, remarked that difficulties of transportation (the World War had not long been ended and there was great lack of steamship facilities) had interfered with the presence of a number of South American members who otherwise would have been there.

"The same difficulty has delayed the arrival of Mr. Kent Cooper, who has been in South America for several months and who has conducted very ably the negotiations so successfully concluded.

"With these disappointments," continued the president of The Associated Press, "came also great compensations, for we have with us a very distinguished member of our organization from Chile, and representatives of two of our most important Buenos Aires members. We give them a most hearty welcome.

"In our Chilean membership is a group of very fine newspapers known as the Edwards group. The Edwards papers, the Mercurios of Santiago, Valparaiso and Antofagasta, are very extraordinary papers. They are represented here today by their head, Señor Agustín Edwards, the Chilean minister to England, himself the great-grandson of an Englishman, and by his associate, Señor Vildo Sola.

"Señor Edwards, it will gratify us very much if you will say something to us this afternoon."

The audience rose and greeted Señor Edwards with hearty cheers. This distinguished publisher and diplomat then paid one of the most striking tributes to The Associated Press ever made in its long history:

"We are, gentlemen, living in wonderful times. The people at large have taken into their own hands not the details of diplomatic negotiations, because that would be utterly impossible and most certainly detrimental to their own interests and to the assurance of peace of the whole world, but the broad lines of the policy they consider best suited to their national purposes. And the press constitutes really and truly today the channel of communication which conveys to those in power the impressions and thoughts of the people, and to the people the difficulties encountered by and the patriotic warnings of those in power. As long as that channel of communication is kept clear and clean, the press is nobly using power that destiny has thrown into its hands.

"The Associated Press has done perhaps more than any other human agency to keep it clean and clear. The news it spreads throughout the world is unbiased. It flows in every direction as crystalline water springing from the purest fountain. This institution, The Associated Press, has to my mind raised the profession of journalism to a high moral level, in which it begins to lose the appearance of a trade and to shine with the glory of a priesthood.

"The Associated Press has just come through a test, perhaps the most severe that it is ever to undergo, in these four and a half years, in which the quality of every institution—and perhaps the quality of every single individual—has been tested.

"Ancient empires have fallen; crowns and thrones have crumbled; systems of government have disappeared, showing their dangers and immoralities and even the machinery of international intercourse has had to undergo repair.

"Yet The Associated Press stood the test and stood it well. It has today, as it had before the war, the respect of the whole world.

"It is easy to understand it. There are things, gentlemen, which never die. The worship of truth is one, and from the standpoint of Chilean journalism I would like, Mr. Chairman, to say in conclusion that it has joined The Associated Press because it embodies its own ideals and above all, because it feels that a new tie, and a very powerful one, has been created in the ever growing friendship of the Chilean and American people."

President Noyes then introduced Señor Romeo Ronconi, New York representative of *La Prensa* of Buenos Aires, who declared that "no other service better than The Associated Press could be had in the world."

"So let us hope," he said, "that many other newspapers from South America will join. They have a taste of the service now. They have 'got the goods,' as you say in this country. They can see it. There is nothing better to join together the North and the South and make for the welfare of both North and South America."

W. W. Davies, New York representative of *La Nación*, followed and concluded his remarks by reading a message addressed to Mr. Noyes by Señor Jorge Mitre, who was back in Buenos Aires and had reviewed the service he had received from The Associated Press. Mr. Mitre left no doubt that he was proud and happy in The Associated Press membership which he had sought so long and earnestly.

"Permit me to express my congratulations and felicitations for the present service you are giving us," he cabled to President Noyes. *"La Nación* and Argentina alike appreciate your conscientious effort to furnish news that is news and which has back of it no ulterior motive, such as propaganda."

When I had returned and read the stenographic report of the speeches at the lunch, I felt that I had been a crusading knight in foreign lands. What was said in those speeches was an immediate reward given during my lifetime for the cause that I had advocated. The press of a whole continent had come to know that, although the United States was a foreign country, The Associated Press principle of true and unbiased news without a tinge of propaganda could be accepted trustfully. Our neighboring Canadians had long before accepted it.

The greatest original American moral concept that had ever been exported from America had been welcomed in a new continent. The European news agency combine had every reason to fear competition from America because America had news agencies that, being backed by a free press, without even a word of benediction from the United States government, were not compelled to operate under government orders.

In the ensuing twenty-five years both The Associated Press and the United Press, as well as the International News Service, have had ups and downs in their fortunes in the matter of news dissemination in foreign lands. Except for Canada and Mexico they all got their start in South America in the matter of exporting news. An ill-advised policy on the part of Havas had started it all. If Havas had furnished the German war communiqués to *La Nación* in 1914, Dr. Mitre would not have sent that little message to The Associated Press and the crusade that I started in the organization might not have been begun. If The Associated Press could have answered it favorably and had done so, it would have been The Associated Press and not its competitors that got away to South America first. But the crusade would have had to come sooner or later.

Meanwhile none of the news agencies of the United States has ever yet had to depart in the operations abroad or here from the moral principles that have made the American press the soundest and strongest in the world. Surely no government here will ever move to jeopardize that standing. And—I *was* glad I found that little unanswered cable and that I was interested.

XI

Peace Depends Upon A Free Press

HAVING made a start in South America, and the Board of Directors' acceptance of my idea having been not only vindicated but praised at The Associated Press annual luncheon, I felt the time opportune to disclose my belief that The Associated Press venture into foreign lands in the matter of disseminating news should not stop with South America.

In the six months while I was traveling to, in and from that continent I had plenty of time to think of what might happen to The Associated Press if a break with the agencies, which Mr. Stone so greatly feared, should come to pass. I thought it might come and that we should prepare for it. I began discussing that necessity at the same time I projected the matter of entirely removing the international news barriers that confronted The Associated Press.

I had begun to suspect that, if Havas could so definitely impose upon a continent its own ideas of the nature, extent and even the morals of the news one continent received, Reuters, with a more dominating position, could impose, jointly with Havas, its ideas of the nature, extent and even the morals of the news service that would be restored to the European continent after the first World War was over.

Using as a pretext my dissatisfaction with the onerous conditions of the new Havas contract respecting South America and wishing to look into transmission difficulties through which The Associated Press was suffering in a Europe after the war, I went abroad in May, 1919, immediately after my return from South America.

In Paris I was very much impressed by what I was able to observe of the methods by which the peace treaty was being put together. I wondered if anyone had thought about the matter of the inclusion of an article declaring for a free press and freedom of international news exchange. I had heard about the Utopian approach on every other subject affecting the welfare of the peoples of the world: there were consideration of how to protect their physical health, their right to live; also about the suppression of their right to wage war and what not. But I could not find that anyone had projected for consideration the welfare of the people as to guaranteeing that they could have true, unbiased news to read in their newspapers about either world or domestic affairs.

Believing in a free press, I felt that a world peace treaty, in the writing of which America had a part, could do no less than declare for that principle throughout the world, especially in the matter of guaranteeing the international transmission of truthful news.

This thought—that good will among men depends on untrammeled exchange of news and views—seized upon me with such force as to become the dominating idea of my stay in Paris. I knew that any step I took to gain freedom of action for The Associated Press in Europe would not be to the liking of my chief if it resulted in a break with the European news agencies.

So I naïvely conceived the idea that if the peace treaty tore those barriers down no one, not even my chief, could object. After all, I really thought that they ought to be torn down. All this brought a decision that I should try an avenue of approach to Utopia on the subject that interested me most of all.

The fact that the World War Peace Conference was then in full swing in Paris was the opportunity that might never again occur in my lifetime. I had been told that Colonel Edward M. House, President Wilson's adviser, was at the Hotel Crillon.

I became acquainted with Colonel House before I went to South America the first time. I had then told him about the project of opening up the southern continent in the matter of news dissemination, and I had found in him a listener who not only was interested but was anxious to help.

Roy Howard carried to South America a letter of introduction and good wishes from President Wilson himself. Colonel House did not offer to get me a similar document, nor did I ask him for it. Nevertheless, he wanted to see my mission successful.

When I returned to New York from my first South American visit I happened again to see Colonel House and told him enthusiastically of the prospects I visioned. I related the whole story of The Associated Press relations with the great European news agencies and its subordination to them in respect to any activity abroad. Colonel House again wished me good luck as I returned

to South America with full authorization of the Board of
Directors of The Associated Press to establish the news
service there.

By the time I had finished this job, the colonel already
was in Paris for the Peace Conference. So I went to see
him at the Crillon, headquarters of the American delegation. He was enthusiastic over the South American
development, but I told him that I felt the task had only
begun. This naturally revived the former discussion of
the obstacles that The Associated Press had to meet in
the matter of free exchange of news.

All the European news agency tentacles into Central
Europe had been broken by the war. I had not yet come
in contact with the managing directors of the Central
European news agencies and I wondered what was going
to happen to them. I asked Colonel House if he knew
whether anything was going into the treaty respecting
the freedom of the press and freedom of international
news exchange. He asked me to explain exactly what I
thought ought to be done, and I told him. He said he
would make inquiries, and with high hopes I left him.

A week later, not having heard from him, I saw him
again. He told me he had raised the question but that
he was answered somewhat cryptically to the effect that
the "matter had been taken care of privately." I gathered the impression that the European agencies themselves were going to handle the affair.

Naturally this meant that Reuters and Havas would
impose their will on Wolff and the agencies of all the
new countries that were being created by the peace
treaty. Also that whatever control Wolff had of the
agencies in the countries bordering on the North Sea

before the war would be replaced by Reuter control. I guessed this because in all political matters the spirit that was dictating what was going into the Treaty of Versailles indicated that would be the result in the private negotiations on news agency matters. My assumption proved to be a good guess because that is exactly what happened.

Anyway, whatever were the details as to what was done "privately," the subject of freedom of the press was not dealt with in the peace treaty. I was disappointed and I wondered then whether in my lifetime The Associated Press would gain the freedom of action abroad that its chief competitor, the United Press, had always enjoyed. I wondered whether in an expanding world The Associated Press could always remain domestic plus only a restrained expansion of its activities in the Western Hemisphere. Already I had seen the United Press get a start in South America two years before The Associated Press was able to free itself from the agency ban.

I wondered what, the war having ended, the United Press would start to do in Europe where the Havas strength, as I had come to know it in the South American negotiations, would be buttressed or manipulated by the more powerful Reuters, both of them probably resolute in their determination to keep The Associated Press out.

Confronted with speculation as to the future I felt I could only get militant inspiration from the idea that a free press would foster peace. I guess I never stopped talking about it whenever opportunity offered. Mr. Stone again felt I was seeking the impossible. Mr. Noyes was much more attentive and interested.

Now it so happened that after the signing of the peace treaty at Versailles in June, 1919, I took a trip into Germany and later went to London, where for the first time I met Sir Roderick Jones of Reuters. I was the second executive of The Associated Press whom Sir Roderick had seen. Mr. Stone had met him when he made his futile trip two years before to obtain a change in the Havas contract.

Sir Roderick was unable to place me in any official position in The Associated Press and his attitude appeared to be one of wonderment as to why I called upon him. I was, I told him, only chief of the Traffic Department of The Associated Press, but mischievousness moved me to add that my duties included dissemination of The Associated Press news abroad.

There was a pause in the conversation during which I thought Sir Roderick might have suddenly recalled that it was I who had gone to South America twice in a successful effort to establish The Associated Press news service there. It was not my idea to keep anything from him and so I volunteered to tell him what I had done in South America, but he said: "I am fully informed by our good friends of Havas."

I was impressed by Sir Roderick's comparative youth and envious of the tremendous field of opportunity before him. My chief was then seventy-one years old and he had confined his activities to the United States. Sir Roderick was forty-two, and the entire world was his field. I felt I wanted to talk to him of my hopes of the future in news agency matters. I felt quite certain he could tell me if he would what were the "private" arrangements outside of the peace treaty to which Colonel

House referred. And then, filled with the glow that here was the man who was in a position to dictate then and there the fate of my dreams, I made a dreadful mistake by saying:

"Sir Roderick, you have a more wonderful opportunity in your position than any I shall ever have to advance the cause of freedom of the press and freedom of news exchange. We are young. We are almost the same age and I would consider myself fortunate if I, on behalf of The Associated Press, could work side by side with you in the development of modern plans for news agency intercourse."

Sir Roderick did not seem to know how to take my surprising suggestion so frankly expressed. He made no answer and his attitude truly made me feel that I had transgressed.

I then held a comparatively minor position with one of the twenty-nine news agencies which Reuters dominated so far as concerned world relations and I had never before been that near the throne of Reuters Rex. There was a little mutual embarrassment which I ended by changing the subject—and then bade him adieu.

I used a couple of weeks in London to get all the information I could regarding the status of Reuters, and it was then that I learned about the Press Association of Great Britain. This organization was established in the early seventies of the last century by the newspapers published outside of London, known as the provincial press.

One member of the Press Association told me that it was organized originally to protect the papers in the

provinces against domination of the entire British newspaper enterprise by the great London newspapers, as it
served for seventy years to weld the newspapers outside
of London and to protect them. While its form is not
exactly like the membership corporation form of The
Associated Press, it is the British prototype of the earlier
American mutual organization. Its methods a quarter of
a century ago were antiquated. Its news was often hand-
written by stylus, a carbon copy method that had not
been used by The Associated Press in America since the
middle nineties. The employees of the Press Association
all seemed to be men past middle life. It was facetiously
said of the association that it did not install typewriters
for fear the whiskers of the reporters and editors would
get tangled up in the keys.

However it may have been then as to lack of progres-
sivism, I formed an admiration for the Press Association
which I had occasion to put into documentary expression some fifteen years later when a crisis came between
The Associated Press and Reuters.

The Press Association by way of protecting itself had
made what amounted to a perpetual contract with Reuters for the use of foreign news in return for the news
that the Press Association collected outside of London.
Being organized effectively, the Press Association was
never slow to protect itself against any possible assault
from the great London press, which had only the Newspaper Proprietors' Association of London to hold it together in a loose sort of way.

The London newspapers apparently felt they needed
no protection whatever against the Press Association.
Nevertheless, it was the Press Association that absorbed

the London News Agency, a medium through which the local news of London was collected for all the London newspapers as well as for the Press Association. Thus the London papers awakened to the fact that the Press Association not only controlled the collection of news in the provinces for itself, but had its own instrument in the form of the London News Agency to collect the news of London. The name of the London News Agency has disappeared but the Press Association carries on the work that the news agency once did.

On my return to America I think I talked more about the Press Association than I did about Reuters. I remember telling Mr. Noyes that I had a real respect for the spirit that dominated that organization in the matter of looking out for the interests of the provincial newspapers, its members. I told him and the members of the Board of Directors about Sir Roderick Jones, and what I had heard of plans Reuters and Havas had for the news agencies in continental Europe.

XII

Isolating the Vanquished

INFORMATION on what had happened in the European agency relationship as a result of the actions of Reuters and Havas after the signing of the peace treaty was given to the Board of Directors by Mr. Stone in the spring of 1920.

Early in that year the board had sent Mr. Stone abroad to negotiate a new treaty with Reuters, Havas and Wolff which would cover the advancements in its world relationships that the board wanted The Associated Press to attain. Among the things the board asked Mr. Stone to try to get was larger freedom in dealing with individual newspapers, especially in the matter of an exchange of news between The Associated Press and the papers. This was one of the things I had advocated in my talks with Mr. Stone. The board also asked for similar rights in respect to co-operative news agencies abroad, if such were established.

The big three, Reuters and Havas having let Wolff resume its status only in respect to The Associated Press, still complacent in their strength and alert against any encroachment on their prerogatives, looked down their noses at The Associated Press and sent Mr. Stone back home empty-handed. The great Reuters, of course, was in command. The way of it was this, as Mr. Stone told the board on his return:

"When I went over I had no idea that our relations would not be resumed on the same pleasant terms that existed for twenty-five years. When I arrived in London I found that the weather was not 'fair and warmer' at all. There was perfect politeness, and I was welcomed very cordially, but there was an entirely new atmosphere.

"In 1902 when I demanded a free hand in the Caribbean Islands and in Central America and in the Philippines, and the Havas people objected, Baron de Reuter, who was then the head of the Reuter Agency, flatly told the Havas people that he would stand by me and that Reuters would back up any suggestion that I made. As a result I got what I asked.

"I found when I went back this time, as I say, a very cordial welcome and a very polite and a very agreeable relation, but when I undertook to talk about the situation with Sir Roderick Jones, who is the head of the Reuter Agency, well, he said: 'Oh, of course we want pleasant relations.' "

Such was Mr. Stone's report of his meeting. Jones was much Mr. Stone's junior for Mr. Stone had then, at seventy-two years of age, been the executive head of The Associated Press for twenty-eight years. He had known the founder of Reuters and he had long known the son, Baron Herbert de Reuter. Sir Roderick was some thirty years younger than Mr. Stone and he had headed Reuters less than five years.

Mr. Stone didn't comment further to the board on Sir

Roderick's reply, but it could need no explanation to make the directors see that such an offhand retort from an old ally was deliberate and intended to put The Associated Press in its proper place. This attitude appeared to be emphasized in a further response from Jones. The Reuters chief was about to leave for Paris to meet the representatives of Havas and Wolff, and Mr. Stone expressed the intention of going over also.

"I think it will be well for you to do so" was the answer.

"So," continued Mr. Stone, "I went over to Paris supposing that I would be taken at once into the confidence of our colleagues. When I arrived I found that they had held private meetings for several days. Although they continued them, I was not invited to participate at all. I was rather surprised, and I asked about it and they said:

" 'Well, do you want to come into a union with Reuters and the Havas people? Of course that is a question to be considered—whether you want to continue your relations with these organizations.'

"And they said that they had some impression that we did not want to. I asked:

" 'Where did you get that from?'

"Well, they had read Director McClatchy's statement, and Sir Roderick was very pronounced in his view. He was ready to give Mr. McClatchy a very high honor as chairman of the House Committee of the Ananias Club. He was very positive in his declaration."

Mr. Stone did not identify the McClatchy statement in question, but there is small doubt as to what he had in mind. Mr. McClatchy, who was noted as a two-fisted crusader in affairs relating to the Western Pacific and was known as California's watchdog against intrusion by the Japanese, made a trip to Japan, Korea, China and the Philippines in 1919. He was particularly interested in transpacific communications, and his investigations brought him to the widely proclaimed conclusion that news between the United States and its Philippine possession was all exchanged by way of London—"controlled by British influence."

On his return home he went before Congress and declared that foreign control of news channels was prejudicing American interests in the Western Pacific. This resulted in Congress directing the Navy to open its transpacific radio circuits to news at a rate low enough to permit of competition with British and Japanese transmission charges.

Now, when Mr. McClatchy talked about "British influences" I assume that he had Reuters—and quite likely the government—in mind because his views on the subject of British influences in the Western Pacific were well known. Sir Roderick was vexed. He did not think it proper for an Associated Press director to speak of Reuters in other than complimentary terms. Mr. Stone quoted Sir Roderick as saying:

"We had very pleasant relations for years, and a very serious charge has been made against us by one of the directors of The Associated Press."

"And then," continued Mr. Stone, "Sir Roderick called attention to the fact that they were offered more for an alliance than we were paying. He said very frankly that they could get more from the United Press than we were paying."

After consideration, the big three reaffirmed that The Associated Press was in the alliance. However, Mr. Stone said that when he took up with them the question of whether The Associated Press "should have the right to traffic with individual newspapers in Europe to get news from them and to give them a certain amount of news," the alliance replied:

"Well, we'll take up each case and see what we can do. If we can do it without injury to the general situation, we will be glad to meet your views, but if we cannot, we won't."

"There has been practically no change whatever in the situation?" asked Director Rathom.

"Well, perhaps, gentlemen," replied Mr. Stone, "I blundered the whole matter, but I feel very keenly that we were in great jeopardy of losing our whole relations with those agencies and that would have been a distinct loss. . . . I think it would be a disaster, an absolute disaster for this organization to break with this combination. Their attitude is this: if we want to break with them we can break. If we want to break with them we can go. They can get more money anyhow than we would pay them."

So that was the end of the 1920 effort of The Associated Press to make arrangements whereby an independent news report could be secured from Europe by means of an exchange with newspapers.

Many, many times I heard repeated the threat that if The Associated Press was not careful Reuters would sign up the United Press for more money than The Associated Press was paying. The possibility of this did not harmonize with the contemporaneous actions and talk of

United Press executives and salesmen in this country. In public speeches the foreign agencies were denounced and Associated Press members heard from United Press salesmen that The Associated Press foreign news was tainted because it was based on the news of the foreign agencies "which were propaganda services."

After the board meeting at which the threat was quoted I told Mr. Stone I did not believe the United Press would buy the foreign agencies' news and that it certainly would not exchange news with them. I said I thought an offer from Mr. Stone to the president of the United Press to share the news of the foreign agencies might be made. If accepted, the United Press would be putting on itself the stigma it was trying to place on The Associated Press. If not, it would stop the threats by Reuters.

"But," said Mr. Stone, "if the United Press accepted, it would give it the same facilities abroad The Associated Press now has."

"And," I replied, with a smile, "it would result in freedom of action for The Associated Press abroad. It would also benefit The Associated Press because, in order to be different, The Associated Press would more than ever intensify on establishing its own independent news sources."

Mr. Stone had become tolerant of my insistence and returned my smile. Without saying anything he indicated that he thought I was—mistaken.

Mr. Stone's report to the board that day, however, gave some details of how Reuters and Havas fixed matters after the Versailles Treaty by which they dominated the situation abroad. His report was a partial story of the isolation of the vanquished.

"Originally," he said, "the whole news business of Europe was established by Baron de Reuter and by Havas, and they appointed their subordinate agencies in other countries. They appointed an agent in Belgium. They appointed an agent in Holland. They appointed an agent in Denmark, and they appointed agents all around.

"The Stefani Agency of Italy is controlled financially by the Havas Agency. The Fabra Agency of Spain is owned by the Havas Agency. The Portuguese agency is owned by the Havas Agency. The Belgian agency is owned one-half by the Reuters service and one-half by the Havas people. The Dutch agency was known as a Reuter agency until the war broke out, and then the name was changed to the Nederlandsch Telegraaf Agentschap, but the manager of it is on the payroll of the Reuter service in London.

"There are no competing agencies, and these organizations absolutely control the field. Moreover, the situation is this, as to any of those smaller companies: if they were not owned, if they were not financially under the control of these larger agencies, they would still be at the mercy of them.

"The Belgian people thought they could free themselves from the Havas control and the Reuter control, as the war seemed to have broken down all existing contracts, and King Albert himself was deeply interested in it. They found they could not do it.

"There is no monopoly in the world equal to it.

"There is not one of these agencies [the smaller ones] that could make an arrangement with anybody else. For instance, take the Swiss agency. We could not make a contract with the Swiss agency unless we were allied to Havas and Reuters, because the Swiss could not get the world news from us over there by cable. It would be perfectly hopeless for us to undertake it."

Mr. Stone said that Havas had an immense advertising agency, as did the smaller organizations, which gave them a great hold on the newspapers. The point was that the papers paid for the news in advertising space and received cash payments for advertising in addition.

"I doubt," said he, "if there is a paper in Europe anywhere that does not on a balance receive more money from those agencies than it pays to the agencies. You see what I mean? The papers pay in advertising space. And they do in China. That is one of their strong points with the vernacular press that ties these people absolutely to the agencies.

"When I was in Italy and when I was in England, a year and a half ago, I had a dream that perhaps there would be a chance to have the papers in those countries organize something akin to our association."

Mr. Stone was referring to the trip he took after my talk with him when I urged him to go abroad and advance the idea of co-operative news associations that would permit the newspapers to gain their freedom from the agencies.

"There is a very rich man, who has the leading paper of Italy, named Luigi Albertini," Mr. Stone continued. "He is the editor of the *Corriere Della Sera* of Milan. He is about forty-five years old. I went to Milan and had a day with him, and I said to him:

"'Now this is a most extraordinary situation. Your

news agency, the Stefani Agency, is controlled by France. There is none too good feeling between Italy and France, but the managers of it are two Austrians, and you are at war with Austria and are in the position of having your news filtered out to you by two Austrians.'

" 'Yes,' he said, 'that is true.'

" 'Well,' I replied, "isn't there enough self-respect among the Italian newspapers to break away from that? Now you are a young man, you have abundant means. Why don't you take up this thing and organize? Of course as everybody knows—the Reuters service people know and the Havas people know—The Associated Press was founded as it stands today on a fight against private ownership of a news organization.'

"Well, we talked the matter all over. He studied the situation and came back to this question of advertising.

" 'Why, Mr. Stone,' he said, 'it would cost millions to do it. It cannot be done. We are in their hands, and we cannot get away from it. Suppose we broke. How are we going to get the news of the world? Here is a combination of twenty agencies dominating twenty different countries.' "

Mr. Stone said he discussed this same question in England and in France. However, "the job was too big for all of them."

The general manager then told of how Reuters and Havas (the Anglo-French allies) emasculated Wolff (the German agency) in the first postwar conference among the three former friends. Relations between Wolff and the other two agencies had been severed, of course, during the war.

"They took away from the Wolff service all control of

the Scandinavian and Russian and Austrian services,"
said Mr. Stone, "and limited it absolutely to Germany.

"They spent several days over the question of the Saar
Valley and of the Palatinate and all Rhenish Prussia
and the territory west of the Rhine, and Dr. Heinrich
Mantler, head of the Wolff Agency, was fighting very
hard to keep that and they were fighting very hard to
take it away. It was perfectly obvious. There was not any
question what they wanted—and Sir Roderick Jones admitted it to me—that the French Government wanted to
render the news service to that territory.

"They have got fifteen years before they have a plebis-
cite to determine whether that territory shall go back to
Germany or stay with France, and they wanted that
fifteen years to be devoted to propaganda, and under the
influence of the French Government the Havas Agency
was fighting for it. Finally they made a compromise by
which the Wolff Agency might serve there, but a copy
of Wolff service should go to the Havas Agency, and if
it was not satisfactory Wolff could be removed from
there."

One other important point was developed in this
memorable session of the Board of Directors. Director
Rathom asked:

"Mr. Stone, have these people [the European agencies]
got any conception of our attitude with regard to a news
service at all? Do they see anything in their service that
is improper or wrong?"

"No," Mr. Stone replied.

"They think it is part of their function to do what
they are doing? Is there any appeal to a higher ground?"

"Not the slightest."

"You are convinced that there is no hope ever to get them along on our line of thought as far as our conception of what a news agency ought to be?"

"I certainly am."

"Then when are we going to come to the evil day when we must dissociate ourselves from that kind of an effort?"

"I don't know. That is for you to answer," Mr. Stone concluded.

The peace treaty of Versailles having been signed without anything in it about a free press or unfettered exchange of news, there was then no appeal to a higher ground.

During the next ten years I heard a great deal about how European news agency matters "had been taken care of privately," as Colonel House had put it.

Reuters and Havas, matching the political terms of the Versailles Treaty, built their own news agency "cordon sanitaire" around Germany. All the political states bordering on Germany were allowed to have only news agencies owned or controlled by either Reuters or Havas or both, in some such alliance against the German news agency as were the political alliances of those border states with England and France.

In other words, the position of the news agencies in those border countries was harmonious with the determination of England and France to keep Germany hemmed in by little nations mostly pro-Ally, such as Finland, Sweden, Norway, Denmark, Holland, Belgium, Switzerland, Austria, Czechoslovakia and Poland. I was also told that Havas undertook to control the news that was to be disseminated to all the Balkan States except Greece and Turkey, which were reported to have fallen into Reuters's sphere of influence.

I do not know the exact form which this Continental agency relationship took in the matter of control by Reuters and Havas, but I was some time later told by several of the directors of these smaller news agencies that they were indissolubly linked to Reuters or Havas or both through ownership or contractual control.

I was also later told by the managing director of the Wolff Agency that it was only after all the private arrangements with these news agencies in the states bordering on Germany had been concluded that Reuters and Havas sent for the managing director of Wolff to tell him where Wolff would stand in the news agency world. In other words, the "private arrangements" as to "freedom of the press and international news exchange" concerning which Colonel House had told me were carried out.

In the same spirit that cried "Hang the Kaiser!" the German news agency was isolated by every agency of every country in Europe. The quarantine was complete —so complete that it was bound to be broken. It didn't work against Germany and it did harm to every country that bordered on Germany. This for the reason that no agency of any of those countries was allowed to serve its newspapers freely and according to its own ideas and resourcefulness. Always orders came from London or Paris—foreign control of what the press of those new and old little countries could obtain from their news agencies in the way of foreign news.

The evidence seems strong that these news barriers

around Germany contributed to the cause of Hitler's rise to power and the eventual outbreak of World War II within the short space of twenty years. Surely in another peace treaty there will be something about freedom of the press and international news exchange—or will there?

XIII

A Knight Convinced

WHILE the Board of Directors at nearly every session continued discussing this vexing but momentous question of how The Associated Press might carry the torch of mutual co-operation as the basis for the press of any country to operate, Sir Roderick Jones was busily engaged in after-the-war rehabilitation of Reuters and tightening the cords that bound Reuters' dominions beyond the seas to the great English agency that still had its offices in Old Jewry. The gains with the agencies in Europe were already showing results, although each year made Wolff more and more unhappy in its confinement strictly to serving the press of Germany.

With all this fixed, Sir Roderick in the fall of 1920 set out on a trip around the world to bring Reuters' world dominions into acquaintanceship with the new managing director, but primarily to enlarge the financial payments to Reuters. As Sir Roderick had gained control of Reuters at Baron de Reuter's death while the war was on, he had never surveyed its world activities personally. He knew South Africa, where he had long been in charge. It was said that South African friends had financed his taking over of Reuters after the baron's death.

The managing director's first stop was New York City, where he met President Noyes and the Board of Directors of The Associated Press. As diplomatically as he could, Sir Roderick broached the matter of increasing the payment to Reuters. President Noyes took charge of him. I have never seen so complete an envelopment of the thought and activities of any man as that which resulted from Mr. Noyes's contact with Sir Roderick.

But no man could then have changed Sir Roderick in his determination to make Reuters immensely profitable. Mr. Noyes had been president of The Associated Press for twenty years. He knew what a non-profit-making, non-money-making institution was, and he believed, as he still does, that such a form of organization is essential to the press of every country. Over and over again I heard him emphasize this point. A few months before Sir Roderick reached New York I had been appointed assistant general manager and fortunately for me I was present at the more formal discussions with Sir Roderick.

Any approach that Jones made to the matter of obtaining more money only gained from Mr. Noyes a reply that "I am not interested in that; I am interested in having you know the desirability of converting Reuters into a mutual organization with which the co-operative Associated Press could work more harmoniously than with a company interested only in selling news at a profit."

Sir Roderick did not then or at any time afterward get any more money from The Associated Press, but he did get an education on the co-operative news agency form.

In things he said and in actions he took, he often

thereafter gave evidence of what he had learned from Mr. Noyes. Probably the first time he worded it was at a dinner given to him by the Board of Directors of The Associated Press at the University Club of New York in October, 1920. In his speech he saluted The Associated Press, praised Reuters, and added an expression of hope that he could so arrange matters that if he were "run over and killed by an omnibus, Reuters will have by that time been owned by the British press."

A sincere and devoted friendship between Mr. Noyes and Sir Roderick had begun. Both have since retired from their high positions, the friendship as strong as ever. But Sir Roderick left New York for the Western Pacific and other parts of Reuter dominions thoroughly convinced in his own mind that Reuters would never permit The Associated Press to enter any of its domain to disseminate news. The approach to that by me met a stern rebuff. This fact, however, did not constitute discouragement.

But there was still some unfinished business in South America and after Sir Roderick had left New York in the fall of 1920 I returned once more to South America to see after a period of eighteen months' absence how The Associated Press was getting on in that continent; also, the two influential Buenos Aires newspapers, *La Prensa* and *La Nación,* were at sword's points in the matter of competition, *La Prensa* demanding that The Associated Press discontinue service to *La Nación.* I had expected this would happen. In refusing exclusivity to *La Prensa,* The Associated Press gave the United Press an opportunity to begin a lively and successful competition, but the Board of Directors rightly would not give a preference to *La Prensa* over *La Nación.*

Another reason for my trip was to see whether Havas was injuring The Associated Press in the matter of transmitting our news to South America in competition with us. I felt that the Havas contract covering South America, which then had been in force for two years, needed amendment and I advocated that Havas be stopped from sending Associated Press news from New York to South America. To this proposal Mr. Stone once more told the board:

"Well, I certainly should have no objection to Cooper's going to Paris and talking to Mr. Houssaye or anybody else on the subject, and if he can accomplish it I should be very glad to see him do it. But at the same time I would not want any action of his over there to put in jeopardy our relations with these foreign agencies, which I regard as vital. That is all I have to say about it."

That was all he had to say about it at the moment, but the following day he reverted to the subject. Again he applied the brakes in fear that decisive action might do irreparable damage. He said he thought the differences between Havas and The Associated Press could be adjusted, but not "if we are going to try and force it on terms that give us a distinct advantage.

"I don't think we can stay in South America," he said, "and make a success at all until we can co-operate with the Havas Agency. . . . I say if we are going down there in competition with Havas, we are going to have trouble. We have a difficult problem at best, and if we are going down there at all, I think we have got to go down there on some form of agreed relation with the Havas people that they will be content with, and I think it is worth infinitely more to us to have our world relation than to have something in South America.

"I don't want to go on the theory that we are going to compete with Havas in any way. I want to say to them:

" 'Here now, let us work jointly, and let the Havas Agency and The Associated Press serve South America jointly. Not that we want such a free hand that we can beat you out of South America, but that we want to work together. Let us divide our service to such an extent that you will know what to send, and we will know what to send, and we won't conflict with each other, and we won't be racing to beat each other, and we will not serve anybody who does not take both services."

I pointed out that I was making just two recommendations. One was to get rid of the clause in the contract whereby The Associated Press guaranteed Havas the income the latter had from papers which left the French agency and came into Associated Press membership. The other was that Havas stop sending our own Associated Press news from New York to South America in direct competition with us.

I went to South America and was unable to convince Dr. Paz of *La Prensa* that he should continue in The Associated Press membership even though, in order to have an individual *La Prensa* service, he might take the United Press. Dr. Paz made a most generous financial offer in the way of the assessment he would pay if he had the service exclusively.

I told him I was sorry but that The Associated Press Board of Directors had committed itself not to give exclusivity in Buenos Aires. *La Prensa's* director felt that in taking the same Associated Press service received by *La Nación* and the cost of the service being divided equally between the two papers, *La Prensa* was in effect reducing the cost of the service to *La Nación*. With *La Prensa* out of Associated Press membership the cost to *La Nación* would be doubled, and Dr. Paz felt that *La Nación* could not meet that increased expense. As a result *La Prensa* withdrew from the membership, Dr. Paz telling me that if it eventuated that *La Nación* did not continue The Associated Press service I might take the matter up with him again. However, *La Nación* came nobly to the front and shouldered the expense involved and has done so for the last twenty-three years. This time Dr. Luis Mitre, a cousin of Don Jorge, saw to it that The Associated Press got proper financial support for its policy. Dr. Luis Mitre was president of the company owning *La Nación* when I called upon him in 1918. He is still president in 1942 and member of The Associated Press for *La Nación*. With the necessary assurances from Dr. Mitre, I was not in a position to resume discussions with Dr. Paz.

My trip impressed me with the grave necessity of changing our contract with Havas, with the result that I proceeded from that continent direct to Paris to see if any change could be effected in Havas's position by which Havas service in South America would stand on its own merits without access to the report of The Associated Press. Mr. Houssaye did consent to send only news of North America to South America, and that in small quantity, but he resolutely refused to accede to more than that. As he gave instructions to his staff, it was unnecessary to include his concession in a new contract at that time.

The next year Havas further agreed that The Associated Press should no longer guarantee the French agency for losses in South America if newspapers dropped the Havas report through becoming members of The Associated Press. Havas at that time incorporated in the contract the verbal agreement that I had made the year before, that it would stop filing to South America the foreign news which The Associated Press brought into New York.

In the fall of 1922 the Board of Directors was considering approval of this newest contract with Havas. I said that if this approval were given I hoped it would be for the shortest term possible and, because there had been changes in the personnel of the board since I first outlined my views in detail, I continued with this presentation:

"Now, it is necessary just for a moment to look in retrospect as to why we went to South America in the first place. We did not go to South America to drive Havas out. We went to South America for two reasons, first as a practical and patriotic thing to do, second, as an expedient, because the United Press was displacing Havas in South America, and the United Press was getting the advantage that went with so many newspaper connections in South America. What was going on, so far as The Associated Press was concerned, prior to our entrance into South America was this:

"Up to 1914 the Havas Agency sent such news of North America as it chose to South America from London, not from Paris but from London, out of the Reuter report. In 1914, because the All America Cable Company reduced the rate to ten cents—first fifteen cents, then ten cents—and because the English cable from Europe to South America was congested on account of the war, Havas came to this office and sent all its reports from this office to South America.

"But for forty-five years Havas has been discrediting North America in South America. It did it from this office by giving a twist to the news and it did it from here to Mexico, our next-door neighbor. That is the way it repaid us in return for The Associated Press permitting it to operate here under our roof.

"The United Press went into South America before we did. We refrained because of our agency connection. When finally we got into South America the United Press had done a good deal in the matter of exploiting North American newspaper and press association methods.

"The Associated Press built there with the best Associated Press principles, and those principles were accepted in South America—the principles of co-operation—but we never have been able to explain why Havas, of which they had such a poor opinion down there, held us back, and it is to this that we have been addressing ourselves. We got a temporary adjustment by which we could begin a service.

"But the South American angle is only a very small nibble at a very large cracker. This discreditable presentation of North American news is against our journalistic principles. Havas was and is a pro-French agency. It has discontinued a part of its service, because the French Government has discontinued its subsidy. It may resume it tomorrow and it would then enlarge its service and resume discrediting the United States in South America.

"I contend that the Havas Agency must not take our news and pervert it, that if it serves South America it must go there on its own news, and I contend that ultimately we shall have to come to that with any agency: that in a foreign land, foreign to them and foreign to us, we must each serve our own news and let the character of the news reports determine.

"If this means ultimately breaking with the agencies, I have no fear of it whatever, with the provision that we thoroughly understand in advance just what we are undertaking.

"I want to repeat what I have said several times, that so far as the agencies are concerned, they have no news from their clients in Europe unless they take it from the published newspapers and, to that extent, their method of operation is entirely different from ours. We can take it from the published newspapers there, but so can our competitors, and the day will arrive—I anticipate this and I hope for it—if it can be done with the agencies agreeing, all right, but it must be done—when we must exchange news with some form of a co-operative newspaper organization.

"I do feel that we are none too young and it is none too soon to begin to anticipate the day when the newspapers of France and England will have to adopt the same principles of news exchange that we have in this country, and I do not think there ought to be a proprietary agency that can bar that exchange. If it must be an individual paper and not an association of papers I would rather have one individual newspaper giving us the news before publication than the Havas Agency giving it to us after publication. And I want to discount, as much as I possibly can, the efficiency of the agencies today. They are not efficient. . . .

"But there is much to be done in this foreign field, and I want to approach it cautiously—but I certainly want to approach it vigorously—within our organization, and prepare for the day when a change must come. We cannot go on indefinitely permitting others to misrepresent us abroad. It is claimed Reuters misrepresents us in Japan. I have never been in Japan. I have been in South America, and I know that the best newspapers in South America are convinced that Havas did misrepresent us for fifty-five years, because they say to us down there, 'Now you send the good and the bad news. We used only to get the bad.' "

"I am in hearty accord with what Mr. Cooper said," Mr. Ochs commented: "the Havas Agency would find it more important to have a connection with The Associated Press than The Associated Press with Havas. It is the greatest asset that they have in France, and the French Government would never have them break their connection with The Associated Press. So I don't feel that severance of relationship is a danger. The situation in South America is an intolerable one."

The solution ultimately was found—but not for several years.

XIV

In the Western Pacific

AT THE earnest solicitation of the Board of Directors Mr. Noyes went to Japan and China in 1922 to learn the status of news agency matters in that part of the world. The director who was probably the happiest because Mr. Noyes undertook the mission was Mr. McClatchy, who had joined earnestly in support of the proposals that the The Associated Press extend its service to South America and to Europe. He gave this preference in spite of the fact that his prime interest was in the extension of the service into Japan.

Curiously enough, it was the revolt against the overlordship of Reuters in the Western Pacific that was the indirect though not the immediate cause of the ultimate approach to a definite break between The Associated Press and Reuters. The clash that almost led to the break was practically inevitable anyway, but developments in Japan gave impetus to the movement for the removal of restrictions upon The Associated Press in the foreign field.

Prior to Mr. Noyes's departure on the trip across the Pacific, Director McClatchy expressed himself vigorously:

"There is a situation in Japan and China which in my judgment calls for most serious consideration by the board. We have had for many years in the Western Pacific the most undesirable reputation as a news association. You cannot communicate with any newspaperman or Chinese, Japanese, English or American, who is familiar with the facts, who does not say in straightforward language, if he speaks his sincere convictions, that The Associated Press continuously misrepresents the news of the Western Pacific."

Now that was strong language, especially as coming from a member of the board. However, it was a fair exemplification of the fact that The Associated Press is its own severest critic, as its annual and state meetings constantly demonstrate.

It should be said, however, that Mr. McClatchy was charging the organization not with deliberate misrepresentation but with allowing itself to be made the victim of designing people. What he brought out in effect, through testimony in the form of letters, was the allegation that The Associated Press got much of its Japanese and Chinese news from Reuters and, as one writer put it, that Reuters in turn bought "ninety per cent of its stuff from the Kokusai Agency, the Japanese agency controlled by the Japanese Government."

"In other words," erroneously wrote this informant, "there is no cable news from Japan and China that gets to the United States without going through Japanese hands and influence, and it is all garbled."

Mr. McClatchy also called attention "to the fact that at this time we are being very seriously injured" by the way in which The Associated Press report, as carried through the mediumship of Reuters, was being handled by Kokusai. Of the operations of Kokusai he declared:

"For years now it has been deliberately misrepresenting news and spreading propaganda throughout the Western Pacific, not only Japan but throughout the Western Pacific generally, for the express and manifest purpose of injuring the interests of this country and bettering the credit of Japan."

Mr. McClatchy was reminded very quickly that his informant was wrong in saying The Associated Press got all its Western Pacific news from Reuters. As a matter of fact, The Associated Press maintained bureaus in Tokyo and Peking and had representatives elsewhere. However, it was equally true that it was mainly dependent upon Reuters, because the Reuters domination of the Western Pacific under contractual relations precluded The Associated Press making any arrangement for a free exchange of news. The fundamental basis of his argument thus remained firm.

"One reason that I am bringing this matter to your attention now," he said, "is that I regard an arrangement with Reuters, which would prevent us from convincing the people of the Western Pacific that The Associated Press is a fair and decent and reputable and unprejudiced news association, would be most unwise.

"You know from statements that have been made before you that Japan has thorough control of the incoming and outgoing news of Japan. They get that through an arrangement made with Reuters many years ago.

"You know from statements that are before you that Japan has endeavored to capture supreme control of the news of China in various ways—by establishing a news agency of its own; by controlling the vernacular press; by selling the news service at a low rate to all Chinese papers that would take it.

"You know that the American Government, in order to protect itself from that sort of Japanese propaganda during the war, did the extraordinary thing of establishing a news service in China, and distributing to nearly three hundred vernacular papers a report sent over the wireless.

"Now briefly that is the situation that I present to you. The American interests over there, the standing of The Associated Press, the prestige of The Associated Press and its reputation are at stake.

"I realize fully the value to this association of the Reuter service and of the Havas service for world news, but I submit that the conditions over in the Western Pacific supply an additional reason why we should not so tie ourselves up with Reuters that we may not be able to secure news through interchange."

Mr. Stone gave Director McClatchy some support with this:

"Now you have said—and you have said correctly—that Japan controls both the outgoing and the incoming news. That is perfectly true."

"I feel," said Mr. McClatchy, "that the interest of the association and more particularly the interest of this country demand a free and practically uncensored news communication between this country and the Western Pacific; necessary protection for the interest of our country; necessary protection for the interest of The Associated Press; necessary protection for the interest of our members.

"We want fair statements of the news of China and Japan, as well as the distribution over there of a fair statement of current news here. I feel that it is not practicable to secure entirely a free hand through the distribution of our news by Reuters. And I make no criticism of Reuters for that.

"Reuters represents in a measure—and particularly at times of crisis—the British Government, the British Empire, and very properly looks after their interests, and it would not be to the interest of the empire to have certain news distributed over there at certain times, although it would be correct and would represent the facts.

"Within the past two months I have seen specific instances of the failure of Reuters to distribute throughout China portions of The Associated Press report which were sent by wireless to Manila and from there broadcast and received by Reuters in Shanghai. These specific instances were such as in the judgment of Reuters it was not to the interest of the British Empire to have circulated in China. As a member of The Associated Press and as an American citizen—I want to insure the distribution in China and the Western Pacific of a fair representation of The Associated Press report. That is what I want.

"My suggestion is that through some kind of a friendly relation with Reuters, we have something of a free hand in the Western Pacific such as we have in South America."

"I would say," Mr. Noyes began, "that the ideal ultimate solution that we would be working for would be a gathering of associations such as The Associated Press throughout the world, and interchange arrangements between them, exactly as we have with Canada.

"I have been approaching the matter with Houssaye and Sir Roderick Jones, on the theory that we had no desire to establish an organization of the world in news distribution, but that we wanted to arrange so that we could come into closer contact with Italy and Spain and Norway and Sweden and Czechoslovakia and Russia than through the three agencies, that our desire was to get into immediate connection with them. We did not care how they divided up their balance of power as between themselves but what we want is to be able to get the news out of these countries for ourselves."

"Mr. President," Mr. McClatchy said, "this situation seems to me to have clarified itself now. My suggestion all along has been that if it could be done with propriety, an adjustment and modification of the Reuters contract be made, so that if it seemed desirable some interchange of news could be had with China through some organizations over there. Now then, the president tells us that he is attempting precisely that sort of an arrangement, not with regard to China but with regard to all the world. That is all I urge."

Again, this time respecting countries in the Western Pacific, The Associated Press board heard a charge as to the operation of the principal agency with which it was allied. Again it heard recited another charge of the insistent policy of governments or outside business interests to foster and control the dissemination of news.

In the United States the press has controlled its own

affairs, with the result that it is not only the strongest press in any country in the world, but the people of the United States are better informed and more accurately enlightened. Left to its own ingenuity as here the press does its greatest service. Curbed or made to say what its own government or some foreign news agency source makes it say, it sadly fails to fulfill its mission. No wonder that I want to see American news standards recognized and understood to the fullest.

Again no formal action was taken to correct the general situation with the news agencies. But the program of The Associated Press to secure international freedom of the press was given a decided fillip by this discussion.

XV

Without Government Influence

THE fall of 1925 saw a decided hardening of The Associated Press policy toward the overlordship of the European agencies and the organization was ready to request a revision of the four-party alliance. I had become general manager in April of that year. The question of changing the allied agency contracts continually cropped up. Mr. Noyes was always receptive to any discussion of the matter. Mr. Ochs, with whom I had discussed my dreams and who frequently accepted my views, voiced the idea at least twice that a free press would foster peace. The first time he said:

"I don't think The Associated Press could do any greater service for the peace of the world than to encourage and develop agencies that would cover the news of the world, and that would not be under the domination of privately owned corporations."

The second time he said:

"I don't know any larger contribution we could make to the peace of the world than to have a free circulation of the news—free from the influence of the governments."

It is significant that these statements were made at a

time when The Associated Press campaign for rights abroad was taking on fresh momentum. Moreover, they were made just after I had been made general manager. This title was a better entree to the closed doors of the European agencies. For the first time it definitely fixed my position as a negotiator. Sir Roderick Jones was among the first to congratulate me, as "the worthy successor to Melville Stone."

The relations I had with Charles Houssaye, of Havas, had grown mutually cordial. Houssaye seemed never to tire hearing me talk about my practical ideals on the press. It was, he would say, a complete mental vacation from his own stressful work in keeping Havas like it always had been and as far as he was concerned like it always would be.

"When you shall have changed French temperament, my friend," he said to me one day, "you still cannot change Havas. When you change the French Republic to something else, you still cannot change Havas. Nothing can change Havas. Come war, come peace, Havas will be the same!" It did indeed not change. It just disappeared during the German occupation in 1940. And Charles Houssaye died while that occupation was still in force.

Poor Charles Houssaye! Gravely wounded in the first World War, and devoutly determined to apply every ounce of his energy and ability to hold Germany down in a news agency way after that war so that she could never rise again, he must have died of a broken heart. He did his part in establishing the "cordon sanitaire" of news agencies around Germany and he lived to see it all break down.

Since it was impossible for me to get word from him after Germany invaded France in 1940, I don't know what were his thoughts until his death two years later— a few months after Havas itself was no more. Perhaps had he lived in a resurgent France he might have helped in another way this time to make a more lasting peace. And then again, perhaps not.

At any rate I felt, having assumed the general managership, that I could count upon Charles Houssaye's friendly co-operation in the matter of modernizing the agency relationship. Havas had already conceded the most important thing it could concede to The Associated Press—a free hand in South America. Reuters had conceded nothing.

I thought that Reuters, being managed by an Englishman whose home country knew what a free press was, should not, if pressed, stand in the way of the reasonable ambitions of The Associated Press to extend its service to countries where it was wanted. I, therefore, said "that the agency relationship as it stood should be modernized because the present situation is not one of dignity for The Associated Press."

One thing that particularly concerned me, I said, was that The Associated Press had no direct communication whatever with the small foreign agencies which were in alliance with Reuters, Havas and Wolff. The only relations between The Associated Press and these little agencies had been by sufferance of the big three, and I maintained that The Associated Press ought to have more direct contact with them.

President Noyes cited the case of Kokusai, the Japanese agency, which had desired to make a direct connection with The Associated Press but was fearful of a break with Reuters, despite encouragement from The Associated Press.

"The truth was," said Mr. Noyes, "that Reuters was
in there and Kokusai wanted to get Reuters out, but
they apparently thought that it was better to deal with
Reuters than to deal with us. Both Count Aisuke Kabayama, president of the Kokusai Association, and Iwanaga, manager of it, talked to me. I went so far, I am
sure, when I visited there a few years ago as I could go
in propriety in suggesting the desirability of their connection being with the United States and with The Associated Press, and that if this was their desire and if they
would make that clear to Reuters, so that it would be
something not of our initiative, I would be very glad to
take it up with Reuters myself.

"I have told Sir Roderick Jones in conversations a
number of times that, so far as I was concerned, I felt
there could be no possible reason why The Associated
Press should not have a direct connection with Japan
and that frankly it was my hope that something of the
kind would be brought about.

"I told him that it was my own theory, and the principle that we followed, of allowing each country to manage its own affairs; that we did not wish to deal in Asia,
for instance, as being a subject country; that we did not
look on Japan or on China as being in the category of
subject countries to any other agency; that it was just as
in South America, where we refused to recognize Havas's
overlordship; that so far as we were concerned, we had
no desire to sell news to anyone in any country but that
we did desire to have an interchange.

"I said that we would like to see the same thing in

Japan as had been done in South America, and that there would be nothing revolutionary in indicating to Reuters that the time had come when we wanted to deal directly with these countries. I added that we are concerned in countries where there is now an overlordship and that we propose to exercise freedom of action and insist on establishing a situation such as we have in South America.

"I have never had any difficulty myself with Sir Roderick in making myself entirely clear to him. He said he hoped we would not come to that, but that he recognized the apparent possibility of it."

It was further brought out that there were important individuals in France who were anxious to organize responsible newspapers for an exchange of news with The Associated Press.

"There is no question," said President Noyes, "but that the powerful newspapers in France are very much at outs with Havas. They regard Havas as an advertising agency, and as a publicity concern subsidized by the government."

The upshot of this debate was that the board adopted a resolution requesting President Noyes, in view of the unsatisfactory general situation as regards the allied agencies, to study the question with a view to bringing relations into line with present conditions.

What amounted to a continuation of this session of the board came on January 29, 1926, some three months later. This second meeting was the one in which I spoke more definitely than I ever had before, and I did so at the request of Mr. Noyes. A prelude was President

Noyes's statement that Reuters had been bought by the British Press Association.

"The Press Association of England," he said, "has taken over Reuters, in a technical sense, but Sir Roderick Jones remains in charge of the organization. The Press Association does not include the London papers. I had the hope when the first announcement came that it did include the London papers and that this would make easy something we had been trying to accomplish for some time, and that was to get access to the news of the London papers."

The Associated Press relations with the Press Association always had been through Reuters. With the amalgamation between Reuters (the foreign agency) and the Press Association (the domestic agency) there appeared some hope that The Associated Press might get access to at least the provincial English papers, but this had not materialized.

The debate made it clear that Mr. Noyes and I were as one in respect to a desire to deal directly with newspapers in foreign countries, so as to secure an exchange of news. There was, however, some difference of opinion as to the methods to be employed in achieving this. In short, I was for direct and vigorous action whereas Mr. Noyes did not wish to take any step which might produce a violent rupture in the relations between The Associated Press and the "big three."

Mr. Noyes truly believed that access to their news was absolutely necessary to The Associated Press, though he wanted them to give us the freedom of action we sought. I did not believe their news was important enough to The Associated Press for it to continue with its hands tied while our competitor was free to take to the world the principles of news treatment which The Associated Press had established as the press association code of ethics in the United States.

XVI

A Great President

"IT HAS been perfectly evident," said Mr. Noyes on that occasion, "that Mr. Cooper has an idea of a very much more sweeping revision of our relations than I have had in contemplation, and that in writing to me and speaking to me there has always been an indication that his personal view was one of a good deal more radical tendency than mine was in the matter. He has also made it clear that he felt there was some loyalty due to me in my personal views and that he thought he should not press his views before the Board in opposition to mine."

"I have come to the conclusion that it will be absolutely necessary for me to ask Mr. Cooper to make clear to the board exactly what his recommendations are, because if the board desires some other course to be followed than what I naturally would follow, I want to be advised of it.

"If there should be the most radical difference between Mr. Cooper and myself as to the treatment of this subject, I think the board is all the more entitled to have the benefit of the general manager's advice as to what this difference is and what ought to be done in the matter, and so I want to say that I do not want Mr. Cooper to withhold from the board any thought which he has on this subject, on account of any supposed deference that he is paying to any view that I have."

If Mr. Noyes had no other trait to admire, his great character was unintentionally disclosed in the quotation just cited. I have never known a more broad-minded concept of a position of trust in a co-operative institution than he showed while president of The Associated Press. Always he wanted anyone who had a view to give it to the entire board—not to him alone, no matter how violently opposite it might be to the view he held. He fully recognized that the by-laws of The Associated Press gave all authority to the board and that the president's intervention in Associated Press matters was always "subject to the direction of the Board."

Nevertheless, in such a long experience in the presidency he could have superseded the board in its prerogatives and taken authority unto himself to act or decide matters without the board ever objecting. He never did so. His policy of bringing to the consideration of any matter the thoughtful judgment of all his fellow directors had the effect of avoiding the creation of a dictatorship in this great co-operative. He kept it co-operative and it was successful during the years he was president. All of which in this instance refutes the claims that no co-operative can be successful unless it is headed by an individual who assumes dictatorial powers.

"Mr. Noyes," said Director W. H. Cowles, "just pursuing this thing to get your view, is it the fact that we want to try and get in the first place direct communication with the news service of each country rather than going at those countries through Reuters?"

"If we had an agreement with the allied agencies," Mr. Noyes replied, "that gave us the right to make exchange arrangements with the newspapers in these various countries, it is immaterial to me whether our relation is direct to them. I will say what I did not say a little while ago, that so far as Japan and the countries that are outside of the European sphere are concerned, I have not made any secret with Sir Roderick Jones or any of them that I do not consider that there is any proper overlordship of Reuters or Havas in countries that are foreign and alien to each of us.

"Mr. Cooper attaches a great deal of importance to direct contractual relations between The Associated Press and the Polish agency, or the Spanish agency, or the Italian agency. Now my own theory is that if they choose to group themselves together as they have with an overlordship, that this is of very little importance to us provided we have the right in those countries to have full access to their news and to be able to make exchange arrangements with the newspapers in those countries.

"It is what we want to do after we have the right that I think is important, and not the question as to whether we have an independent arrangement with each of them. I am not desiring to argue the question at all. I simply want to urge that Mr. Cooper state perfectly frankly to the board any view he has which he thinks is for the good of The Associated Press in our relations with the gathering of foreign news, without any thought that there is any offense on my part if it is a view that is entirely opposed to a view that I have expressed."

"All right," I said, "I will make it as brief as I can. I must say it is partially a personal statement."

My memory of this moment in my quest for liberty of action is that I felt I had reached the crisis. I wondered whether I had better speak with restraint or open the floodgates and speak of my convictions with finality. Mr. Stone was not present. He had retired with the title of counselor, but he was not at all active. Nevertheless, I thought of him and his convictions. I also knew, as Mr. Noyes had indicated, that my ideas seemed radical to Mr. Noyes. I came to the conclusion quickly that a radical attack on the problem would retard favorable action. I decided to speak with restraint. "It must be," I had said, "partially a personal statement."

"Several years ago I saw no future in The Associated Press for myself unless I could evolve something of an unusual character and when I went to Europe in 1919 I became fascinated with the idea that there was an opportunity to put the leaven of Associated Press idealism into operation in Europe.

"I came back and talked to Mr. Stone about it and told him I thought the crowning event of his life could be something of that kind: that as the dean of American journalism he could go over and sow the seed.

"I also talked to Mr. Noyes and told him I would be willing to give the rest of my life to it—that I would undertake to learn French to do it, because that would be very necessary. I had learned one language for The Associated Press, but I would learn another. So as we went along with this thing a greater opportunity in The Associated Press came to me and I became general manager, and I considered that there was a very active and large field which I could occupy accordingly.

"It may have been presumptuous, but I urged upon the board last October that they impress upon the president their interest in the allied agency matter and leave it entirely to him. And since then I have thought nothing of it, except that I expressed to Mr. Noyes my own thoughts about it, but I did not want to come to the board with a disagreement of my own with Mr. Noyes. That is a personal statement. You have told me to be entirely frank. If it is your desire now, all right.

"It is this: That I feel that either we are right or we are wrong in this country as to our methods in obtaining from our members before publication the news we deliver to other members. If we are right, I wanted to impress that upon the foreign agencies as to what they should do, with all the weight and force that we could possibly muster.

"Also, I went farther as to the ethics, that no overlordship in England should be over any other country, even though Reuters, for instance, owns the Dutch agency; that for respectability The Associated Press should ask to deal directly with the Dutch agency rather than with an individual at London, and that if the newspapers served by the Dutch agency wanted true, unbiased news of The Associated Press as to what goes on all over the world they should have it. And if we asked to do that it would at least acquaint Reuters with our idea of the proprieties in our international relations as to news.

"I thought that anything that we left out of the situation in that way would put us in the position of being smugly self-satisfied with the agency situation in Europe. I had the hope—I am frank—that I could talk to these people and get the leaven of our own ideas, which plainly are more efficient than theirs, into their minds and carry this allied agency relationship into an effectiveness where it would be worth something to us, attending their meetings and inviting them to have their meetings here, and letting them see the imposing operations of this organization and learn its principles.

"And, after all, my plan and my thought was one of mutual progress toward the light. Now, the other view of that is that we should not be ambitious—that we should be satisfied with what we have. We could be if we want to continue to stay in our shell, except that our competition, in this country, is bound in no such way. It goes up and down the world doing as it likes. We have seen it in various ways.

"And we go as far as we can until we are up against this stone wall of the agencies, which we meet then face to face, with no previous kindly consideration by them of our situation or by us of theirs. I do not think there is any of the leaven that I speak of in that. They do not know what our viewpoint is. They do not know my thought in the matter, for example.

"Now I have expressed the feeling that there is a way, and a proper way, to bring the entire situation to one of harmonious accord and effectiveness where the agencies would really be allied to us. You tell me I am hostile to the agencies, whereas I feel I have a very broad and kindly feeling toward the agencies. But I feel that we have got something so much better than theirs that it is really unkind not to acquaint them with these facts.

"With that I would like to leave it."

"In a nutshell," said Mr. Ochs, "the proposition is that Reuters controls these agencies and we deal through Reuters with the agencies, and what you have in mind is to deal more directly with the subordinates of the Reuters Agency so that you would be more in contact with them."

"In order to reach the newspapers," I said. "Our relationship with Spain should take on the flavor of Spain rather than the flavor of London or Paris. I would consider it an unfinished piece of business until we did get the news of the newspapers for publication. I would put pressure and all the activity I could put into it to do that, because there is the real advantage. Anybody can take the news from the newspapers after they are published. We prosper because we get it before it is published."

"But, of course, to do that," said Mr. Noyes, "you have got to get the consent under our present arrangement, first of the agencies—whether of the three allied agencies or of all the agencies—if it is preferable to deal with twenty-nine instead of with three. We have got to get their consent, and then after that we have got to get the consent of the newspapers themselves, because none of these organizations has any power whatever over the newspapers."

"I would carry it to the point," I said, "that if the agencies cannot do it, we can for our own purposes."

"There is no question," said Mr. Noyes, "so far as I know, as to the desire. Everybody in interest with this board feels that we desire to have the opportunity to make exchange arrangements with the individual news-

papers to get news for ourselves and in exchange to offer
to give them news that we have got over there, or to give
them access to news over here, and to do that we have
got to get the consent of the allied agencies."

"Why not pursue that," said Mr. Ochs, "and see what
obstacle we run across and then we can cross that bridge
when we come to it."

"There is no question," replied Mr. Noyes, "but that
to do it in an orderly way we should give them notice of
the termination of our present arrangement."

"Is that necessary?" asked Mr. Ochs.

"It will run without being changed unless you give
notification," replied Mr. Noyes. "But I have got the
idea that Mr. Cooper will be insistent, from the point of
view of The Associated Press, on the dissolution practically of their present grouping. That is, so far as we were
concerned, they would have to cease their present grouping and each deal with us separately."

"But I don't understand," said Mr. Ochs. "Is it urged
that this be done yet?"

"It is very desirable."

This last sentence was mine. What I was driving at
was, as Mr. Noyes thought, a redetermination of matters
that would let in the leaven of The Associated Press
ideals, with more freedom, no profit and a more generous attitude each to the others. I had seen all of the
Reuters overlordship that I wanted to see.

Also I had observed the methods of all the agencies
abroad. They were extremely antiquated and they were
slow in action. In the United States delivering the news
is always as nearly as possible simultaneous with obtaining it. The action is fast, for speed is an element of the

operation that is always stressed. Not so in Europe, where at that time, lacking even typewriters, leased wires and adequate telephone facilities, the agencies were being thrown into confusion by the rapid methods used by the United Press. And on top of this speed was our competitor's application of our ethical principle that news from everywhere must be true and unbiased.

European governments could still influence how the local agencies told the news of neighboring or distant countries but to have it come directly from those countries to the newspapers from an American news agency was something that not even Fascist Italy, where the United Press was doing it, seemed to want to try to stop. Thus the position of the agencies allied to The Associated Press was pitiful. Some of the smaller ones wanted The Associated Press to come to their aid but their contracts with Reuters and Havas forbade! They could not save themselves.

"There is another question involved that is much bigger," Mr. Ochs resumed, "and I have no doubt that Mr. Cooper has got it in the back of his head that these agencies are entirely inconsistent with the spirit and purpose of The Associated Press. They are privately owned and are simply propagandists for governments and under their influence.

"The Associated Press would like, if possible, to secure its news from all sources direct and free from that contamination and association. Whether we are quite prepared to have to go beyond the organization now controlling the news sources is another question.

"I believe a step forward would be, possibly, to get in contact with local papers by consent of the agencies now controlling their news service, and then to go a little

slow. It could not be done suddenly. We are quite un-
prepared to enter into these foreign countries while
there are forty or fifty different agencies perhaps and endeavor to get service from them."

"Mr. Ochs," I said, "the difficulty is this: If Wolff, for
instance, could decide this question without having to
get Reuters's consent, it would be an entirely different
matter, but everybody waits upon Reuters—Wolff,
Havas and everybody. Reuters stands as the dominator
of the news of the world so far as the agencies are concerned. I do not want The Associated Press to be under
that domination.

"The Associated Press is one of those that contribute
money to Reuters when there is a sufficient quid pro quo
in the value of our service. The whole situation is one
where the world control of news rests with Reuters
today, and if Wolff could deal directly with The Associated Press, and if Kokusai could deal directly with The
Associated Press, they would do it, because I know they
would prefer to deal directly."

"I agree with Mr. Cooper," said Mr. Ochs, "that we
should move for having our news free. The fact is that
Reuters does control or dominate the news of the agencies throughout the world. . . . It seems to me the best
plan is to go ahead under our existing contract and first
to get the news ourselves and as to the future relations
let them develop when the gathering of our news is interfered with."

The discussion of the board developed along the line
of Reuters control of the small agencies, and their inability to make contracts without permission of the British concern. I finally interposed with this:

"Well, my point, gentlemen, is this: That Reuters with one hand holds back The Associated Press from getting news it wants in the way it wants to get it, and with the other holds Wolff and all the rest of them to what Reuters wants them to do and exacts so much money from them that they cannot afford to develop for them selves the local news which we want. Their managing directors have told me so.

"That is what happened in Japan and in Germany, and it is happening all over the world. Reuters is a vast, profitable institution by doing that, and it is making the dependent agencies struggle for their very existence in order to pay Reuters what it must have to make it a profitable institution."

I did not then disclose the developments in Japan because I had not sufficient information on which to make a presentation. I had been told of what had been happening in Japan since Sir Roderick Jones made his visit there after calling upon The Associated Press in New York in 1920. In the ensuing months I learned considerable about it.

Japan furnished an excellent example of the policy of the Reuters management. As a result of Sir Roderick Jones's first visit there the Japanese press resolved that it would have to appeal to The Associated Press.

XVII

Nippon Shimbun Rengo

WITH the studied thoroughness with which he analyzed any subject, Mr. Noyes obtained in China and Japan a true picture of matters in 1922. For instance, he found no member of the Japanese Government who had any interest in receiving American news, or indeed any foreign news.

"As a matter of fact," he said, "while I came into contact with a very large number of Japanese men of prominence I think none of them had this in mind in any way. On the other hand, I found that many of these same men were greatly interested in the export of news from Japan, and in this I think Japan, its government officials and its leading men in private life, do not differ from other civilized nations, including our own. Every government with which I have come into contact wants to acquaint the rest of the world with its merits and is primarily interested in the export and not the receipt of news.

"The group of Japanese who own the stock of the Kokusai News Agency are businessmen of high standing who I think are actuated by a natural desire to have the premier news-gathering organization of the country in

Japanese hands. There is apparently a purpose to make it as distinctively a Japanese organization as Havas is French or Reuters British. The relation of the government to the business interests generally is extraordinarily close, but I received the impression that it was only a question of time when the larger newspapers themselves would take over the functions of Kokusai, probably in an organization on the lines of The Associated Press and this with the cordial acquiescence of the stockholders of Kokusai."

Mr. Noyes reported matters to the Board of Directors in great detail. But my own conception of the value of his visit was not in what he learned but in what he taught. He had expounded in high places the principles on which The Associated Press operates and what he said there had a lasting influence.

The Japanese had within a space of two years met and discussed matters with the managing director of Reuters and with the president of The Associated Press. The visit of the managing director of Reuters was to clinch the Reuters News Agency hold on Japan and China. The visit of the president of The Associated Press was for the purpose of obtaining information. He also eloquently portrayed the moral concept of news presentation as it has been developed by American news agencies.

There was one Japanese, however, whom both men met while in Japan. This was Mr. Yukichi Iwanaga, who until shortly before Mr. Noyes's visit had no public connection with the Kokusai News Agency. He did, however, as he told me several years afterward, observe with interest the differing approaches of Sir Roderick and Mr. Noyes.

So interested did Mr. Iwanaga become in what Mr. Noyes said as to the principles of The Associated Press in not seeking any selfish advantage and in endeavoring to portray truthfully, without bias, the points of view of all governments, and without any American government direction, that he later decided to undertake their adoption by the management of Kokusai.

It should be remembered that up to 1914 Reuters had been the only news agency in Japan. Japanese businessmen, more than Japanese newspapermen, became convinced that the British Reuters News Agency should not be the national news agency of Japan.

The Japanese Government apparently had given the matter no consideration. Japanese diplomats abroad had made no protestations of the anomaly by which Reuters presented Japanese news to the world and the news of the world to Japan. It was, therefore, Japanese businessmen who took the matter in charge. Reuters was approached to see what arrangement could be made by which Japan would have its own national news agency with a Japanese name.

The story, as it was afterward told to me in Japan, was that Reuters set an evaluation of what were called its "franchise rights" to Japan. The Japanese conception of what these "franchise rights" really were was vague, but they were led to believe that they stemmed from the fact that all the other news agencies of the world, which were linked with Reuters, had conceded to Reuters exclusive rights to the commercial sale of news in Japan.

The Japanese never clearly understood this, but thoroughly understood that in order to receive the Reuters news and to have Reuters vacate Japan in perpetuity, they would have to pay Reuters a principal amount which represented the Reuters appraisal of its "franchise rights" in Japan, and additionally they would have to pay Reuters a service charge for the right to receive Reuters news for use in Japan. The service charge was to be named by Reuters and was to be accepted by the Japanese, as was the payment of the principal. A deal on these lines was consummated, Reuters probably feeling that the principal amount specified was in payment of its Japanese business. Again Sir Roderick Jones had arranged that Reuters, selling its Japanese business and continuing the service charge, ate its cake and had it, too.

Backed by Japanese businessmen, who put up the money, Kokusai came into being with a British-born, naturalized American, J. Russell Kennedy, as managing director. As no Japanese at the time ever had had any world news agency experience, Kokusai also retained for a while some of the British employees who had previously worked for Reuters in Japan. When some time later Mr. Iwanaga took charge, he felt that the Japanese agency should be Japanese and that its policy of approach to the world should be upon the high principles which Mr. Noyes had delineated.

Mr. Iwanaga became an ardent admirer of The Associated Press when he came to the United States shortly after taking over the management of Kokusai. He was, until his death in 1939, one of the really great men of Japan and he became enthused with a determination to raise the standards of the press in his country. Indeed, he spent a large part of his very considerable private fortune in this effort. He was of the Japanese school which

believed that Japan could make its way in the world
without military aggression, and he had an unquench-
able thirst for knowledge and acquirement by the press
of Japan of the high moral concept of the American
press in respect to unbiased news. He was an uncle of
Hiroshi Saito, the Japanese ambassador who died in
Washington in 1939. The family of which both were
members were not adherents to the military party which
was rapidly taking over control in that country. President Roosevelt recognized that fact and bestowed the
highest post-mortem honor he could on Saito by sending
his ashes home to Japan aboard an American cruiser.

Iwanaga was not, however, the first news agency man
from Japan I met personally. Before Mr. Iwanaga came
to New York in 1925 I had a visit from Mr. Mitsunaga,
president and principal owner of Nippon Dempo, which
had become a vigorous competitor of Kokusai and received a small budget of world news from the United
Press. Mr. Mitsunaga was not satisfied and he wanted to
make a contract with The Associated Press. I told him it
was not possible at that time, but that an arrangement
for an exchange of news might be effected if he was in
no great hurry. I had in mind the length of time it had
taken for The Associated Press to negotiate a free hand
with Havas as to South America.

Mr. Mitsunaga said he wanted The Associated Press
connection more than anything, but that unless something could be done at once he was confronted with no
other alternative than to make a perpetual, or at least a
very long-time, contract with the United Press. Otherwise, he said, the United Press had indicated it was going
to begin a service itself directly with Japanese news-

papers. As it undoubtedly had been the efficiency of the United Press service that had launched Mr. Mitsunaga's Nippon Dempo agency upon a successful career, he felt that Nippon Dempo while morally obligated to continue the United Press was also at its mercy unless it could by a quick stroke displace the United Press with The Associated Press.

He left my office and went to the United Press offices and there made the contract which bound Nippon Dempo to the United Press until several years later Domei became the only Japanese news agency permitted to operate in Japan, permanently displacing not only Nippon Dempo but all other Japanese agencies.

When Mr. Iwanaga came to me there began a friendship which, because of our mutual adherence to the principle of a free press and freedom of international news exchange without governmental control, lasted until Iwanaga's death. I introduced him to Mr. Stone, who spent several hours with him advancing the idea that Japan should have a co-operative news service owned by the newspapers.

Iwanaga never forgot that talk with Mr. Stone. As a result he and I later talked of the formation of "The Associated Press of Japan" and for the first time that I had heard it, he gave me what the name would be in Japanese —Nippon Shimbun Rengo. Shortly after his return to Japan I received an announcement that Nippon Shimbun Rengo had been organized as a co-operative news association in succession to Kokusai, which had been dissolved.

On April 26, 1926, The Associated Press cabled this explanatory news dispatch from the Japanese capital:

"Dissolution of Kokusai, Japan's national news agency, and the formation of a new non-profit, mutual news association, similar to The Associated Press in America, was announced today following a meeting of representatives of the empire's largest vernacular newspapers.

"The Japanese name of the new association is the Nippon Shimbun Rengo which, translated into English, is 'The Associated Press of Japan.' Eight newspapers, having 75 per cent of the total newspaper circulation of Japan, compose the charter membership.

"Yukichi Iwanaga, who has been managing director of Kokusai, was elected to a similar position in the new organization. Regarding the plans of the association, Director Iwanaga said:

" 'We wish to follow as far as possible the general idea of The Associated Press of America, which undoubtedly is the greatest news organization in the world today. Owing to the peculiar conditions in Japan, however, we cannot hope for attainment of this ideal for some time to come.

" 'The newspapers of Japan want their news unbiased and uncolored, and it is believed that only through a mutual non-profit arrangement can such news be exchanged. It will also mean, eventually, a tremendous saving of money in news gathering.' "

On the same date a great Osaka newspaper, *Mainichi,* printed an editorial which said in part:

"It is welcome news that a national agency under the name of The Associated Press of Japan has been organized under the joint enterprise of eight of the greatest newspapers of this country. We have long cherished the hope that a truly national news agency, such as exists in

Europe and America, would also be established in Japan, not as a commercial enterprise as our news agencies have generally been, but as a non-commercial, cooperative association similar to The Associated Press of America, the most ideal organization for this sort of news service.

"The birth of the new organization, The Associated Press of Japan, most decidedly opens a new era in the history of Japanese journalism, as Japan will henceforth have a strong news agency with so many powerful newspapers of the country as its associated members—the real suppliers as well as consumers of the news collected and distributed throughout the world. It is our expectation that the newly organized agency will prove to be one of the most powerful agencies of the whole world. Japanese news will find better and wider circulation all over the world and the foreign news will be supplied to the Japanese press in a far better way than before, and this to the benefit of millions of readers of the papers that use this service."

Rengo under the Reuter ban could make no contract with The Associated Press. The relationship legally was still necessarily under the aegis of Reuters. But from that time forward until Rengo was absorbed by Domei as was Nippon Dempo, the idealistic aspirations of Rengo were joined with the idealistic aspirations of The Associated Press in the matter of foreign news exchange.

Those principles were held impractical in the onrush of Japan to a destiny that was sought by force of arms. The leaven of idealism had too little time to work. That it was given a chance, however, was due in the first place to Mr. Noyes's trip to Japan. It was because of that trip,

Iwanaga once told me, that Japan looked toward the United States in news agency matters.

Another incident was that the Australian press approached The Associated Press with an earnest request that Associated Press service be made available to Australian newspapers in competition with Reuters. The appeal could not be consummated, what with Reuters in complete control of news dissemination in the British Empire.

There was, however, established there The Associated Press of Australia, owned by Australian newspapers. They merely took the name of The Associated Press, in compliment to the world's oldest news agency, just as the newspapers of New Zealand had done. Then in India Reuters service went under the name of "The Associated Press of India." Reuters did not begin the use of the name there. A Bengali named K. C. Roy started competition against the Indian News Bureau, which had been surreptitiously financed by Reuters. Roy put up such a good fight that Reuters openly acquired his organization, which he called "The Associated Press of India," as well as the Indian News Bureau, so that since 1911 Reuters has had control in India under the name of The Associated Press of India. Thus, while it carries the name of The Associated Press, it still is Reuters— Reuters-managed and Reuters-owned—and is not an association of the newspapers of India any more than the United Press Associations is a union of the newspapers it serves. The latter is an amalgamation of press associations—the Publishers Press, the Scripps-McRae Association and the Scripps News Association—all of the United States.

Reuters has done very well with the venerable name of The Associated Press in India. Educated leaders like Gandhi, however, know that the original Associated Press is American. But in Australia there was the anomaly that The Associated Press of that country, unable to contract with The Associated Press of America because of Reuters interdiction, made a contract with the United Press. Not until many years later could The Associated Press of Australia also make a contract with The Associated Press of America. It then did so.

After years of consideration, the Board of Directors of The Associated Press voted unanimously in April, 1927, to denounce the four-party treaty—The Associated Press, Reuters, Havas and Wolff—for the purpose of making a new contract.

I was instructed to proceed to Europe to try to get acceptance from the other three of the first basic alteration ever made in this generation-old pact. But I was also cautioned not to bring the negotiations to the point of a break. All I could wish for under these circumstances was that I might suddenly be endowed with tremendous powers of persuasion and that the directors of the great European news agencies would be generous. At least I was going to talk to them about the matter regarding which I had for twelve years argued with Mr. Stone and harangued the directors.

XVIII

"Conference of Press Experts"

THE extent of the solidarity of the twenty-nine agencies that were in the international alliance in 1927 was entirely unknown to me so far as personal investigation and observation were concerned. In preparation for the negotiations with Reuters, Havas and Wolff, I decided to visit as many European capitals as I could to observe the agencies in action. In two and a half months of that summer I went to sixteen European countries. The managers of the agencies in the countries in which I did not visit appeared at the conference of allied agencies held in Warsaw in May. That meeting was a rare opportunity for gaining information on what I did not know and confirmation of what I had been told.

The conference was to have been held earlier in that month, but I was extended an unusual courtesy in that the meeting was postponed until I could get there. Some friends I had made among the directors of the various news agencies were responsible for this. Sir Roderick Jones and my friend, Mr. Houssaye of Havas, felt it very important that they wait for my arrival so that I could observe the solidarity and see the members of the alliance in session.

The visit being my first abroad since I was appointed general manager of The Associated Press, Sir Roderick most graciously invited me to visit him in London en route to Warsaw. He entertained me in a most cordial spirit and gave a lunch for me at Claridge's, which was attended by several members of the British Cabinet including the Foreign Minister, Sir Austen Chamberlain. Several of the great London publishers were there.

On being introduced by Sir Roderick, I refrained from being specific in that company as to my ideas of freedom of international news exchange but I did say that I hoped before the summer was over there would be a liberalization of any fetters that prevented the extension of the institution known as a free press which had bulwarked and strengthened our two great democracies.

At the meeting of the other agencies in Warsaw, Mr. Meynot, one of the directors of the Havas New Agency, presided. He is a linguist. Sir Roderick had the place of honor and was kept fully informed through translation of every important thing said. It was not difficult to observe that Reuters and Havas had the conference very much in hand. The subordination of all the other agencies to Reuters and Havas was marked, although Wolff (now D.N.B.) of Germany figuratively sat on a step of the throne above the rest.

The discussions had practically nothing to do with news availability. No speeches were made about the moralities of news presentation. Practically everything was about traffic arrangements for the transmission of reports, with the greatest stress upon the manner of reception, coding and decoding of the Reuters great commercial service covering market prices throughout the world. It was these commercial services that prospered all of the agencies, even Rengo of Japan being a recipient of Reuters wirelessed market reports.

I had several private discussions respecting the principles of news collection and dissemination and the betterment thereof. I even discussed privately my feeling that there should be greater freedom of action, that there should not be dominance by one or two agencies such as there definitely was. Some seemed fascinated with my ideas in private discussions. Others shrank from them as if I had brought a bomb to the conference. No one wanted me to light the fuse and no one wanted a discussion of idealism in news work included on the agenda.

I gave a dinner to those in attendance, and because there was an important matter pending affecting The Associated Press I spoke only vaguely of putting idealistic principles into effect. The important matter that precluded any positive declaration was the impending negotiations with Reuters, Havas and Wolff, in which I was to represent The Associated Press. That was the big business in hand. After a modern contract had been obtained would be time enough to be specific in my hopes as to international news exchange.

At any rate, as most of the agency representatives were merely direct or indirect employees of Reuters and Havas, it would have done no good even if I had convinced them, unless the managing directors of Reuters and Havas were convinced. I saved my voice and my prayers for the later negotiations with the "big three" which it had been mutually decided would take place later in the summer, preferably at Geneva. Attendance at the Warsaw conference of allied agencies was merely an interlude.

That summer I received an impressive invitation from the League of Nations to attend a "Conference of Press Experts" summoned by the League to meet at Geneva on August 24. The invitation explained:

This conference is called as the result of a resolution adopted in September, 1925, by the Assembly of the League of Nations, which invited the Council to consider whether it was opportune to convene a conference of experts representing the Press of different continents in order:

1. to determine methods of insuring the more rapid and less costly transmission of press news with a view to reducing risks of international misunderstanding, and

2. to discuss all technical problems the settlement of which would be conducive to the tranquillization of public opinion.

This resolution of the Assembly was the subject of an inquiry and of several preliminary meetings during the following months. The preparatory work having been concluded, the Council decided, on the report of the representative of Belgium, at its session last March, to summon a Conference of Press Experts.

The Conference will consist of proprietors of newspapers and agencies. There will also take part in it as assessors, Directors of Government Press Bureaux, the President of the Committee of Journalists which participated in the preparation of the

Conference, and representatives of certain international press organizations.

The essential business of the Conference will be the examining of technical international problems affecting the Press, in the solution of which the organization of the League of Nations might usefully collaborate.

Naturally, as practically all the news agencies of the world had been invited, including three from the United States, together with many publishers of newspapers, and the real intent of the League of Nations being altruistic, attendance there gave an opportunity to speak in terms of practical idealism.

I knew also that anything I said on this score would be supported by the executive heads of the United Press and International News Service of my own country, just as I would support what they would say inasmuch as there has been since 1919 unanimity among American press associations as to the idealism that is the real subject of this story. Though I knew that the three American news agencies would be outnumbered, I felt, as did my American associates, that it was a good place to put our American news principles at work.

We were delighted to find that others in the business from other countries had ideas for the improvement of international news exchange that were in harmony with our own. By way of emphasis we confined the presentation to only two matters: first, the principle of the so-called "property right in news" and, second, to the principle that there be no exclusivity in the availability of news at its source. They were combined in one resolution.

My associates of the European allied agency monopoly were with me on the first, and were prepared to speak favorably. The second proposal bestirred less enthusiasm since the allied agencies long had prospered through their exclusive access to the news of governments, many of them indeed being merely departments of governments. But I still had my American associates besides a few well-wishing friends among the international figures present.

It was at the Geneva sessions that I first found out that the Newspaper Proprietors Association of London was not very happy over the fact that Reuters had been acquired by the Press Association, which I have identified as owned by the British provincial newspapers. Lord Riddell, owner of the *News of the World* of London, and representing the Newspaper Proprietors Association of London at Geneva, spoke with some asperity in opposition to the resolution which I proposed, which read as follows:

"This conference affirms its acceptance of the principle of the property right in news, but emphasizes that there be no property right at the source in official news emanating from governments."

Speaking on the resolution, I said:

"I should like to say that, although this resolution comes from the New World, it comes from an experienced journalist, for I undertake to speak for my illustrious predecessor as general manager of The Associated Press of America, he who today is the recognized dean of American journalism, Mr. Melville E. Stone, now retired. The establishment of the principle was the last great important work of Mr. Stone's active life.

"Newspaperwork is to be pursued upon ethical and practical principles. From an experience of ten years under the practical principles covered by this resolution, we in America can report to you that, apart from the ethics, which are hardly open to dispute, in practice the thing is not only workable but has contributed to the prosperity of every newspaper and news agency in our land. All three of the great news agencies in America operate under this principle, and so does every daily newspaper to the number of over two thousand. In such a fraternity of interest in this common principle journalistic enterprise has under its protection taken on greater ingenuity. In the last ten years journalism has progressed tremendously.

"Finally, let me say that the interest of the League of Nations in this conference, as I understand it, is to promote international understanding through greater international exchange of news. Let me remind you that in the nature of things the international exchange of news on any pretentious and wholesale scale actually is and must be carried on by the news agencies. They cannot properly develop their international work or bring it to the highest point of efficiency unless protected in the expenses which they incur. Given this protection, it is conceivable that any other obstacle can be surmounted, and not only the news agencies but the newspapers of the world will benefit."

Both Sir Roderick Jones and Mr. Meynot, of Havas, seconded the resolution, whereupon Lord Riddell said:

"Mr. President, before dealing with the merits of this question I should like to point out that the position is rather humorous. This resolution has been proposed by an American friend of mine. Now America is the only civilized country that has not yet confirmed or ratified the Berne Convention regarding copyright. The first Berne Convention was passed in 1886 and the second in 1908, but notwithstanding the lapse of time America has always declined to ratify this convention and is, as stated, the only civilized country in the world which has not done so. Therefore, what reason have we for thinking that if this conference commits itself to this proposal, and if the other civilized nations of the world adopt it, that America will do the same. America is not even a member of the League of Nations.

"Of course, I shall be told that in America they already have this law in operation, but that is not the point. The law in operation in America is of a very nebulous character. The question is whether America is prepared, if the conference agrees to this resolution, to adopt the same legislation as will be necessary and as will be adopted in other countries if they ratify these provisions. Well, I am quite sure that my American friends will agree with me that there is no justification whatever for the belief that America will adopt any such resolution by passing the requisite legislation. I have had the pleasure of sitting in conjunction with an American representative, President Wilson, for six months in dealing with certain matters which you are all acquainted with, and, of course, the whole world knows that when President Wilson got back to America, America said: 'No, we are not going to confirm what President Wilson has done, because it is not our policy to enter into an international arrangement of that sort.' That is one humorous branch of this question.

"The other humorous branch of the question is that my friend, Sir Roderick Jones, who seconds this resolution, represents Reuters. Now Reuters is a British company owned chiefly by the British newspapers. Well, the British newspapers who are the controlling shareholders in Reuters have sent me here today to say that they emphatically disagree with the proposals made by Sir Roderick Jones. Well, of course, in other words, the proposer and seconder of this resolution are both tainted in different ways by different disabilities which are of a very serious character when we come to consider a subject of world-wide importance such as this.

"With great skill Mr. Cooper talked in general terms and invoked the ghost of my friend, Mr. Melville Stone, as justifying his procedure here today. Well, of course, that is a common method of argument. When you have not got a very strong case you bring in some great man who was formerly connected with the trade, industry or line of thought involved and you say: 'This great man believes in what I am now propounding; do not examine the merits, but take it on his name.' So far as I am concerned I have a great respect for Mr. Melville Stone, but he is an American too and, of course, there is a tendency at the present time on the part of America to formulate policies for the benefit of benighted Europe and then to walk home and say: 'We have put Europe right but at the same time we are not going to be put right ourselves; let Europe mind their own business.' Well, I admit that a new, energetic and progressive country like America is entitled to take up that line of action, but at the same time, even a worm will turn, and the British worm on this occasion is turning very vigorously."

Lord Riddell, whom I had known during the Peace Conference days in Paris in 1919, gave voice to the great difficulty confronted in an international idealistic approach. I have quoted him thus fully to emphasize the point which was on that occasion brought home to me with considerable force. I was not concerned about anything the Conference of Press Experts did or said but Lord Riddell was a newspaper publisher. I began to see what difficulty there was going to be in opening up the avenues of unimpeded international news exchange, and I even thought that probably before the principles which The Associated Press had accepted as its own could be cultivated and flowered, there might be another world upheaval. But as sparring with my friend Lord Riddell was never anything that I avoided, indeed, it was something I had enjoyed, I was given an opportunity at the meeting next day to comment on his remarks as follows:

"I pass over his lordship's allusion to the presence here of Americans and their offer to bring here their experience. I rather prefer to accept the invitation of the League of Nations as being sincere and, of course, as to Lord Riddell, every conference must have its 'funny man' to provide the humor and Lord Riddell has not failed us on this occasion. But since yesterday he admitted that America is a civilized country—an unusual admission for an English lord to make—I forgive him all.

"As I said yesterday, we have had an experience of ten years with this principle and we sincerely hope that there will be a common ground on which we can meet. Without it I repeat that I see no hope of any pretentious scale of interchange of truthful, international news. If there is no protection afforded the business only those will risk it who have some selfish master who can afford to pay for it—a government, for instance. Private enterprise cannot always compete with a government-subsidized effort.

"I have been asked one question as to what is meant by 'news at its source.' It simply means this: News at the spot where it happens or is disclosed belongs to anyone who is there to get it. My point is that there should be no appropriation or utilization by the rest of us of that upon which one of us has expended enterprise and money in obtaining and delivering to newspapers.

"The event itself, of course, is open to all, but it is altogether unfair and hinders the development of the very thing we all seek to bring about if any of us appropriates and resells another's news that has cost us only a penny or nothing at all to get. Such a procedure, improper and really dishonest, is bound to hinder the development of international news exchange, as money will not be invested in that which cannot be protected. I repeat there is no property in the event. No one has ever claimed that.

"Perhaps 'property right in news' is a misnomer. Very well, put it this way: All of us should be energetic and enterprising with regard to the event at its source and do the best we can to get it to our newspapers first, but none of us should lie back and let others do the work and then appropriate it after the expense of transmission and the expense of gaining the news at the source have been borne by others."

Karl Bickel, then president of the United Press, supported the resolution eloquently, and both he and Mr.

Koenigsberg, then president of the International News Service, were made members of the committee to which the resolution was referred. It came out of that committee and was adopted in the following form:

"The conference affirms the principle that newspapers and news agencies and other news organizations are entitled after publication as well as before publication to the reward of their labor and enterprise and financial expenditure upon the production of news reports.

"But the conference holds that this principle shall not be so interpreted as to result in the creation or encouragement of any monopoly in news."

Both points, the advocacy of which I undertook, were thus disposed of. Other resolutions, the advocacy of which was undertaken by others, were adopted by the conference. Some of them have a little of what I call the European journalistic flavor, but others were very important. They dealt with the following matters:

1. Lower press rate communication.
2. Priority for news dispatches.
3. Improved communications, especially with the Far East.
4. Coding of press dispatches.
5. Improved facilities for the transportation of newspapers.
6. Protection of both published and unpublished news.
7. Travel tours, schools and scholarships for journalists.
8. Exemption of foreign journalists from double taxation.

9. Reduced railway and steamship fares for journalists.
10. Special passport and visa facilities and identity cards for journalists.
11. Protection of journalists against expulsion and other repressive measures.
12. Equality of treatment for all newspapers, agencies and journalists in the distribution and transmission of official news.
13. Special facilities for foreign journalists in conducting investigations.
14. Abolition of censorship, if possible, but otherwise fixed rules covering the application of censorship.
15. Creation of an international institute for journalists at Geneva.
16. A request that the League of Nations council convoke a periodical press conference.
17. Measures for suppressing publication of exaggerated news calculated to endanger world peace.

The "conference of press experts" at Geneva ended, and nothing has been heard of it since or of the resolutions it adopted. It was the second interlude of the summer for me, since my presence in Europe really had to do with making a new agency contract.

The experience, however, emphasized my conviction that news activities, whether they be of press associations, of newspapers or of individuals, cannot be legislated upon or controlled by governmental powers and still result in a pure stream of news. Not even a league of nations should make the rules, even if it has the authority to see that the rules are carried out. The business of getting news to the public cannot be regimented by government action without either damming or tainting the stream. It should not carry the flavor of government favor. The personality and character of the press association, newspaper or the individual can count as much as the news itself. The public will always want to know "Who said so?"

This perishable thing that we call news can be relied upon when each press association, prospered by a public that wants the news, carries its own standard just as far as it wants to carry it, international boundaries not impeding its progress.

If the people anywhere, for example, want to know what Reuters thinks is news, then their newspapers should have Reuters. If the people anywhere want to know what The Associated Press thinks is news, then their newspapers should have The Associated Press.

The sooner government, business and other extraneous powers learn that the most wholesome-minded people live where the news reporting activities are in the hands of news men whose sole responsibility is to their public, the stronger the government, business and other extraneous powers will be—if they should be in power at all.

And of course a world free press must be the basis of it all.

XIX

A Step Towards Freedom

WHILE the Geneva conference was in session, the new Reuters-Havas-Wolff-Associated Press contract was taking form. It was, as I have said, the first basic change in that contract since it was made thirty-four years before.

In conformity with the injunction under which I worked, the contract had to be acceptable to the agencies. Sir Roderick Jones sensed the fact that The Associated Press had no idea of breaking with the agencies. Therefore, the contract was in effect what he was willing to give under as much argument for a broadening of the rights of The Associated Press as I was able to offer.

In the previous year, when Sir Roderick visited the United States, Mr. Noyes had negotiated with him a tentative preliminary memorandum which might have been the basis of the new contract but for the fact that Sir Roderick said that his Board of Directors had called for many important changes. As a result, Sir Roderick found it necessary to depart considerably from the preliminary arrangement, thereby increasing my dissatisfaction with the whole business.

I was reminded with emphasis that The Associated Press was at the mercy of the good will of the other three, and that The Associated Press had no relation even by inference to any agency except the three others mentioned in the contract. I was told there existed at that time a prior contract by which Reuters, with the consent of Havas, had divided the world, and that the other two gave the United States and Canada to Reuters under that contract. Reuters, Havas and Wolff consenting, gave the United States and Canada to The Associated Press in 1893.

Reporting to the Board of Directors upon my return I said I was irked every time I discussed anything with the European agencies because of the fact that this prior contract existed between them. When I asked for something, I presented my request and was asked to retire while they gave it consideration. They had to inform themselves mutually as to their individual attitudes before they would give me an answer. In other words, I was at the bar and they disposed of my proposals jointly as against me because of this prior contract. So it was in 1927 with me as it had been with Mr. Stone in 1920.

It seemed to me that if The Associated Press wanted to be in on a division of the world as between the other three agencies the contract should specify what territories were allotted to each. In other words, it should be in on the ground floor so that it might know specifically what was going on between the others and what rights each had as against the other.

So the contract, for the first time, gave territorial specifications; for instance, "Reuters shall have the exclusive exploitation of the following territories: The British

Isles, Holland, Egypt, India, the Straits Settlements, Dutch East Indies, the Far East, Australia, New Zealand, North America and all other parts of the British Empire and the British mandated territory, with the reservation that The Associated Press shall have a free hand in British North America and the British West Indies."

Then in an amazing piece of verbal legerdemain Reuters consented to The Associated Press having the exclusive exploitation of the following territories: "North America and United States possessions with a reservation that Reuters and Havas shall have a free hand in Canada and Mexico. Further The Associated Press shall have a free hand in Central America, South America and Cuba."

There were no contradictions as to the territory allotted to Havas, which caused me to conclude that Reuters indeed held all of North America for itself as against Havas and Wolff. The exclusive exploitation for Havas included "France, Spain, Morocco, Portugal, Italy, South America (subject to the right of The Associated Press as previously mentioned) and the possessions, colonies and protectorates of these countries and French mandated territories."

It did not take many words to specify Wolff's territory. It was simply that "Wolff shall have the exclusive exploitation of Germany."

The word "exploitation" attracted considerable attention among the members of the board of The Associated Press when I returned because the word has taken on a stigma in the United States which it does not have in Europe. So that was changed. I was asked what territory this gave The Associated Press that it did not already have. The answer was that neither Reuters nor Wolff had ever conceded any rights to The Associated Press in South America. Havas had.

Sir Roderick emphasized that Reuters had never consented to our going into South America and that he considered that something was due Reuters because of our activity there, and Mr. Houssaye brought up at that late date the question of remuneration to Havas for our entrance into South America now that our rights were to be specified in a four-party contract. He suggested a differential because of the grant. So far as I could make out, neither was joking, although they may as well have been because I gave the question no serious consideration.

The specifications of the contract permitted any of the parties to enter into direct relations for the exchange of its own territorial news with any agency affiliated with one or more of the other three members of the alliance, with the knowledge and consent of the others; it gave the right "so far as existing contracts permit, that each party have the right of supplying supplementary services to newspapers in the territories the other parties" in consultation with the agency that controlled the territory where the newspapers were published.

I was unable to get any mention in the contract respecting Japan in spite of the fact that in the tentative agreement made the year before with Sir Roderick there were specifications which, though rigidly restricting The Associated Press, nevertheless constituted a mention of the subject. Indeed Sir Roderick asked me not to mention Japan before the other two, and told me, not in the presence of the others, that he felt that to save face the arrangement as to Japan should be merely an exchange of letters between The Associated Press and Reuters. He did not like to admit to the other two in any document which all four signed that The Associated Press had gained any entrance whatever into Reuters territory, such as Japan. The exchange of letters was made.

My own conclusions as to this meeting were that it was an experience. The contract changed nothing at all except that it wiped out the money differential that The Associated Press was paying the other three. After thirty-four years Reuters, Havas and Wolff conceded by waiving the money differential that the news of The Associated Press was worth as much to them as their news was worth to The Associated Press.

Then, too, all three of the heads of the other agencies heard for the first and at the same time an account of The Associated Press attitude. They may have concluded that The Associated Press was no longer to be a silent partner in the matter of allotments of news territories. While the declaration of attitude was not a welcome one, and it could not be worded forcefully, they nevertheless knew an attitude existed and within seven years they learned how deeply it was rooted in the minds of those who were conducting the affairs of The Associated Press.

The most lasting impression I have of the meetings in Geneva was the pathetic figure of Dr. Heinrich Mantler, managing director of Wolff. I had met Dr. Mantler in Berlin some months earlier and he had given me an idea of what had happened to his agency as a result of the war. He said that, on the one hand, he could not, figuratively speaking, address a newspaper or an agency in one set of neighboring countries except in the presence of a gendarme—Havas; likewise, he said that he could not address a newspaper or an agency in another set of neighboring countries except in the presence of a constable—Reuters. The story he told of the plight of his agency was materially the same as that which Mr. Stone had recounted to the Board of Directors of The Associated Press some seven years earlier.

Dr. Mantler was the dean among the representatives of the contracting parties. He had told me in Berlin that it probably would not be practical for him to discuss matters with me privately in Geneva for fear he would raise suspicion of undue friendliness toward The Associated Press which, however, he said he greatly admired. This was in the days of the struggling German Republic which felt that France and England were throttling it. Dr. Mantler said he felt that the actions of France and England imperiled their own future safety as much as the German Republic itself was imperiled; that it was a pity that, owing to a change of political administrations in the United States, the latter country was no longer interested in European developments and that much as he would like to see the German Republic become solidly established he had grave doubts about it.

Dr. Mantler was a peace-loving man, an internationalist, and had been for forty years the head of Continental Telegrafen Bureau, commonly known as Wolff, because of the name of the founder. He was much interested in my proposals because he felt the time might come when his own agency might once more be accepted in a full fraternity, but at Geneva he said nothing nor did I see him alone at any time.

Devoutly wishing that Germany could be the friend of

and be befriended by all nations, Dr. Mantler lived barely long enough to see the effort in Germany at the republican form of government completely fail. In his place a spirited, aggressive, militant management set out to break down the barriers that Reuters and Havas had created, and the name of the concern was changed to Deutsches Nachrichtenbüro, or simply DNB, as it still is. Dr. Mantler was of the late Victorian era and as unhappy as any man I have ever known over the break of tradition and family ties between Germany and Great Britain.

As notice had been given of the termination of the 34-year-old contract and as the date of its expiry was approaching, the board in October, 1927, approved the Geneva contract which I brought back with me. It took the place of the older document. No one thought it was satisfactory, but everyone seemed to think it was best to put it into force in substitution of the old one as it was at least some advance over the 34-year-old agreement which did not recognize that The Associated Press had any foreign rights whatever. Technical clauses were included, which were insisted upon by the big three undoubtedly to prevent The Associated Press from extending its service abroad, and they actually did prevent any increased foreign activity on any practical basis.

I felt it was merely the beginning of an advance to real freedom of action and so it proved to be. In the ensuing year there were constant references to the need for The Associated Press to go to any extreme, even to breaking completely with the agencies if necessary, to make its service available to any newspaper in the world that wanted it.

XX

Reuters Hears From Japan

BETWEEN October of 1927 and the spring of 1929 a number of events emphasized that The Associated Press could not continue relations with the agencies without the world field being open to it. The demand for its services came from unexpected quarters—all of them being in territory which the contract recognized as Reuters—India, Australia, China, with increased insistence from Japan and finally from England itself.

Rengo of Japan was edging closer and closer to The Associated Press from the time in 1926 when it supplanted Kokusai. Mr. Iwanaga visited America, absorbed more and more of The Associated Press ideas through his contacts with Mr. Noyes and myself, and on one occasion when he told me good-bye with a warm handshake he said: "Please consider that so long as I have anything to do with Rengo it is an ally of The Associated Press before all others."

As might be expected, this attitude, which The Associated Press welcomed, put on it the chief burden in any negotiations with Reuters for, while Mr. Iwanaga was possessed of unlimited courage, his agency was in its infancy and not strong enough financially to battle successfully with the mighty British concern. Indeed, Rengo had started out with a serious handicap as was evidenced by what Mr. Iwanaga told me on his visit: Rengo was heavily burdened by payments it made to Reuters. Details of these arrangements as outlined by him were that, in the first place, Rengo was paying yearly installments on its assurance of a large total payment which Mr. Iwanaga said was the unpaid amount of what Kokusai had originally agreed to pay for Reuters rights in Japan. In the second place, Rengo paid a service charge of £6,000 (normally about $30,000) yearly plus approximately $18,000 as a service charge for the commercial service.

Mr. Iwanaga and his troubles in Japan were very much in mind at the time of the exchange of letters between Reuters and The Associated Press at Geneva in 1927 affecting The Associated Press relationship with Rengo, but the stipulations in those letters by no means gave The Associated Press a free hand in Japan. The wording, however, was euphonious: "The Associated Press shall have free entry into Japan to serve only Reuters ally in Japan (Rengo) and/or its members and/or clients with the consent of Reuters ally."

That would have been something if the agreement had stopped there. It went right on with: "If Reuters' ally in Japan should elect to replace the Reuters service wholly or in part with The Associated Press service, then The Associated Press shall pay Reuters the whole or proportionate amount of the service charge as the case may be, which the Japanese agency pays Reuters at the time of the replacement, and The Associated Press will continue to pay wholly or proportionately this service charge to Reuters as long as the Japanese agency continues to take The Associated Press service. Any news that The Associated Press sends to Japan shall be available to Reuters in Japan for Reuters to disseminate elsewhere in its Far Eastern territory."

That, of course, was tantamount to a reiteration of Reuters sovereignty in the Western Pacific and offered no practical basis upon which The Associated Press and Rengo could make an agreement. Nevertheless, the Reuters claim to sovereignty or exclusive rights in a country foreign to it, which country happened to be Mr. Iwanaga's Japan, spurred Mr. Iwanaga in November, 1928, to make a bold move.

Rengo's contract with Reuters was due for renewal and revision, and Mr. Iwanaga presented to Sir Roderick some points for a new treaty which made these demands.

1. The right to make an independent contract with The Associated Press.

2. A free hand in China (which was part of Reuters domains).

3. A reduction of Reuters service charge.

Mr. Iwanaga probably didn't expect to get far with his claims. As a matter of fact, in a letter he wrote to me at the time he said it appeared that the "two sides were pretty far apart in their ideas." And confirmation that Reuters-Rengo were indeed far apart came to Mr. Iwanaga the day after he wrote the letter to me, for he received a letter from Reuters which proposed to raise the news service charge against Rengo from £6,000 ($30,000) to £10,000 ($50,000) annually.

Mr. Iwanaga's and Sir Roderick's letters crossed in the mails but immediately on receiving Iwanaga's letter Sir Roderick rejected Rengo's proposals and countered with the suggestion that Rengo and Reuters continue their existing friendly and economical relationship with only minor changes in the contract. As The Associated Press was not free to meet Mr. Iwanaga's needs because it had not gained from Reuters freedom of action in Japan, and there being no alternative, Rengo renewed its contract with Reuters for four years—until July 1, 1933—a date which proved to be memorable.

Back in America and a meeting of the California members of The Associated Press in Los Angeles. There a representative of the Hearst newspapers called upon the Board of Directors to authorize the availability of Associated Press news to Australian newspapers and urged that any contract preventing this be changed so that Australian newspapers might receive The Associated Press. Any such authorization meant, of course, that Reuters consent would have to be gained.

I felt at that time that Sir Roderick might with insistence from Mr. Noyes grant The Associated Press a free hand in Japan that would permit operation there on a practical basis. I was quite certain then, however, that there could be no contract between The Associated Press and Reuters that would permit The Associated Press to enlarge its relations with the press of the British Empire except in Canada. Canadian publishers had long put their loyalty to The Associated Press ahead of Reuters. and in more recent years second only to their own Canadian Press.

Here, though, was a demand voiced on behalf of William Randolph Hearst, who owned more Associated Press newspapers than anyone else ever has, and who, because of that fact, has always been the largest financial contributor to its support without ever having had a representative on its Board of Directors. Never before, or since, so far as I know, had he ever suggested what The Associated Press do in matters affecting its foreign relations.

Mr. Hearst's representative insisted that the Pacific Coast was deeply interested in the news of the countries on the other side of the Pacific and that the countries on the other side were deeply interested in the news of the United States. He said that The Associated Press news by the time it got to Australia through Reuters could not be recognized as Associated Press news, after having been sent to Reuters from New York to London and from London to Australia. The old, old charge that the news that Reuters transmitted as representing the activities of the United States covered nothing but lynchings, murders and other crimes was reiterated.

Another development between 1927 and 1929 was that in China and Japan Reuters, having refused the right of an ally, The Associated Press, to serve its news there on a practical basis, had begun to find some keen American competition in the activities of the United Press. It was even said that the United Press service in China was a livelier service and more representative of wide coverage than was Reuters. Reuters was frankly disturbed by this competition and wanted to know what The Associated Press was going to do about it. The answer was that The Associated Press could not do anything about it unless Reuters allowed a free hand in that part of the world. Moreover, I was not interested in helping to put stone and mortar in the Reuters wall built up against The Associated Press around a foreign country like China or Japan.

As all this was discussed by the board, it was again Adolph Ochs who spoke:

"I hope that the management may be able so to adjust its arrangement with Reuters that it will enable us to go ahead and serve American news to foreign countries where it is desirable."

Colonel McCormick of the Chicago *Tribune* then expressed himself:

"I agree very thoroughly with Mr. Ochs on that. Reuters is a national propaganda news service in China. I have had a great many letters from people in China complaining of the quality of news that gets over there— nothing about America except lynchings in Alabama and gang murders in Chicago, and financial and critical news about New York—about the kind of things I used to read about America when I lived in England thirty years ago.

"It is the same way with Australia. It seems to me that we ought to stretch every point we can. We are the representatives of the American press much more closely than anybody else—infinitely more closely than any second party. I have an idea or a conviction that it approaches a duty for us to put our news service all over the world, as far as we can afford to do it without taxing our members too much.

"I would like to see us accomplish for this country in the news what the movies have done for this country in the newsreels. I would like to have them get a good American service abroad, whatever it may be—political news, economic news, fashion news, if you will—anything that is American and represents the real country, instead of having it strained through this filter that it does go through now.

"There are few people in China who read the news, but for that reason they are correspondingly more influential. I suppose one reader in China is worth a thousand readers in the United States. Only one man in a thousand has any influence.

"I had a friend recently come back from Australia and he said the Australians were personally friendly to Americans, but always had a sneer in their attitude. Well, that may have been hereditary, it may have been due to rivalry, but it also is constantly being fed by the fact that the news which gets out there is always turned against us."

XXI

Volcanic Material

PRESIDENT NOYES had been absent from the room when Colonel McCormick made his statement, and I asked him to repeat his declaration after the president joined his colleagues. Colonel McCormick did so, and because he employed different language and amplified his earlier remarks, I quote him again:

"A nationalist news service such as Reuters and Havas and the German one is always a propaganda agency. It is unavoidable that this should be so. The three nations were in competition all over the world and the national viewpoint was such as it was. And their treatment of news is not the American treatment. I have lived abroad a good deal and have been irritated constantly by the fact that the news we got abroad was always unfavorable news—murders, lynchings, railroad wrecks, crooked politics, and so forth—and very little of anything else.

"Well, in a previous generation there was nothing to do about it. We were a small country, without much consideration of us by the world and without much consideration of the world among our own people. But now there has been a great change.

"We are much the most important country in the world and much the richest country in the world, and in comparing America with foreign countries the press stands probably higher in America, compared even to the press in England, than any other institution stands. I think it is a pretty good guess that American newspapers print and supply two-thirds of all the world's news, and I think that the revenue of the American newspapers is probably three-fourths of all the revenue of the newspapers of the world.

"Now I have been approached a number of times by people living in China and people living in Japan who have asked me to establish a newspaper over there so that they could get the American viewpoint. Well, I have not been able to do it. But the criticism is constantly made that Reuters news is one-sided and distorted—Reuters news from America.

"I would like to see The Associated Press, if it is practical and if it is within the contract obligations of The Associated Press, have its foreign news service everywhere. I would like to have The Associated Press be the great gathering organization of world news.

"I think it is a patriotic object. Although I am not an internationalist, I think it is an international object. I think we would make a fairer presentation of world news than any other news service.

"If this effort is to be undertaken by an American organization, certainly The Associated Press is much the greatest news-gathering organization in America and obviously it is almost 100% representative. When I use the word 'almost' I am referring to the fact that we do not have among our membership quite 100% of all the newspapers, but we come near enough to it.

"In general I would favor very much The Associated Press doing whatever its financial and contractual ability permitted it to do, to extend its foreign service to be a complete world-wide news service."

The April, 1929, session of the Board of Directors ended. Once more I went to England to see Sir Roderick to impress upon him the fact that The Associated Press was determined to take action, with Reuters consent if possible; if not possible, to do it anyhow. At the same time I looked into a plan of mine for the creation of subsidiary companies abroad named "The Associated Press."

After my return from Europe I was again visited by Mr. Iwanaga who, although he had signed a contract with Reuters, was most unhappy and urged The Associated Press to modernize the entire agency relationship. Only The Associated Press, he said, could do this, but he was willing to put Rengo side by side with The Associated Press for whatever value that would be.

I told him that, since his contract with Reuters had some three years to run and as something might happen to him or to me in three years, we perhaps had better put in writing an expression of attitudes which could be approved or disapproved by our respective boards of directors.

Accordingly, on January 7, 1930, I presented to the Board of Directors of The Associated Press a rather volcanic memorandum which Mr. Iwanaga and I had drawn up. The document flatly provided "for the contingency of a break" with Reuters. Its terms follow:

"1. If Associated Press decides to break with Reuters at any time before June 30, 1933, Associated Press shall notify Rengo in due course of its intention to do so.

"2. Upon the receipt of this notification, Rengo shall immediately take necessary steps to conclude a primary contract with Associated Press in regard to mutual exchange of news service.

"3. The above mentioned steps shall be taken by Rengo on its own responsibility, but Associated Press shall also render all possible assistance to enable Rengo to so adjust its contractual relation with Reuters as to cope with the terms of the primary contract it entered into with Associated Press or, if necessary, to enable Rengo to sever its relation with Reuters altogether with the least damage.

"4. If the contractual relation between Associated Press and Reuters still exists on July 1, 1933, when Rengo's contract with Reuters terminates, Rengo can make a primary contract with Associated Press to replace its present contract with Reuters.

"5. Primary contract which may be concluded between Associated Press and Rengo shall be based upon the following principles:

a. Each party shall recognize the territory of the country of the other party as its contractual territory.

b. Mutual supply of domestic news services shall be rendered free of charge. However, if either of the parties asks the other to supply it with foreign news as well, then a reasonable amount of service charge as is agreed upon shall be paid by the one receiving such service.

c. Each party shall be at liberty to conclude with any news agency or newspaper outside United States and Japan any kind of contracts of mutual news service, provided they are not inconsistent in any sense with the terms of the primary contract between both parties and provided such other news agency agrees not to make its news available in Japan to anyone but Rengo, and in the United States to anyone but The Associated Press.

"6. Until such primary contract is made between Associated Press and Rengo the existing co-operative relation shall be continued."

"In explanation of this," I told the board, "there has been a discussion here from time to time as to whether we should deal directly with Rengo, with whom we have no contract, and make The Associated Press news available in the Western Pacific. There is likely to be nothing more important before the Board of Directors in my opinion in the next two years than this question.

"I personally feel and would strongly urge that now, with the existence of this signed memorandum, and knowing that Rengo far prefers to deal primarily with The Associated Press, with or without Reuters—even with The Associated Press as against the world—we notify Reuters that we want a free hand in the Western Pacific as we have in South America. It does not prevent Reuters from still being there.

"The Associated Press cannot go on in my opinion as it has in the Western Pacific with the present left-handed arrangement. We have a certain obligation to our members in Manila which we are not able to meet because we have not the finances unless we impose a charge upon the members in the domestic service which, to my notion, would be entirely inequitable. Because of the free hand of our opposition in the Western Pacific it is able to deliver a very fine and very complete service to American newspapers in Manila as well as to China and Japan.

"I see no reason why we should permit this to continue, particularly in view of this memorandum. The Associated Press must not let Reuters continue to exploit the Western Pacific with our help, which it has been doing, carrying the name of The Associated Press linked with Reuters.

"I feel that if we turn down this extended hand of Rengo—Rengo being co-operative exactly on our lines as near as it can be in Japan—that we will have refused to take a step that is wholly consistent with our principles and will set back the cause of mutual news dissemination and collection the world around for many years.

"I had hours upon hours of talks with Mr. Iwanaga. He says that the interests of Rengo are plainly linked with The Associated Press; that the relations of Japan with the United States should be closer and the two peoples understand each other better and that we are the principal customer of Japan economically."

The board thereupon took two definite steps. First, it approved the statement as outlined in the memorandum signed by Mr. Iwanaga and myself. Second, I was asked to prepare a plan to launch the activities of The Associated Press abroad, harmoniously with the existing agency contract if possible. If not, to make a new contract.

XXII

Crossing the Rubicon

THE next year (1930) I made another extended trip to Europe to study the best possible procedure in connection with plans for launching Associated Press activity abroad. I returned convinced that the time was ripe for action, and on September 30, 1930, I made a definite recommendation to that effect, having come to the conclusion that it was not going to be possible to convince Sir Roderick that The Associated Press meant to do what it had repeatedly said it wanted to do.

The revolutionary proposals were the answer to the board's request for a considered program for development of The Associated Press throughout the world. They advocated the creation of a news-collecting and -distributing company in London to be known as The Associated Press of Great Britain. It was to have a Paris branch, since the French laws made that method of operation more practical than to operate The Associated Press in France. The plan also included the establishment of The Associated Press in Germany. These companies, I felt, would provide a springboard to The Associated Press entry into the foreign field and, so that

they would have something to do until the lines had
been laid for the establishment of news services, they
were to undertake the collection of news photos for The
Associated Press of New York which three years before
upon my recommendation had established a news photo
service.

I was convinced that under the contract then existing
the relationship of The Associated Press to the European agencies was more a disadvantage than an advantage. I felt that The Associated Press was perfectly capable of standing on its own feet and had no fear of the
consequences if relations with the European agencies
were severed.

At that time I had served as general manager for five
years but I had had twenty years of activity in Associated Press work. Also I had been interested in this
matter of foreign news dissemination for sixteen years.
I decided that if, with that background, I could not convince the board that the overlordship of Reuters should
be removed; that if the Board of Directors wanted to
keep the largest news association in the world harnessed
to Reuters and the monopoly and subservient to the decisions of the comparatively much smaller European big
three, I would have to accept defeat of my plans.

The strange thing about it was that all the directors
apparently favored action but a majority of them feared
what Mr. Stone had so often expressed—that a break
with Reuters would be disastrous. Yet, as I was conducting the news service and had no such fears, the situation
seemed to suggest that I should ask a vote of confidence
by the board's accepting or refusing my definite recom-

mendations. Failing such a vote of confidence I knew there was an alternative.

In discussing it again with the board, the personnel of which was constantly changing, I said that any analysis of The Associated Press foreign situation had to begin with a discussion of the foreign news agencies, if for no other reason than that The Associated Press foreign service began with its relations to the foreign agencies, and continued:

"Our entire structure for the collection of foreign news—our entire activity abroad—has been modified and restrained by our relations with the foreign agencies. Let us, therefore, look at the standing of the agencies when we began relations in 1893, and their standing today by way of contrast with The Associated Press of 1893 and The Associated Press of today.

"As President Noyes knows, I began my study of the agency situation in 1914. My first report thereon was made to the general manager. Since then I have taken every opportunity that has been afforded me to study the foreign news agency situation because I recognized in the agencies the bulwark of our early existence and regretfully I assert that what was then a bulwark is today the bar to our greater efficiency.

"I am trying, therefore, to make this recital historical as to the relationship, a fair criticism of it as matters are today and a presentation of a plan for the future. I have come to the belief that the decision of the board at this time may determine whether The Associated Press twenty years from now shall be the comprehensive factor in American journalism that it is today.

"Thirty-seven years ago practically all foreign news collection was in the hands of these agencies. From them came the news of the world for American newspapers. The agencies themselves in those days had no competition and when the present Associated Press contracted with them there was no competition worthy of the name against The Associated Press in the United States.

"The exclusive rights of newspapers within The Associated Press, however, left a field for the development of a competitor of The Associated Press in the United States, which was not the situation in foreign countries because the foreign agencies gave no exclusive rights to newspapers, nor do they today. This was a fundamental difference between the agencies and The Associated Press. A second difference is that each of the important agencies is proprietary and profit-making and more interested in making money than in getting the news. A third difference is that the agencies have remained what they were thirty-seven years ago as to efficiency in the manner and scope of collecting news. The Associated Press has modernized itself and stints itself at nothing in the way of expense to get the news. A fourth difference is that The Associated Press has kept step with the requirements of its members. The foreign agencies have not kept step with the requirements of their clients.

"The only foreign agencies in Europe that are of any use to us in our work are, in the order of their efficiency and importance to us, Reuters (on account of the Press Association), Wolff and Stefani. I do not mention Tass, the Russian agency, because we have a direct contract with Tass independent of the agency relationship. Tass is very important though it is rapidly becoming non-exclusive to us.

"The value to us of the agencies mentioned is for their routine spontaneous news like railway accidents and government pronouncements. This is just what we got from them thirty years ago. Through Reuters we have availability to the Press Association report. The Press Association covers the British Isles and is by far the most efficient agency in Europe and I have hoped its ownership of Reuters would cause it to take an active interest in the administration of the affairs of Reuters and thus bring about an improvement in Reuters report. Apparently, however, it does not intend to do so.

"Reuters coverage of India, Australia, South Africa and Egypt is fair. Its coverage of China and Japan, once sufficient for our purposes, in no way compares to the efficiency that we have through our own staff correspondents in the Western Pacific. We could without any embarrassment cease relying at all upon Reuters for any news of that part of the world.

"We have had to establish a bureau in India, and we must establish bureaus in Egypt, South Africa and Australia, regardless of the continuance of the Reuter connection. We must do this because Reuters is not fast enough from these sections, and has not our ideas as to what is news to meet our needs as against our competition. We can, without any great expense, duplicate in those sections our effectiveness in the Western Pacific and since we must do this we will have at once a product different from and faster than Reuters for use in England.

"Wolff covers Germany better than its competitor, the Telegrafen Union.

"Stefani in Italy is a sort of stepchild to Havas, although owned by an Italian who is a close friend of Mussolini.

"Havas holds the French press in bondage because of its advertising department. A paper that does not take the Havas service cannot get advertising. But the news service of Havas is so inferior that it is not worth considering.

"There is no need to mention Fabra, of Spain, and the agencies of the other small countries, because they have no news of their countries except what they get from governments and what they clip from newspapers.

"All in all, I will say that the value to us of all the agency services we use is showing a decrease each year. My opinion is that the present relationship is more a disadvantage to us than an advantage, not only because it ties our hands against expansion but more because we continue hopefully to rely upon them and they continue to fail us. It is natural for our men abroad to try to avoid expense to get news that they have every right to expect from the agencies. A further disadvantage is that our men abroad, fearing to incur useless expense, constantly repress their ingenuity at getting news in the alert and aggressive manner that they have been taught in America and they become, shall I say, lazy-minded in this respect, because unconsciously they feel that the failure of the agencies to give what we expect of them is a good enough excuse.

"Our costs for the collection of foreign news have been increased largely because of the deficiencies of the agencies. We are spending an average of approximately $500,000 a year for news collection abroad exclusive of cable tolls, as compared to approximately $50,000 a year thirty-seven years ago, or ten times as much. Practically all of this greatly increased expense is for the collection of news in world territory still controlled by the agencies. Thus we have to spend to meet our needs because of their deficiencies. During the same period our wordage has increased probably thirty times. The Associated Press foreign service of today is really of great magnitude. The agencies stand still. We spend more and more in their territories for news, without any return therefrom in their territories either in money or in reputation.

"We do our work so completely at home to meet our own needs that the product more than encompasses their needs. Not only that, but we do our work so well in their territories, better in some respects than they do, that they rely upon us for the coverage of news in their own territories. It is not an uncommon thing for them to send back to Europe from New York news that we have collected through the energy of our own staff right in their home territory.

"No statement as respects the agencies would be complete without reference to the ethics of news work which they follow as compared to our standards. Through our relationship we are supporting, in a way, methods that are abhorrent to the principles of our journalism. We do not receive subsidies from governments, but we are parties of those who do.

"We have always known that some of the foreign agencies are subsidized by their own governments to suppress, carry or distort news and we have paid out large sums to prevent falling victims to these practices. To have to do that is bad enough.

"With the deficiencies of the agencies; with them falling behind the progress of the newspapers of their countries; with their inadequacy in speed and coverage, to say nothing of a rising feeling by newspapers against official news agencies, no wonder our competition here can find and is finding a fertile field in almost any country. Our competition is rapid. Few of the agencies are. It is progressive. The agencies are not. It is free from government influence. The agencies are not. It does not carry propaganda. The agencies do. It endeavors to mold its work upon the very standards of impartiality and accuracy upon which The Associated Press was founded.

"Our chief competitor got its first start in the foreign field in South America, sixteen years ago. And it got it because the request for service which came to The Associated Press had to be referred by The Associated Press to Havas. The inquiry came because there was gross dissatisfaction with Havas in South America and, The Associated Press not being free to act and deferring courteously to Havas, there was nowhere for South America to turn except to our competition which made the most of its South American experience. When the World War ended it branched out ambitiously to compete throughout the world with the agencies that are allied to us.

"We must bear in mind that no newspapers of any country outside of the provincial press in England, the Canadian newspapers and the large Japanese newspapers which financed Rengo, have any proprietary or even good-will interest in the agencies that serve them. Up to now the agencies have been necessary to the newspapers, but I predict that each year will see less and less reliance upon the agencies by European newspapers and their patronage will fall more and more to the progressive press association that is on the spot, whether it be our competitors or any other progressive organization.

"Indeed our competition is today heir to the good will of scores of newspapers abroad, all of them the really important newspapers in their field. I find that the newspapers which contract with our American competition are proud of their connection. And be it remembered that it is the newspapers that have the local and national news, and because they have the news our competition gets the news from them and gets it first.

"I emphasized earlier that the agencies had the official news first. They did at one time. They do not now. Foreign governments feel that they reach The Associated Press with their news through their contacts with their local official or semiofficial news agency with which The Associated Press is allied. The attitude toward us is a detached one, with no special effort for us nor interest in us.

"These governments have not this feeling respecting our competition which comes to them directly and aggressively, and with the assertion that being a worldwide news agency the governments owe it to themselves to take care of our competition's requirements at least upon equal terms with those of the local agencies with which The Associated Press is allied. In this way our competition has established itself with government officials on equal terms with the official agencies, but without any strings tied to it as are tied to the official agencies,

Thus our competitors get the official news and are required to suppress nothing, whereas the official agencies with which we are allied suppress and withhold news from us. It is not difficult to see where our alliance injures us in this respect. Also we get it secondhand.

"Our competitors have not assailed the position of The Associated Press where The Associated Press had always had a free hand to develop according to the needs of its members. They can never assail the position of The Associated Press in its home territory unless they come to this home territory with a superior world news service.

"Thus I hold it to be a strong and farsighted policy for our competitors to strike at The Associated Press at the latter's only vulnerable point—the foreign field. That is where The Associated Press has to struggle to overcome the handicap of the agency attachment in order to make up for the deficiencies of its allies. In these fields one of our competitors goes in as the only worldwide agency and it has got such a start in the matter of distributing and selling its news that if The Associated Press were now free to proceed similarly it would cost The Associated Press untold amounts and years and years of labor to catch up. But if our competitors are to encounter any opposition in the foreign field it will have to be The Associated Press that contends with them there."

As I was talking, I became aware that I was having closer attention from the board than I had ever had before. I began to feel that this would be the last time I would have to appeal for decisive action.

"Now if all this is an alarmist picture," I continued, "it is my firm conviction it is a fair one. And yet we should not think of breaking with the agencies unless they absolutely will not, with a generous and fraternal spirit, let us meet and beat aggressive competitors at their own game. The thing to do now is to prepare for that eventuality and at this time decide upon a plan for the future, which would be followed whether or not the agencies compel us to discontinue the alliance with them."

I looked around the table, noticed that each member was showing keen interest and presented my plans:

"Because The Associated Press structure does not lend itself to the activity of news dissemination abroad, we should proceed as follows, even though I recognize the size of the undertaking and the novelty of the procedure suggested:

"In at least one of the more important countries, preferably in England, and possibly also in France, Germany and Italy, there should be formed a news-collecting and -distributing organization known as The Associated Press.

"Each such company should be organized not for profit, in fact, could never make a profit. Its income at the start would be only from The Associated Press of New York, and as its first mission would be to fulfill the requirements of The Associated Press, its expenses would be just what The Associated Press of New York would be willing to pay.

"These companies would be free to sell to any newspaper or news agency in Europe the news that they collect so long as such news would not be retransmitted by

the recipients anywhere without the consent of the company that forwarded it.

"This procedure would merely mean that The Associated Press of New York would contract with such company or companies to furnish its news, and these foreign
companies would have a free hand to sell such news
locally or internationally and could do anything not inconsistent with their contracts with The Associated Press
of New York.

"By this plan The Associated Press will have erected a
springboard for entry into the foreign field. It should be
done frankly and without conflict with the agencies. In
the end the most each company could do, within present
anticipations, and so long as we maintain relations with
the agencies, would be that it would compete with the
present efforts of our competitors abroad. The name of
The Associated Press and its activity abroad would take
on a new importance and for the money that we spend
there we would have a co-ordinated product and a tan-
gible method of disposing of it, if and when the same
were deemed expedient.

"Eventually each such company might be transformed
into a mutual co-operative organization like The Associated Press. That, briefly, is the plan I favor. If, however, this plan is not acceptable to the board, and if we
are not to plan any actions except through the allies,
then we should by all means require much more of them.
In any event, I think we should have these foreign companies to act as disseminators of Associated Press news."

XXIII

Reuters Gets A Shock

THE fact that the directors broke into applause at the conclusion of this statement—an almost unprecedented method of recording their sentiment —is a fair indication of their enthusiastic approval, which had more formal expression in due course. Not a word of opposition developed to the far-reaching recommendation.

An unusually long discussion arose and ran over into another day's session but this was largely in the nature of inquiry and suggestion. Among those taking a leading hand in the debate was Mr. Ochs, who early made his position clear in this striking comment:

"I think it is extremely important that we should have a free hand in Europe. I heartily approve the idea of establishing an organization in England, and in France and in Germany. I know nothing that would arouse my enthusiasm and interest more than that, and I would be very glad on the financial end of it to be helpful to a very considerable extent."

Colonel McCormick also added his, "I am in favor of it," and later made this contribution:

"In regard to the salability of our news over there, it seems to me this comment can be made:

"The foreign news services were established to spread trade, and while they purported to bring home accurate information for their owners, they brought home propaganda for their people—propaganda against competing countries and propaganda to influence local politics.

"On top of that, the old countries are entertaining most extravagant ideas of the periphery of the earth. So at the present time the appetite for American news or South American news or Chinese news is largely for the monstrosities. And also among a great many readers it is biased politics.

"I think once before I spoke to you about a dispatch I read in London from Athens. The King of Greece delivered a speech from the throne at a time when his point of view was contrary to that of England. And this dispatch came from Athens, paying full rate, and there was less space given to what the King said than what the correspondent thought he ought to have said.

"Now, that is entirely contrary to our views of news, but it is a taste they have got in their mouths at the present time. The only comment I have got to make is this:

"That to begin with our straight way of dealing out news as a commodity may meet with some lack of interest, but if we are willing to go to it and keep it up, just like any other superior commodity, in time it is going to make itself felt."

If further proof were needed that The Associated Press meant business in its attack on the great foreign

news barrier, it was provided six months later. On April
13, 1931, The Associated Press of Great Britain, Ltd.,
was incorporated in London and a little later a branch
was registered in Paris. An Associated Press of Germany
also was incorporated there.

These foreign companies were a mystery—and consequently a source of worry—to the great Reuters. The
only function they performed in their early career was
to handle The Associated Press news photo service for
Europe. Reuters could see this activity all right, but was
strongly suspicious that The Associated Press had something up its sleeve—and how very right the British
agency was! Associated Press employees abroad were constantly bombarded by Reuters executives with inquiries
as to the precise purpose of The Associated Press of
Great Britain. This went on for nearly three years and
the inquiry became as monotonous as must have been
the very truthful answer, namely, that the company was
engaged in handling The Associated Press news photo
service.

Two months after I recommended that The Associated Press prepare for invasion of the foreign field, the
Executive Committee of the board instructed me to give
a year's notice as of December 31, 1930, of termination
of the four-party contract among The Associated Press,
Reuters, Havas and Wolff, which had then had less than
three years of life. Again this notice was for the "purpose
of effecting changes in the treaty and was not calculated
to bring about a severance of relations." I asked that the
new agreement be made operative by January 1, 1932,
or earlier if possible.

This notification was quickly followed by outlines for

a new contract, prepared by President Noyes and forwarded to Sir Roderick. The proposals were far-reaching and firm, the entire operation apparently being carried out in the atmosphere of a letter which I wrote to Mr. Noyes on December 23, 1930, wherein I said:

"Finally, let me say that I greatly hope for a favorable reaction to any letter that you send. I am not wanting the thing approached with the idea that we are trying to sever relations. I stand squarely upon my statement to the Board of October, that we must make every endeavor to get on with Reuters and the others, but without compromise of what are essentials to us. We are not now in the position that we have to compromise."

While I wanted peace I was confident in the strength of The Associated Press and would not stop short of a rupture with the European agencies to attain The Associated Press aims.

Mr. Noyes's proposals to Sir Roderick contained what amounted to pronouncements of policy. He laid down five points, but two of these related to technical matters and only the other three are quoted; in substance they were as follows:

1. Each of the contracting parties shall have the right to make arrangements for an exchange of news with newspapers, or for the sale of its own services to newspapers, which are clients or members of the allied agencies.

This demand was one for which The Associated Press had battled from the start. Agreement to this would mean that The Associated Press could make contracts anywhere in the territories of the other three allied agencies—a privilege which was one of the basic principles involved.

2. The general alliance must be based on the conception that a minor agency, which is allied to one of the four major agencies, must have the right to select the major agency or agencies which it wishes to have for its prime news source.

This point struck directly at the hegemony exercised by the big three over the host of little agencies, none of which could make a move without permission of its master. Specifically, Mr. Noyes was aiming at the Japanese situation. The new Japanese agency, Rengo, preferred that its primary contract be with The Associated Press instead of with Reuters, which considered the Western Pacific its own private preserve.

3. The Associated Press probably will find it necessary also "to form a subsidiary British corporation to which we will delegate the collection and distribution of our foreign news."

This last was indeed a bombshell. If there was any doubt as to the full significance of the first two points, the third certainly left nothing to the imagination. It was a flat notification that The Associated Press intended to proceed abroad.

Sir Roderick's attitude toward these proposals was cordial, though cautious and patently suspicious. He eased into the subject by admitting to Mr. Noyes that the latter's purpose was much the same as Jones's would be under similar circumstances. So in this they started out by being in accord. However, there might possibly be differences of opinion at the outset as to how the purpose of The Associated Press was to be achieved.

In those delicate phrases which were always at his command, Sir Roderick made it known that he had some doubts as to how The Associated Press terms would be accepted by Havas and Wolff. He thought that these two agencies might possibly be a bit suspicious and ascribe to The Associated Press predatory intentions—the last thing, of course, which would ever enter Sir Roderick's own mind, for he realized that such designs were wholly alien to the purpose of his American ally. In short, the Reuters chief thought that perhaps Wolff and Havas would receive in a critical spirit The Associated Press proposals, which all of them really should welcome.

Because of these circumstances Sir Roderick was inclined to suggest that Mr. Noyes state categorically the intentions of The Associated Press. This naturally was not to say that the five points be modified, but just that the American organization should relax and not hold its cards quite so close to its chest.

Specifically Sir Roderick thought Mr. Noyes should state, on the one hand, (1) what liberty of action was desired outside of America, (2) in what territories The Associated Press wished to operate, and (3) what co-operation was expected from the European agencies. On the other hand, and here Sir Roderick really got down to cases, what was The Associated Press prepared to give in exchange for the concessions sought?

While Sir Roderick adroitly placed the burden of suspicion on Wolff and Havas, it seemed natural that it was he who was greatly concerned as to just what The Associated Press had in mind. The establishment of a company in Great Britain would in itself be enough to arouse his anxiety.

Mr. Noyes immediately replied with a letter making it clear that The Associated Press was not asking for anything that it would not grant to the other agencies in return. He then made the remarkable gesture of offering to throw the whole territory of The Associated Press wide open to the European agencies, with permission to supply supplemental news reports to member newspapers of The Associated Press. President Noyes further explained that the desire of The Associated Press was "to be free to supply to agency clients such a supplemental report as will effectively compete with our American competitors or their subsidiaries."

"We have no thought or desire whatever," wrote Mr. Noyes, "that such supplemental service as we propose furnishing would in the slightest degree supplant or injuriously affect the relations of the agencies with their members or clients."

In May, 1931, Mr. Noyes proceeded to Europe for conferences with Sir Roderick to prepare the way for negotiations that I later undertook, and which were exceedingly difficult. But at long last Sir Roderick and the other two allies agreed to The Associated Press terms, and a new contract finally was signed in London on March 8, 1932. The results were summed up in the official minutes of a meeting of the Board of Directors on April 21, 1932:

"The General Manager reported the completion and signing of the new contract with the foreign news agencies, the form of which had received the minute attention of the board at previous meetings.

"The contract grants The Associated Press a right it has long sought, namely, the right for The Associated

Press to serve Associated Press news directly and independently to newspapers in foreign countries. In gaining this concession The Associated Press concedes the right of any foreign news agency to serve members of The Associated Press directly if any member desires such a direct service."

Moreover, as I had not forgotten the memorandum that I had signed with Mr. Iwanaga, there was, I thought, a definite understanding as to the future of The Associated Press-Rengo relations, for Sir Roderick gave me a letter the terms of which I accepted in writing and which said: "The Associated Press shall have a free hand in Japan and China subject only, in the case of Japan, to the expiry of Reuters' contract with Rengo in 1933."

With all the talk there had been respecting the wishes of The Associated Press and Rengo as well as the exchange of letters about them, it would have seemed that Rengo and The Associated Press were free to make an accord with each other to take effect July 1, 1933. But so certain was Sir Roderick that even with this consent to The Associated Press he could still control the contractual activities either of Rengo or of The Associated Press or both, that in May, 1933, he received quite a shock upon learning that I had appeared in Japan to conclude matters there without notice to him and therefore without Reuters being present also as a negotiator.

XXIV

Around the World to London

ON May 8, 1932, Managing Director Iwanaga
gave Sir Roderick Jones formal one-year notice
of Rengo's determination to terminate its contract with Reuters on June 30, 1933. However, like the
phrase that appeared in the notices given by The Associated Press, Mr. Iwanaga said he was giving the notice
for the purpose of effecting changes in the treaty and
that it was not calculated to bring about a severance of
relations.

All the indications were that Rengo had decided definitely that its destiny lay primarily with The Associated
Press. This attitude was made quite clear in the message
he sent to me, which was that it was his firm intention to
conclude an agreement with The Associated Press to go
into effect July 1, 1933, providing for coverage of the
world outside of Japan and China by The Associated
Press for Rengo.

I did not know, however, any more than Mr. Iwanaga
did, why he should then or ever have wanted any abrupt
break with Reuters. I had repeatedly stated that I did not
want to break with Reuters and that this had been
my attitude over a period of twelve years. I well un-

derstood that Mr. Iwanaga held the same view. Very often in our discussions we had talked of the hope that Reuters some day would be in the managerial control of the newspapers that owned it, as both The Associated Press and Rengo then were. We felt that we could make faster progress in gaining acceptance of the practical idealism to which we both adhered if we were associated with the newspapermen who owned Reuters. We thought it might be easier to get the acceptance of our idea that international news, which generates actions upon which the fate of nations depends, should not be sold or bartered, restrained, suppressed or tainted: in short, that the urge to have news agencies traffic in international news for profit was not a wholesome procedure.

Mr. Iwanaga's notice to Reuters started a ferment that worked fast. After the notice was given, he was continuously in touch with Sir Roderick as he was with me. He felt that the happiest relationship would be a three-cornered one so far as Rengo was concerned, but he said he was unable to get Sir Roderick to accept the idea that The Associated Press position should be on a par with that of Reuters. Mr. Iwanaga, a mild-mannered man, really tried to gain the affections of Sir Roderick and in doing so created in his own heart an affection for him. "He needs friends," Mr. Iwanaga once said to me.

Finally, upon the earnest invitation of Mr. Iwanaga, I spent the month of May, 1933, in Japan. Between rounds of Japanese hospitality Mr. Iwanaga and I worked on a direct contract between our two organizations in which neither of us wanted to have a clause that precluded Reuters's right also to make a contract. Being in Japan I was able to get accurate information as to just what Rengo could afford to do and still have money enough left to cover the domestic news of Japan so as to have a better domestic service than its competitor, Nippon Dempo, which was allied with the United Press.

The first time I ever met Mr. Iwanaga I asked him what the Kokusai Agency, as it was then, had in the way of domestic news. He said not much of its own, and I said I didn't see that he had much he could offer to Reuters or to anyone else except in the way of money as an exchange for what any agency would need in the way of a differential to warrant its taking the news of the world to Japan with no news of Japan in return. A reciprocal news report at least covering the domestic news of Japan was necessary in any exchange. Mr. Iwanaga thereupon set about to establish a really comprehensive domestic news service.

By the end of May, 1933, we had completed an agreement which made the entire Associated Press news report available to Rengo. The agreement recognized the ideals of co-operative news service. This was not accomplished, however, without reverberations of thunder from the Reuters head office in London. Sir Roderick apparently was so astounded that The Associated Press had proceeded without notice to him, in spite of the fact that it was no longer barred from contracting with Rengo, that he ordered his general representative in that part of the world to insist upon entering the negotiations between Mr. Iwanaga and myself. The young man he sent was Christopher Chancellor who in 1942 is joint general manager of Reuters in London. He was not, of course, admitted to our conferences, but he had some conferences alone with Mr. Iwanaga which I hoped he would have on behalf of Reuters.

One of the stipulations in the contract with Mr. Iwanaga was that Rengo could also have a contract with Reuters, but that if it did not, the differential for world news that The Associated Press would give Rengo would be doubled. That was my idea of creating an incentive for Rengo to contract with Reuters, thus having two services at no more expense than one.

Having learned that Sir Roderick was incensed, I proceeded to Manila, having decided to return to New York by way of the Suez Canal so that I could confer with Sir Roderick regarding the new alignment in the Western Pacific. As we were still in alliance with Reuters, and my thought was that it was a continuing one, it was due Reuters to know exactly the convictions of The Associated Press and how it came by these convictions.

Accordingly I dispatched a letter to him so that he could know my mind prior to my arrival in London. The essence of the letter was that "The Associated Press can no longer refuse to deal directly with Rengo, jointly with Reuters, if you are agreeable or alone if you are not."

My letter read:

"In the hope that you will receive this in time to give consideration to it before I see you I outline herein the situation of The Associated Press as respects the Western Pacific. Some of the things you know, but to give sequence to the story I relate them here.

"For almost twenty-five years there have been important members of The Associated Press, particularly on the Pacific Coast, who have been urging the Board of

Directors to place The Associated Press service in the Western Pacific. Nothing could be done because of the contract with Reuters. Reuters had always had the Japanese field as far as The Associated Press was concerned.

"About twenty years ago Mr. Kennedy, who was then The Associated Press correspondent in Tokyo, constantly hearing objections from Japanese to a British-owned agency predominating in Japan, presented the idea of a Japanese-owned agency entering the field. He first talked with a group of Japanese industrial, financial and political leaders, and found in Count Kabayama a leader. Kennedy was commissioned to present the idea to Melville Stone because even at that time the Japanese felt the necessity of an American connection, just as the members of The Associated Press in the United States were feeling the necessity of our news activity in Japan.

"Mr. Stone was deeply interested in the idea, but said The Associated Press could not make a connection because of the Reuter contract. Accordingly Kennedy went to Reuters in London, where the arrangement was made. Kennedy had told Mr. Stone he hoped to be General Manager of the new agency. The Associated Press agreed to help Reuters make the service efficient, and has continued to do so for the last twenty years. There is no doubt in the mind of Mr. Iwanaga and the leading Japanese newspapermen that if The Associated Press had not liberally and unselfishly supported Kokusai and later Rengo, through Reuters, there would have been an end to this Japanese-owned undertaking a long time ago, and Nippon Dempo, the competing Japanese news agency, would have been further ahead than it is today.

"I hope you will appreciate just how much The Associated Press has done. It has made its world-wide service available to Rengo. As an example, when the Zeppelin made its round-the-world trip Rengo depended on The Associated Press for bulletins over the entire trip, and was good enough to say afterward that the service was ahead of all competitors. Hundreds of such cases could be cited.

"In the first ten or twelve years of the existence of this Japanese-owned agency The Associated Press received nothing of value in return for its co-operation. It did have access at London to the news Reuters' correspondent sent from Tokyo to London. After the World War the value of this routing of news was precipitantly diminished because the competitor of The Associated Press was receiving directly from Japan, and more quickly than The Associated Press could obtain it from London, a really efficient report of domestic affairs in Japan. This came from Nippon Dempo.

"As a result, The Associated Press at its own expense had to extend its own news collection in the Western Pacific to meet its own competitor. How well it did this over a period of years is proved by the fact that frequently, and even today, Reuters sends from New York to London a protective service on what The Associated Press has obtained from its own correspondents in the Western Pacific, including Japan.

"At the beginning this was an increased expense to The Associated Press and there was no return whatever. While The Associated Press had access to the news of Kokusai, and afterward Rengo, neither had any domestic news because at that time practically the only function of your ally in Japan was the selling of Reuters' service in Japan which it received economically from Shanghai.

"Loyal day by day, and year by year, to Reuters The Associated Press demurred to the insistence of many of its own members that something be done in the Western Pacific by The Associated Press. It increased its own news collection costs at the expense of those members and other members. All the time the United Press was expanding its service throughout that territory. It got and gets both news and money from its ally. It is the American agency that pioneered in that part of the world.

"How insistent was the demand that The Associated Press do something is shown by the fact that President Noyes volunteered to make a personal study of the situation and reported thereon to the Board of Directors. That was over ten years ago. At that time Kokusai's desire for a direct American connection had not taken much form. Nippon Dempo's competition was not acute. Without an important Japanese connection The Associated Press could accomplish little in the Western Pacific.

"Fully respecting Reuters' rights, no action was taken, but a few years later we made an effort to do something through Reuters. This was found wholly unsuccessful and impractical, so we began to feel the necessity of having a free hand in the Western Pacific. As a result of my conference with you in Geneva in 1927 you gave us permission to deal with your ally in Japan, and five years later when the present four-party contract was made we obtained that for which we had felt an increasing urgent need, namely, an entirely free hand. I considered that concession one of the wisest things Reuters could grant for its own sake, and to strengthen itself in the Western Pacific, so I felt it was no imposition upon Reuters.

"Far better will it be for Reuters to have an American partner dividing the field with Reuters in Japan than it is for Reuters to have an American competitor merciless in its opposition to Reuters. And while we have a free hand I am not proceeding in disregard of Reuters. Far from it.

"Even now I am addressing this letter to you and am proceeding to Europe to urge you to join wholeheartedly in The Associated Press plan to allow Rengo to rehabilitate itself with The Associated Press and Reuters sympathetically and solidly back of it. I am doing this although The Associated Press can see the thing through alone and will have to do so for its own sake as well as for its traditional ally, Reuters, if you will not join with it.

"The Associated Press has too much at stake to be put aside. Rengo has fully accepted The Associated Press interest and I want Reuters to accept The Associated Press as a full partner with equal responsibilities and equal returns.

"While more acute, the situation in Japan is parallel to South America where, because The Associated Press persistently deferred to Havas, the United Press got a strong foothold four years before The Associated Press obtained the right from Havas to enter South America. I have always said that if The Associated Press had not done that Havas would have had nothing left in South America. As it was, the field was divided between three, and The Associated Press divided the patronage that would have gone entirely to the United Press. Havas lost nothing.

"And so in Japan, time went on and both Rengo and Nippon Dempo applied to The Associated Press for a direct contract for an exchange of news. Rengo did this because it was smarting under the increased competition with Nippon Dempo, which competition was accentuated through the militant co-operation of the United Press with Nippon Dempo. The latter made a final effort to contract with The Associated Press before it consented to the United Press plan of a permanent contract.

"Over twelve years ago Mr. Mitsunaga, the president of Nippon Dempo, came into our office in New York and talked with me about making a contract. He did not know then that we would not do this because of our deference to Reuters. I told him that some day we would probably have to be active in Japan but at that time it was not possible for us to adopt his suggestion. He replied then that unless it was done at that time it probably could never be done. I did not know what he meant but I have since learned that he otherwise decided to sign the United Press contract.

"Mr. Iwanaga discussed the direct connection with me as early as eight years ago. At that time I discovered that Rengo really had nothing to furnish The Associated Press in the way of domestic news that was of any importance whatever. Mr. Iwanaga admitted the predominance of Nippon Dempo in the Japanese domestic news field. That meant that our competitor was getting from its Japanese ally what we wanted, and the sale of your news and our news to Rengo by you was netting The Associated Press nothing, either in money or in news.

"I told Mr. Iwanaga that unless he developed a domestic news service I saw no way by which The Associated Press would gain anything by tying up with Rengo. He recognized this fact, and we all know that in the last few years Rengo has developed a really efficient domestic service.

"Having met the requirements of The Associated Press, and the latter having adjusted its relations with Reuters, The Associated Press can no longer refuse to deal directly with Rengo, jointly with Reuters if you are agreeable, or alone if you are not. Accordingly, on instructions from my Board of Directors, I went to Japan and made a detailed study of the situation as it is today, and I tell you frankly and earnestly that it is acute.

"Rengo today is fighting for its life against competition. A number of well-informed Japanese newspapermen whose sympathies are with Rengo declare that Nippon Dempo is a better service both as to foreign news and domestic news. Others say that Rengo has the better domestic service, but none says Rengo has the better foreign service. I was myself amazed to find the magnitude to which Nippon Dempo had grown.

"All of this time Reuters, with the unremunerated aid of The Associated Press, has been receiving a large income from Japan which Rengo has had to meet from sources other than the patronage of newspapers. You know that The Associated Press view is that there is nothing sound nor wise in that procedure.

"Rengo feels that every break has been in favor of Nippon Dempo. At any rate, Rengo is confronted by an emergency and cannot pay in service charges what it has been paying. If it collapses I doubt whether there is anything Reuters could do that would ever bring the Japanese field back to a profitable basis for Reuters. The only hope, as I see it, is that we both consider only a nominal financial return as sufficient and that Reuters join wholeheartedly with The Associated Press in getting behind Rengo.

"I cannot believe you will have resentment toward the plan I propose. I believe you will bear in mind that for twenty years The Associated Press has deferred to Reuters as respects Japan. But The Associated Press has denied itself meeting its own necessities as long as it dares.

"I have written this presentation because I was astonished to learn that you are opposed to The Associated Press sharing equal responsibilities and financial returns with Reuters as respects relations with Rengo. It is due you, therefore, as an ally and friend that you know how fairly we feel we are dealing. You surely will want to know The Associated Press side of it just as I have tried to know Reuters' side.

"With confidence that our minds will meet on this matter, and with kind personal regards, I am," etc.

Several months later Sir Roderick wrote me that there was hardly a paragraph in my letter which he was not prepared to challenge and refute and that his intention for some time was to do so. However, he said he found it difficult to fulfill that intention without appearing to give offense, which he was anxious not to do. He then entered a definite denial of all the statements in my letter. There he let the matter of denial rest, reserving the right to recite matters correctly and in more detail at some future time.

Although I saw much of Sir Roderick in London and New York after that I have never yet had from him his story of the position of Reuters in Japan and China during the twenty-five years to which he referred. My own information, contained in my letter, was given to me by high representatives of Reuters, by Mr. Iwanaga and Mr. Stone.

XXV

Reuters in Wrath

S IR RODERICK JONES was bitterly indignant over The Associated Press-Rengo contract, as was clearly shown by his subsequent actions. While I was still on the high seas en route to Europe from Japan, Reuters served The Associated Press with a coldly formal notice to terminate the four-party treaty. The British agency explained that the object of this notification was to clear the way for the adoption of modifications to bring the contract in line with mutual interests.

Reuters also said it noted that I was traveling back to the United States from Japan by way of Europe, and the agency's directors trusted that it would be convenient for me to stop off in London to see Sir Roderick who, it was made known, had been vested with full powers to carry on negotiations.

The hope that I would visit London was of course fulfilled, as that was my idea. Upon my arrival in London I called on him. We met on terms of cordiality. There wasn't the suspicion of a suggestion that Sir Roderick was displeased with the turn of events. Always Chesterfieldian in courtesy and hospitality, he entertained me in the delightful surroundings of one of England's most exclusive clubs, and invited me to spend a weekend at his Old World home in the country.

One thing, however, he did not invite me to do. He did not invite me to meet any members of his Board of Directors who were then, of course, members of the Press Association. I was very anxious then as I had always been to meet the members of the Press Association, owner of Reuters.

When the managing director of Reuters came to New York he was always entertained at lunch and dinner by the entire Board of Directors of The Associated Press. Once he was asked to sit with the board at its business sessions. All this was a great experience for him and he learned a good deal about The Associated Press which he could learn in no other way.

At that particular time when a break between the press of our two countries as represented by our two institutions was imminent, I was most anxious to become acquainted with his directors, thinking, perhaps, that among them I might find one who would see reasonableness in The Associated Press position and its principles. So I said I would like to meet the members of his board while I was there. He looked at me as if he had not heard me and changed the subject. Thus while he was head of Reuters I was never fortunate enough to meet any of his fellow directors.

It was first in Sir Roderick's oak-paneled office overlooking the Thames River and then across the snowy damask and Georgian silver of the club luncheon table that we dealt with the subject of the Rengo contract. Sir Roderick stated in most friendly terms that he felt

I had rather got out of bounds in my operations of the past several years.

The general atmosphere in which this assertion was made was that Reuters had proprietary rights in the vast territories which had been assigned to it in its treaty with Havas and Wolff, who also claimed their own exclusive rights. I, it seemed, had been inclined to trespass on the prerogatives of the allied agencies, and the case of my invasion of Japan was an illustration of this fact. There would not, I was led to believe, be another case like Havas and South America so far as any Reuters territory was concerned. I was made to feel that with Reuters aroused The Associated Press would cease its activities or else! All this was said with far greater finesse than has been attempted in this record.

While I wondered how long it would be before this bubble of Reuters world domination would burst, I responded in effect that the last thing The Associated Press desired was to be an unwelcome homesteader on ground already being worked by Reuters or the other allied agencies. Still, The Associated Press did feel very strongly that there should be world freedom of operation, not only for itself but for all news organizations. It wished, however, so to achieve its ambition that it would be in truth welcomed by its colleagues of the four-party alliance. In short, The Associated Press believed there was room for all, and it desired nothing more than to maintain with Reuters and the others the most friendly relations and co-operation. I was willing for Sir Roderick to blow his bubble so big that it would burst through his own exertion but I would not puncture it myself.

Sir Roderick pointed out another aspect to the Japanese situation: Reuters had tilled the Japanese soil these many years until it was a fruitful project; now along came The Associated Press and made a contract which deprived Reuters of considerable revenues; Sir Roderick might be prepared to concede to The Associated Press the rights of operation in Japan, but The Associated Press should make good Reuters loss in money. I had known his injured pride was partially responsible. I decided then that if the loss of money could be recouped the injured pride would heal.

I responded that The Associated Press expected Reuters also to make a contract with Rengo, but I could not concede that The Associated Press was under obligation to replace any Reuters losses in what I felt should be the free and open territory of Japan. The contract, I said, had been sought by Managing Director Iwanaga of Rengo. The Associated Press had not bullied its way into Japan and forced Iwanaga to make a treaty. Rengo preferred to have The Associated Press as its primary news source and under those circumstances there was no reason why The Associated Press should pay for the privilege of exchanging news with Rengo.

I asked Sir Roderick to state specifically what his demands were in regard to Japan. He said that he could not do this offhand but would put them in writing and forward them to me in New York. So the matter was left.

Another view of what was beginning to flame was given in a letter to Mr. Noyes telling him of my conversations with Sir Roderick, written July 30, 1933, on my return voyage:

"I waited for Sir Roderick to express the tone of the conversations. He apparently waited for me to do this but in an instant he was all smiles, and in a few minutes had more cordiality than he had ever shown before toward me. I responded with equal cordiality.

"I told him in great detail just what I had found in Japan. He said he was amazed at Iwanaga signing any kind of a contract with The Associated Press without full consultation with him because, he said, 'Rengo is one of my children' . . . When I told him I understood Iwanaga was coming to London he showed real fire by pounding the desk and declaring with his teeth set:

" 'That's his only chance!' "

"Hiroshi Saito, who is the nephew of Iwanaga and is now Minister to Holland, was one of the members of the Japanese delegation at the Economic Conference here this month. At Iwanaga's request Saito had called on Sir Roderick two or three times. Saito told me he had learned definitely that it was 90% a case of Sir Roderick's pride being hurt and that the wound could only be healed by my coming to his office to make amends and, above all, for Iwanaga to come. At any rate I have made my explanations and Iwanaga will be in London shortly."

It was largely a matter of hurt pride that caused Sir Roderick to take such strong action. He was—and I dare say still is—a very proud man. I had every reason to explain matters to an ally but I did not feel called upon to apologize even if by doing so I would have calmed the troubled waters, yet it gave me no pleasure to observe his state of mind. Indeed, because of our many discussions, always amicable, I had begun to have an affection for him. So I was sorry to see him vexed.

My letter to Mr. Noyes gave confirmation on the matter of pride:

"I then told him I could not refrain from expressing my amazement that when he knew I was on my way to see him on what in reality is a minor matter he injected a major matter by astonishing Havas, Wolff and The Associated Press in New York by denouncing the contract; this without any previous discussion as to any requirements that Reuters feels necessary. He said:

" 'You will understand, if you please, that one challenges quickly when one's pride is hurt.'

"I replied that having made my explanations, wouldn't the best thing be to recall the denunciation and then let us negotiate changes, etc. He said he could not do that without discussing the matter with his Board, and the Board did not meet until next month, and that it would be better anyway to wait to see the result of his talk with Iwanaga, since the Rengo matter was, so far as he was concerned, the source of the entire trouble.

"I told him as he had confessed to some pride himself I would have to confess to some personally, although I was not authorized to speak for The Associated Press— that my Board had never clothed me with authority to deal with the matter as he had written us in his denunciation his Board had clothed him. I pointed this out by way of emphasizing that I was merely speaking for myself when I added that my pride would not permit me to beg and plead with him to withdraw the notice or even to continue an alliance with The Associated Press if it gave him great unhappiness to do so.

"It was left this way: After he sees Iwanaga and after he discusses the matter with his Board, he proposes to answer my long letter of June 11. Evidently he proposes to give Reuters' side of the matter with as much force as I tried to give The Associated Press side."

Mr. Iwanaga came to New York in August, 1933. He told me that he had no intention of going to London to see Sir Roderick because he was incensed that Reuters had canceled the four-party contract while I was en route from Tokyo to London to discuss the matter with him. Iwanaga told me that he felt Reuters had been extremely discourteous both to The Associated Press and to Rengo.

Whatever influence I had with Iwanaga I used to induce him to make the trip to London and to use the ability I knew he had to satisfy Sir Roderick. The latter had told me that he could not determine the future relations of Reuters with The Associated Press until he had seen Iwanaga. As I wanted Sir Roderick to make up his mind, I insisted that Iwanaga make the trip. Finally he said he would go and the day he sailed I wrote to Mr. Noyes:

"Iwanaga sails this evening. He is going to Reuters, willing to make any concession other than for Rengo to break with The Associated Press. In other words, if Reuters tries to get him to accept a contract that would supersede a Rengo-Associated Press contract, he says he will decline.

"I told him I wanted him to go, convinced as I am

that the best results, most easily obtained, will come from his contracting with Reuters in addition to his Associated Press contract. That would involve a continuance of the Reuters-Associated Press relationship, which I want to see continued unless Reuters demands such modifications in the present contract as would nullify all that we have gained through these years of association.

"I had misgivings when I first saw Mr. Iwanaga. He felt keen antagonism against Reuters because Reuters denounced the four-party contract without warning. He told me that he came to New York to tell me that he was going to return directly to Japan without going to London, and stand upon his relationship with The Associated Press. He was sincere about this, and thus convinced me of his appreciation of and loyalty to The Associated Press. However, I started slowly to persuade him that he must go to London for the good of the common cause. Finally he said that he would go because I wanted him to. Through the three days I have had with him I have been able to build up enthusiasm on his part that he go there determined either to settle the matter for Rengo or to settle the matter for both Rengo and The Associated Press in such a way as the continuance of the Reuters-Associated Press relations shall be effected."

Sir Roderick did await the arrival and departure of Iwanaga before writing me. Then in a letter to me, the introduction of which I have quoted, Jones said that a situation had been created "which might have developed disastrously but (a) for Mr. Iwanaga's response to

my suggestion that he visit London, and (b) for that gentleman's statesmanlike and honorable conduct throughout the negotiations which followed upon his arrival
here. These negotiations, I am happy to say, produced
covenants which I believe will reinforce and consolidate
the close relationship which has existed between our
Japanese ally and Reuters from the beginning. They
leave Rengo free to make their arrangements with The
Associated Press."

With the ability that I knew he had, Iwanaga had
healed Sir Roderick's pride and satisfied Reuters with
a five-year contract, carbon copies of which Iwanaga gave
me when he returned to New York. Then he went to
Washington where, with true Japanese ceremony, he
laid a wreath in the Washington Cathedral on the tomb
of Melville E. Stone, my beloved predecessor as general
manager of The Associated Press.

I asked Byron Price, chief of The Associated Press
bureau in Washington, to assist Mr. Iwanaga in the com-
mission. Price told me that as Iwanaga was about to
carry out the ceremony he felt he owed Price some explanation and he offered this with the simplicity which
was one of his characteristics:

"I have always looked upon Mr. Kent Cooper and
Sir Roderick Jones as my very dear brothers. When the
trouble arose this summer and it seemed that the long
friendship between these two was about to be ended,
I was deeply distressed. I came to New York and saw
Mr. Cooper. Then I went to London and returned to
New York. I talked with both of them. Now that I have
done what I can to keep my two brothers together, I
wish to lay this wreath upon the tomb of the one whom

I call my second father—the man who gave me lessons in the great principles of mutuality and co-operation in the collection and dissemination of the news of the world as exemplified by The Associated Press."

So Iwanaga laid his wreath in reverent memory of the great journalist. Later I had told him that there was no personal feeling on my part against Sir Roderick —that he merely represented a school of thought in the methods of international news exchange which was not my concept of what such methods should be; that I had directed my efforts to obtain free and open operation internationally in the hope that all peoples through their newspapers everywhere would benefit.

"And, of course, I know what you say is true," Iwanaga replied.

XXVI

An Answer Is Given

THE crisis between the nineteenth century Old World principle of monopoly in international news exchange as represented by Reuters and its twentieth century New World antithesis was brought to a head in the winter of 1933 by Reuters. Until that year, Reuters for three-quarters of a century had actually controlled access to the greatest pool of international news in existence. Reuters knew of the determination of The Associated Press to extend its service to every country in the world that would accept it and that it proposed to do this without profit to itself. With Reuters owned by a portion of the British press The Associated Press hoped that Reuters would share in this twentieth century progressive movement which constituted the most important change in world news agency approach to its task since The Associated Press, the first news agency, was created.

Reuters decided to penalize The Associated Press at an unusual time, since the resources of the latter had for several years been many times greater than those of Reuters. Moreover, it decided to do so in spite of the fact that it knew that the Canadian Press, the co-operative that served every newspaper in Canada, had given its adherence to The Associated Press as against all others, including Reuters. It did so in spite of the fact that Havas, Reuters's great ally, had thrown open the entire South American continent to The Associated Press. It did so in spite of the fact that the press of Australia and other parts of the British dominions was asking The Associated Press to make its world-wide service available to it either alongside of Reuters or to displace Reuters if the latter withdrew its service as a penalty. It did so after Rengo by preference had firmly bound itself to The Associated Press with a five-year contract.

The presentation by Reuters of its proposal to penalize The Associated Press was positive in its terms and firm in its demand. It assessed against The Associated Press a large sum of money to be paid by The Associated Press as a differential for its right to have access to the Reuters service. Not for six years had there been any payment of a differential by The Associated Press to Reuters. That differential payment went out with the first change in the basic contract, which was made in 1927. As a matter of fact there was the firm conviction of many of the executives of The Associated Press that Reuters was getting vastly more from The Associated Press than the latter received from Reuters. Reference was made to this many times before the Board of Directors, but since The Associated Press is not a profit-making concern there was no disposition to make a demand for a differential.

Sir Roderick's astonishing proposals for future relations were answered by a letter from President Noyes:

"I have read your letter to Kent Cooper dealing with the proposals made by Reuters as to future relations between your organization and The Associated Press.

"I think that these letters constitute a major, if not the major, disappointment of my life in that, to me, they seem to indicate a very low estimate on the part of the directors of Reuters and of yourself of the value of The Associated Press in the close association that has existed so many years between our respective organizations.

"I will, of course, submit your proposals to our Board of Directors at its next meeting on January 9.

"I would appreciate it if you would cable me before that date whether you and your board of directors have definitely concluded that it is not desirable to continue operating under the four-party treaty now under denunciation."

In response to this letter Sir Roderick cabled confirmation of the Reuters decision not to continue the contract. He then confirmed this by letter.

Whether Sir Roderick expected Mr. Noyes to reply that The Associated Press was prepared to accept his terms would be pure conjecture. Be that as it may, the answer was even more sensational than the demands had been. That development can be told in no better way than to quote the succinct letter of January 12, 1934 (no cable was sent), which conveyed this announcement from President Noyes to Sir Roderick:

"Our Board of Directors has given detailed consideration to the proposals made by you in behalf of Reuters in your letters of November 21, 1933, and January 1, 1934, and has reached the conclusion that our point of view is so entirely divergent from that expressed and reiterated by you that the two cannot be reconciled.

"It has, therefore, been voted to accept as definite your denunciation of the four-party treaty as of April 1.

"I greatly regret that this situation has developed and that the two organizations must hereafter travel separate paths."

While I was not astonished that the ultimatum came from Reuters I could scarcely believe that after nearly twenty years of consideration The Associated Press was at last going to face the world on its own. In those twenty years the Board of Directors had tried to find a method that would bring The Associated Press and Reuters into complete harmony. It was difficult to realize that the great day had come and that when it did come the board reached its decision so quickly and in such a determined mood.

If The Associated Press had been depending on the Reuters service there would have been much to do. However, for almost nine years I had been developing the staff abroad with the possibility that sometime The Associated Press and Reuters would have to travel separate paths—not that I wanted them to, but that I intended to be prepared for The Associated Press to do so rather than to have it give up its operations abroad or to pay a penalty to Reuters. There was nothing left to do by way of preparation except to enlarge the coverage for British territory.

There were, however, some expressions of sentiment to be made. First was one to my friend, J. F. B. Livesay, general manager of the Canadian Press, who for many

years had been at my side in this matter of idealistic
approach to our work; another was to Mr. Houssaye
of Havas; and another was to Mr. Otto Mejer of DNB
of Berlin. A brief quotation from the letter to Mr. Houssaye follows:

"The thing about it that is preposterous is that unless The Associated Press consents to meet an exorbitant
and unwarranted demand from Reuters, there can be no
treaty between The Associated Press and the others. It
seems altogether incongruous in this age of civilization
that an agency in one country can disturb the alliance
between two friendly agencies, located in two other
countries which have been associated for over forty
years. . . .

"Reuters appraises its service to The Associated
Press at so high a value and The Associated Press service
to Reuters at so low a value that it was wholly out of
the question for The Associated Press directors to accept any such proposal. Reuters, therefore, has cut the
tie. The annulment of the contract by Reuters is to be
allowed to stand.

"We have no ill feeling, either because Reuters cut
the tie or because of the appraisal Reuters makes of The
Associated Press. We are certain of our own security just
as Reuters seems to be certain of its security. There is
no antagonism involved nor intended so far as The Associated Press is concerned. We can understand that
Reuters has a position and a dignity to maintain, and
you can understand that The Associated Press has the
same. Our resources are ample, and I hope Reuters will
find elsewhere an ally that will be as loyal to Reuters
as The Associated Press has been and that such an ally

will supply Reuters with the financial help Reuters feels it needs, as demonstrated by its demand upon us.

"I do not know whether you are compelled to permit Reuters to decide the future of the Havas-Associated Press relationship. If you are at liberty to deal with us as to our respective national territories and as to the Latin-American situation, I would be glad to know that fact and it would give me a good deal of personal pleasure to be able to negotiate with you."

At the same time I wrote to the Press Association of England, the owner of the capital stock of Reuters, inviting it to make a direct contract with The Associated Press since there was in my heart a feeling that something sometime would be evidenced by the Press Association that its principles and its operations were not alien to those of The Associated Press. Sir Roderick had not given me an opportunity to meet Mr. H. C. Robbins, its general manager, or Mr. Henry Martin, its editor in chief. The Associated Press could, of course, get along without the Press Association. Likewise the Press Association could get along without The Associated Press. Nevertheless, I felt that the two associations were blood brothers and had much in common. Also I felt the time would come when they would have a great deal more in common because even then Germany, no longer a republic but approaching a Hitler dictatorship, had begun to exert itself not only against the articles of the Versailles Treaty but likewise against the restricting contract that Reuters and Havas imposed upon the Wolff (later DNB) news agency of Berlin.

So I wrote to Mr. Robbins of the Press Association, my letter saying in part:

"While The Associated Press never has had any direct contractual relations with the Press Association, I cannot let the development by which Reuters has made it necessary for The Associated Press to accept denouncement of Reuters' treaty with The Associated Press pass without writing you.

"The Associated Press will find itself in no need of any of Reuters' service as The Associated Press already has a world-wide news collection staff capable of delivering what it believes to be a prompter and better news service than any in existence."

After explaining something of the break and the situation arising from it, I continued:

"With this explanation let me frankly state that for the fifteen years during which I have been acquainted with the work of the Press Association, I have come to have for it a high regard. I would be glad indeed if a way could be found to have a direct relationship with the Press Association, although I fear that Reuters would not permit that.

"I would be obliged to you if you would let us know what, if anything, we may expect so far as concerns the Press Association, and in any event rest assured that we shall always have the highest regard for the work the Press Association has done in its field from which The Associated Press has received large benefits, just as we have enjoyed and appreciated the relationship with Reuters through which the Press Association report reached us. The real important element contributing in recent years to our satisfaction with Reuters connection, however, has been the availability of your service."

Last but not least I wrote to my friend Livesay on the day The Associated Press advised Reuters that it accepted the termination of the contract. Not until eight years later did the letter again come to mind. And that was when I started to write this story. But here it is:

"I want to assure you that The Associated Press, which has less and less been relying upon Reuters, will have a far better service by virtue of its independence than it has ever had before. When I think of the way we have protected Reuters and given it beats from everywhere, through its sending our news of Europe and the world at large from here to London, I could be more fearful as to the efficiency of Reuters' service in the future than I am of our own.

"I am establishing bureaus in each of the chief countries of the British Empire. It is about this that I want to talk to you when I see you. Out of it I hope there will be an advancement of your marvelous idea of some co-operative news activity in the British Empire. If The Associated Press could join in that I would be most happy.

"As for myself, Fred, I am more confident as to a grand development, improvement and perfection in the work of The Associated Press than I ever could have been under the restraining and forbidding hand of an ally who maintains position of arbiter, controller and fee collector of the activities, hopes and aspirations of news agencies in countries other than his own. Once and for all The Associated Press can pronounce, with entire freedom, its attitude in the international agency situation. It has long been a liberal one, its cardinal principle being that each agency should be free to contract directly with an allied agency in any other country, without getting the permission of a third agency in still another country.

"I personally believe that the overlordship of Reuters in the matter of consenting or denying agency connections between agencies of two other countries than Great Britain is not only antiquated but is wholly inconsistent with the progressive thought of today. Indeed, I personally believe that such overlordship may eventually lead to serious international misunderstandings. Certainly such overlordship can, and I believe has, acted as a deterrent to the widest possible development of news exchange upon a salutary basis.

"But why preach to one who shares religiously this feeling as to the work to which we have both devoted our lives—co-operative, non-profit making news collection and dissemination, honestly collected and truthfully written!

"For many years I have been telling the Board that freedom of action, which meant freedom from Reuters' territorial control, would be like a breath of fresh air to the executives of this organization. I have told my executive staff that we shall no longer submit to Reuters in our foreign activities and if you could see the happiness and confidence with which this move has inspired them you would have no doubt as to the future."

The reverberations in Europe to the terse letter Mr. Noyes sent to Sir Roderick and my letters to Havas, Wolff and the Press Association were considerable. The reaction of the Canadian Press to the position taken by The Associated Press was one of the finest compliments ever paid to the latter. The Canadian Press could have been expected in all loyalty to have cast its lot with Reuters in spite of the fact that if it did so it would have had to put aside memories of its beginnings, briefly sketched as follows:

Until a little after the turn of the century it was The Associated Press that served the Canadian newspapers. In harmony with the trend of thought on both sides of the border and with the idea of Canada adopting the mutual co-operative plan of news collection and dissemination without profit, the Canadian Press was born. It came into being with the benediction of The Associated Press, and while during most of the life of the Canadian effort there have been contracts respecting the arrangements between the two mutual co-operative organizations, matters run so regularly between the two that neither of them seems ever to find it necessary to refer to any written contract. The Associated Press withdrew from Canada because it felt that the Canadian newspapers should have their own national organization, which would exchange news with The Associated Press.

The status of the great news agency of Canada, therefore, conforms to the idea of The Associated Press that every nation whose press can afford independent operation of its news agency should have its own co-operative for its newspapers and owned by them. Each such co-operative should have exchange relations on an international basis with all the others.

The press of some units of the British commonwealth of Nations has long wanted to have a co-operative news exchange with all the units of the commonwealth, but according to those who would foster the idea, Reuters has opposed the development. One of the things expected of Reuters under its ownership by the British Press Association is the development of these co-operatives, and that they will ultimately work as harmoniously together as have the Canadian Press and The Associated Press. Those who hope for this ultimate development believe that, with no overlordship, the press of the nations that accept the plan will effect a system that will at the same time be both ideal and practical.

XXVII

Melodrama by the Thames

I HAVE said that the stir in Europe caused by the position taken by The Associated Press was considerable. Indeed, for a time the developments over there were somewhat melodramatic. Fleet Street, the newspaper area of the British capital, was the locale of one of the incidents and a drab London café in that vicinity saw one of the little scenes enacted. The season being January, one of those yellowish, gray fogs was rolling up the Thames. Into the dimly lighted café from this shrouded mist slipped a figure whom the customers of the soup restaurant had never before seen in the place.

Lorin Johnson, chief of the United Press bureau in London, at the time had his head in a bowl of soup when he was astounded to be accosted by a Reuters executive who had served under all three managing directors. The executive was Mr. Murray, the secretary of Reuters, and a confidant of Sir Roderick. Murray said to Johnson with a wink:

"You had better tell Mr. Bickel [president of the United Press] to get in touch with Sir Roderick quickly."

Whether Mr. Johnson learned any more from Mr. Murray as to what it was all about I do not know. I was told that he communicated to Mr. Bickel what Mr. Murray had said, and that as Mr. Bickel did not respond to Murray's suggestion he received direct from a mutual friend another cablegram which was a bit more specific. It said that if the United Press wanted to displace The Associated Press with Reuters, Bickel had better rush over to London.

I did not believe that Karl Bickel would rush over to London. I had then known him for twenty years and of course I had not forgotten that we stood foursquare together on the code of principles discussed at Geneva in 1927. Also, though the United Press had grown into a strong competitor of The Associated Press, it could not have done so if it had sought and embraced the idea of monopoly as represented by Reuters.

Since the days of its incorporation in 1907 the United Press has been headed by individuals each of whom I have known intimately and each of whom I have rated as men of unusual ability. There was John W. Vandercook, who died shortly after the news agency was incorporated. There were H. B. Clark, Clayton D. Lee, and then in succession Roy W. Howard, W. W. Hawkins and Karl A. Bickel.

Roy Howard was so much the dynamo of the United Press and so projected it into its greatest development that, although he has not been president of the United Press for more than twenty years, there are scores of newspaper publishers and many people in public life who still think the names of Roy Howard and the United Press are synonymous.

The silent partner in Howard's dynamic activities with the United Press was Hawkins, who for many years served as vice-president, then president. I sometimes wonder whether the United Press ever would have amounted to anything had it not been for these two men. Hawkins is sure it would have been successful without him and Howard has said he could not have succeeded in his work in the United Press without the friendly and dependable Bill Hawkins at his side.

The two constitute one of the most amazing teams I have ever known. Titles as such have meant nothing to them in recent years. Howard became the partner of Scripps in all the enterprises in which the Scripps fortune was invested. I never have kept account of their titles because the titles meant nothing to me since I know them so well. It may be that at this time Hawkins is chairman of the board of the United Press and Howard is chairman of the executive committee. It was probably the reverse at one time. I have not followed the mutations by which they have identified themselves corporately with the Scripps organizations.

I do know that in them the newspaper business of America gained recruits who know the depth of responsibility that the press and news agencies have, and who have always adhered to the highest principles. They admired what Melville Stone did for American journalism in setting the standards of truthful, unbiased news and they inculcated these principles in the minds of the officials to whom they entrusted the operations of the United Press, which of all the many Scripps institutions is the one closest to their hearts.

When their opportunities and responsibilities in the

great Scripps organization increased, and it looked as if they were not longer to be active in the United Press, Howard cast around for someone who might ultimately carry the fuller responsibility of the news agency. He considered two.

One, who shall be nameless, declined and thus passed up an opportunity to become wealthy. Bickel accepted and later became president of the organization. This was before I became general manager of The Associated Press. Bickel fought for the continued ascendancy of the United Press with all that he had and he carried it forward. In my opinion he would not, any more than Howard or Hawkins, accept the dominance of the European news agency monopoly. It was as repugnant to him as it was to them.

While all the presidents of the United Press made it a point to be on personal terms with the managing directors of the leading European agencies, I am told that Bickel never seriously indicated any desire on the part of the United Press to displace The Associated Press in the world-wide allotments of news agency territory.

By the time he became president of the United Press, The Associated Press had already gone through a turbulent ten years of trying to modernize its relationship with that monopoly. This fact was rather common knowledge. I always felt that Bickel enjoyed the fact that The Associated Press was in the meshes of monopoly and that the United Press was profiting by that fact. If this was true, it could be understood that Bickel would not care to have the United Press change places with The Associated Press which up to that time had made very little progress in freeing itself so that it could carry abroad the American principles of news dissemination.

When I heard that a message had been sent to Bickel I was not astonished. But knowing Bickel's background and everything for which the United Press stood, I would have been very much astonished had he rushed to London to see Sir Roderick Jones in response to that message. I asked him about it, and he said in a nonchalant sort of way that he had not decided what to do except that he was going to Cincinnati to make a speech and then leave for Sarasota, Florida, where he had just purchased a home and where he hoped to spend a month's vacation.

A week passed and out of the London fog came another even more astonishing development. On January 31, Mr. Noyes received in his office in the Washington *Star* Building the following radiogram from the managing director of Reuters:

"Granted your good will, I am determined, my dear friend, to settle this trouble. I am sailing Berengaria Saturday to see you, I could not cable sooner as impossible to assemble all my directors."

I would not give the impression that the United Press did not give some consideration to the possibilities of a contract with Reuters but I have the conviction that if one had been made it would have left the United Press free in the world field.

The news agency did want the news of DNB from Berlin, of Tass from Moscow, and possibly of Stefani from Italy. Also it probably would have been interested at that time in having access to the Press Association news. However, it apparently wanted nothing of Havas or Reuters, and as Havas was a full, though perhaps what might be called a junior, partner of the monopoly, it would not have been possible for Sir Roderick to have got the consent of Havas for a contract with the United Press.

Indeed, I was told that as a result of my letter to Mr. Houssaye, Reuters felt the formidable power of Havas applied for the first time. Mr. Houssaye let me know beyond doubt that so far as Havas was concerned Reuters would continue on the terms that had existed in the four-party treaty that the four news agency heads signed in London, in February, 1932.

So Sir Roderick's message may have come as a dramatic turn in his futile efforts to gain the assent of Havas to install the United Press in the place vacated by The Associated Press. Then, too, he apparently was getting no encouragement from the United Press, which may not have wished to make any contract at all with Reuters —certainly none that would include Havas. As up to this time the head of Reuters had been doing all the negotiating, probably only he knows the whole story. Nevertheless, because of the information I had as to what was going on, I commented to Mr. Noyes: "The bubble of Reuters domination has burst," and added that the star of The Associated Press is ascendant in world news relationships.

Then, as though by way of confirmation of this statement, I received the next day a communication from H. C. Robbins, general manager of the Press Association of London, deploring the break between Reuters and The Associated Press and offering his services to mend the breach. This was fair evidence that things were beginning to boil in London, since Mr. Robbins would send no such message without the consideration of the directors of the Press Association, which in turn owned Reuters.

Mr. Robbins's message read:

"Confidential your letter January twelfth. Press Association deplores prospect of break between Associated and Reuters. We convinced no good whatsoever can flow therefrom for either organization and only long standing rivals of both can benefit. As cooperative body of British newspapers Press Association has strong affinity with Associated. In view of our mutual ideals we be most happy to continue in relationship with you. We regret however our covenants with Reuters make this absolutely impossible if break becomes effective.

"Wishful as we are that two American British cooperative enterprises Associated and Press Association should continue together instead of being in opposition camps we prepared use our influence with Reuters with which we feel we could with satisfaction negotiate. We cannot but think that Reuters would be prepared to withdraw their proposals and return to statusquoante if coupled with early meeting in New York or elsewhere to clear up all causes of misunderstanding.

"Press Association would welcome solution now suggested as means of maintaining link between American and British newspapers through our respective associations."

Simultaneously another offer of mediation came from Otto Mejer, managing director of the DNB in Germany, whom I had also invited to make a direct contract. Mejer cabled me:

"I urgently commend an agreement with Reuters as a break with Reuters is impossible. I offer mediation."

A commentary on this message came a few days later from Louis P. Lochner, chief of the Berlin Bureau of The Associated Press. He had been dining with Mejer and relayed to me the following:

"Reuters are apparently flabbergasted at your taking them at their word, and are importuning Mejer to mediate on their behalf. There have been long distance messages between Sir Roderick and Mejer and evidently letters have also been interchanged. I showed Mejer a copy of the contract which you authorized me to offer DNB. Mejer was delighted with it. He told Sir Roderick that he considered it a model contract and an 'excellent one which all of the agencies ought to be glad to sign,' to which Sir Roderick replied that he, too, saw no reason why it should not serve as a model between the various agencies.

"Moreover, while during Mejer's mid-month visit to London Reuters had still been quite offish about liberating DNB from its fetters, they apparently now on learning through Mejer that you were negotiating a separate contract, were ready to give DNB anything it wanted."

With the background I had as to the attitudes of the Canadian Press, Rengo, DNB, Havas and the Press Association, I was ready to proceed with a step I had wanted to take for a long time, but which until now had not appeared opportune.

I knew that the United Press had always followed the

news principles of the older Associated Press and I felt that the owners of it would be no less interested in a statement of principles of mutual conduct of American news agencies addressing themselves to the world at large. There had never been any occasion that seemed to call for a discussion of these principles with the United Press, which was then and always had been, and probably always will be, in sharp competition with The Associated Press everywhere.

If, as was reported concerning Sir Roderick's visit, he was coming to America either to mend the breach with The Associated Press or contract with the United Press, his visit to these shores was a matter of mutual interest to both The Associated Press and the United Press. The crisis was at hand.

Personally I cared not at all whether Reuters made a contract with the United Press or with The Associated Press because in either case a contract would give The Associated Press the freedom of action it wanted, since the Board of Directors had definitely decided that the organization must have a free hand so as to extend its operations throughout the world.

With nothing to lose so far as The Associated Press was concerned, and with everything to gain so far as the advancement of practical idealism was concerned, I took up with our competitor the matter of making a contract unique in the history of press associations, if not unique as a contract between two competitors in any business.

XXVIII

A Stroke Against Monopoly

WHILE Sir Roderick was rushing to America
to try to repair the ravages of the hurricane
he had let loose, The Associated Press and
the United Press made a treaty which, so far as these
strenuously competing organizations were concerned,
threw the whole wide world open to all news agency
enterprises.

The pact was unique because it was intended not to
establish monopoly or exclusivity, but on the contrary
to ensure that neither would obtain or accept exclusivity. This was a thrust at the Victorian news agency
monopoly which hardened into the contracts that were
made by Reuters and Havas during the peace negotiations that led to the Versailles Treaty.

The Associated Press and the United Press pledged
themselves to keep the door open to each other or to
any other competitor who wished to adhere to the contract. It specifically provided that if the third American
news organization—William Randolph Hearst's International News Service—wanted to join the other two,
all it had to do was to sign the contract.

The contract was signed without ceremony in the

rooms of President Noyes at the Ritz-Carlton Hotel in New York City. Mr. Noyes had willingly accepted the idea and I was proud to have his name affixed with mine. Karl Bickel and Mr. Hawkins signed for the United Press. And the lawyers were there—John W. Davis, for The Associated Press, and Thomas Sidlo, for the United Press.

The idealism of this extraordinary pact was summed up succinctly in the introduction. This made the following points:

1. Neither party to the agreement approved of or wished to sustain "the practice of European agencies which, at the dictation of one or more of them, hinders international news exchange by making exclusive arrangements for the availability of their news."

2. Neither party desired "to seek a selfish advantage which, if acquired, would only contribute to prevent the fulfillment of the object herein sought."

3. And so, "for the purpose of obtaining a freer flow of international news exchange," they were uniting "in a common effort to open up a free and unhampered availability of the news of Europe and the British Isles."

In order to put teeth into this declaration of independence, The Associated Press and the United Press pledged that neither would make a contract with any European agency to the exclusion of the other or have relations with an agency which refused to serve them both. Moreover, they agreed that neither would make with any European agency a contract which couldn't be terminated on ninety days' notice, except with the written consent of the other.

They even went so far as to include this share-and-share alike clause in their pact: "If as a result of any action it takes because of this contract either party shall be denied traffic facilities (wire communications) or suffer traffic delays, or be subjected to unfair censorship or to any other disadvantage, the party not thus affected will not seek, accept nor maintain any advantage denied the other party."

There was more along the same millennial lines, and then just to put the hallmark of sincerity on the contract it was written down that whenever either party should make any sort of agreement with a European agency, it should be filed with the other party within sixty days. In brief, both organizations agreed to work absolutely in the open with each other. I felt that stipulations less strong would never break down Reuters domination. The text of this document follows:

This CONTRACT was made and entered into this eighth day of February, 1934,
BETWEEN
THE ASSOCIATED PRESS, incorporated in the State of New York, with its principal office in New York City, N. Y.
AND
THE UNITED PRESS ASSOCIATIONS, incorporated in the State of New York, with its principal office in New York City, N. Y.
WITNESSETH THAT:
WHEREAS both parties hereto not approving nor wishing to sustain the practice of European agencies which at the dictation of one or more of them hinders international news exchange by making exclusive arrangements for the availability of their news, and not desiring to seek a selfish advantage which, if acquired, would only contribute to

prevent the fulfillment of the object herein sought, and for the purpose of obtaining a freer flow of international news exchange, do hereby unite in a common effort to open up a free and unhampered availability of the news of Europe and the British Isles. In order to bring this about, and for that purpose and to that extent only, they both in a spirit of common welfare agree:

DEFINITIONS:

The term "EUROPEAN AGENCY" shall be construed to include, other than the signatories hereto, any news agency or governmental activity located in any European country, or in the British Isles, which collects or issues news of such European country or countries, except that it shall not include THE ASSOCIATED PRESS OF GREAT BRITAIN, THE ASSOCIATED PRESS OF GERMANY, THE UNITED PRESS DEUTSCHLAND, THE BRITISH UNITED PRESS, or any subsidiary or affiliate of either party now existing or hereafter established.

The term "CONTRACT" shall mean an agreement, arrangement or treaty of any kind, whether in writing or not, for the purpose of OBTAINING news in contradistinction to the DISSEMINATION of news by sale or otherwise.

ARTICLE I

Neither party shall endeavor to contract, nor contract nor operate, directly or indirectly, through any subsidiary, affiliate or otherwise, with any European agency for availability of such European agency's news to the exclusion of availability to the same extent to the other party and upon the same terms.

ARTICLE II

Neither party will make a contract with any European agency that cannot be terminated on ninety (90) days' notice, except by written consent of the other party.

ARTICLE III

If a European agency has or makes a contract with an outside party through which outside party one of the parties hereto might have, or may later have rights to or availability of the news of such European agency thus indirectly, whether availed of or not, the party hereto having such rights and availability guarantees that it will either not avail itself thereof in any particular or will obtain equal availability for the other party at any time the latter so desires. Such availability shall be upon terms consistent with the terms of this contract, and the procedure in the endeavor to secure such availability shall be followed as specified herein, but pending satisfactory conclusion of such procedure neither party will avail itself of such European agency's news in any manner.

ARTICLE IV

Either party which may now have a contract or arrangement with any European agency which prohibits the other party hereto equal access will notify such European agency that it waives any objection and cancels any right of protest to the other party having equal access to such European agency's news but upon the same terms. If upon application of the other party hereto such European agency refuses or delays to contract with the applicant in the manner herein outlined, the party having such contract shall, upon the request of the applying

party, promptly proceed in conformity with AR-
TICLE V.

ARTICLE V

If any European agency with which one of the
parties hereto may have, or shall at any time ac-
quire a contract, shall impose such terms or delays
as the other party not contracted therewith and desiring equal availability, asserts to be unfair, the
party having such contract shall seek equal terms
of availability for the other party hereto, and upon
failing to obtain them shall promptly take appropriate action to cancel and discontinue its contract
with such European agency. But if such contract
is cancelled neither party shall thereafter contract
with that European agency without the consent of
the other party hereto in writing first having been
given.

ARTICLE VI

If as a result of any action it takes because of this
contract either party shall be denied traffic facilities or suffer traffic delays, or be subjected to unfair
censorship or to any other disadvantage, the party
not thus affected will not seek, accept nor maintain
any advantage denied the other party.

ARTICLE VII

This contract does not include RENGO or NIP-
PON DEMPO of Japan, unless and until these two
Japanese agencies are merged, or until there exists
a monopoly by a Japanese agency, or unless there is
only one dominating or leading news agency in Japan; when either of those two things happens both
parties to this agreement shall cooperate to see that
each party hereto that desires it shall promptly receive rights and privileges to the news of such Japanese agency in the same manner, and to be affected

in the same terms as apply herein to European agencies.

ARTICLE VIII

THE ASSOCIATED PRESS, party hereto, declares that all of its present exclusive arrangements with European agencies, with the exception of STEFANI of Italy, and TASS of Russia, terminate on March 31, 1934. No provisions of this contract can, therefore, apply to the unexpired terms of such contracts as expire on that date. If, for any reason, the termination date of such contracts is extended beyond March 31, 1934, such extension shall positively terminate not later than June 30, 1934. Thus, the terms of this contract shall apply to relations with the foregoing agencies not later than June 30, 1934. THE ASSOCIATED PRESS contract with STEFANI, of Italy, and TASS, of Russia, may be terminated at the end of 1934, but meanwhile THE ASSOCIATED PRESS agrees it shall notify STEFANI, of Italy, and TASS, of Russia, that it waives objection to THE UNITED PRESS ASSOCIATIONS, party hereto, having equal terms of availability to the news of STEFANI and TASS. Thus, the terms of this contract shall apply to relations with TASS and STEFANI at once, if the latter are agreeable, or in any case, not later than December 31, 1934. THE ASSOCIATED PRESS, party hereto, declares it has no other exclusive news availability contracts in Europe or the British Isles.

ARTICLE IX

THE UNITED PRESS ASSOCIATIONS, party hereto, hereby declares it has no contracts for the exclusive availability of the news of any European agency and that any future contracts shall be made in conformity with this agreement.

ARTICLE X

THE ASSOCIATED PRESS, party hereto, guarantees that its subsidiaries, or affiliates, THE ASSOCIATED PRESS OF GREAT BRITAIN, and THE ASSOCIATED PRESS OF GERMANY, or any subsidiary, or affiliate, that it may create, will not make exclusive news availability contracts for any territory with any European agency; and further that they will not in any respect operate inconsistently with the terms and intent of this contract.

ARTICLE XI

THE UNITED PRESS ASSOCIATIONS, party hereto, guarantees that the British United Press, United Press Deutschland or any subsidiary or affiliate of United Press Associations, of British United Press, or of United Press Deutschland, now existing or hereafter created, will not make exclusive news availability contracts for any territory with any European news agency, and further that they will not in any respect operate inconsistently with the terms and intent of this contract.

ARTICLE XII

Whenever either party shall enter into a contract or arrangement with a European agency, such party shall, as soon as possible and not later than sixty (60) days after the execution thereof, file a copy of such contract with the other party.

ARTICLE XIII

If the International News Service shall at any time desire to join in this agreement its signature hereto shall constitute it a party hereto with the same force and effect as THE ASSOCIATED PRESS and THE UNITED PRESS ASSOCIATIONS.

ARTICLE XIV

This contract shall continue in effect for five years from the date hereof and shall renew itself thereafter unless notice of a desire to terminate it shall have been given by either party to the other by registered mail two years before the expiration of the initial five year term, and shall be terminable thereafter at any time upon two years' notice from either party to the other by registered mail.

ARTICLE XV

This contract is signed in duplicate by the respective President and Secretary of THE ASSOCIATED PRESS and by the President and Vice-Chairman of the Board of Directors of THE UNITED PRESS ASSOCIATIONS, and is subject to the approval of the Board of Directors or Executive Committee of the respective parties hereto.

All this meant, of course, that when Sir Roderick arrived in New York with an appointment to see Mr. Noyes and an assurance that he would see Mr. Bickel, Reuters had lost its only hope of applying what Sir Roderick may have thought would be the coup de grâce to The Associated Press. With the contract with the United Press in existence, things did not look too good for the continuance of Reuters world hegemony.

Word of the contract reached Roy Howard at far-off Honolulu. He cabled me: "Hearty congratulations. I think the foreign news agreement is the most important achievement since the decision in Stone's case to establish the property right to news. [Howard had reference to Melville E. Stone's famous and successful campaign, carried to the United States Supreme Court, to establish the principle of a property right in news.] I hope this marks the beginning of a long overdue era of intelligent cooperation between the two agencies. Please extend my felicitations to President Noyes. Regards."

The pact ran its full life of five years. It then was terminated, notice having been given by me, for two reasons which I stated to Hugh Baillie, successor to Mr. Bickel as president of the United Press, like this: "I personally believe that this primary period has fully met our mutual needs and therefore it has served the purpose for which it was made. In canceling it I only feel that I do not want to tie my successor to the policy if something should happen to me in the next four years." President Baillie replied: "We will regard the contract as ending on February 8, 1939, unless other arrangements are made in the meantime. Perhaps we can reopen the matter later. As I told you on the telephone, I regret that you feel it necessary to terminate this agreement which I believe is an advantageous instrument for both of us. However, I understand the reasons which have caused you to take this step."

So the printed form of the contract passed out, but I believe the spirit of it still lives. Certainly the good which it achieved would, if it could be set down, fill a volume.

XXIX

Emancipation!

IT was not planned to happen that way but the emancipation of The Associated Press which later led to
emancipation of other agencies under contract with
Reuters occurred on the birthday of the Great American
Emancipator—February 12.

President Noyes, having assured Sir Roderick that he
would be glad to see him upon his arrival, awaited him
in New York. The conference between the two took an
hour and a half on the morning of February 10, 1934.
The conversation covered all matters concerning the
rupture, who was at fault, and a mutual expression of
regret. When it came to the matter of what to do next
Mr. Noyes said that the negotiations for the future were
entrusted to me and that he would be very glad to arrange an appointment for Sir Roderick.

As the managing director of Reuters seemed most
anxious to bring the business to a conclusion, we met
that same afternoon in The Associated Press offices. I
had not seen Sir Roderick since the previous August in
London and I had no idea what his attitude would be.

Whatever his feelings were I shall never know. His

manner was one of strictly business as he sat at the side of my desk and drummed the glass top with his fingers. I was quite ready to continue the argument of the preceding August or I was equally willing to forget it. Mr. Noyes had told me that he had left the negotiations to me but as Sir Roderick was asking for continuance of relations after having denounced the treaty, I felt it was his first move. He seemed quite sincere when he asked me what were my ideas as to the form the contract should take or whether I should like to have the existing four-party contract continue.

I told him I did not favor continuance of the four-party treaty under any conditions, as one of the points that seemed important to The Associated Press was that it should make direct two-party contracts with any agency with which it cared to deal and without having to gain the consent of a third agency. In other words, The Associated Press wanted an end to the overlordship of Reuters.

I emphasized that The Associated Press wished a direct contract with the Press Association. I did this because I visualized a powerful coalition that could bring modernity and high principles to the business of international news exchange. This could happen provided The Associated Press, a co-operative news association and dominant in the United States, the Press Association, also a co-operative and dominant in England, and the Canadian Press, co-operative and dominant in Canada—all of them using the English language and being beneficiaries of a free press—would form such a coalition. Under such an entente the progress that could be made in advancing the cause of freedom of the press and freedom of news exchange the world around would be inspiring.

I insisted upon a free hand for The Associated Press everywhere, including the British Isles, all of which meant that The Associated Press would have the right to serve newspapers and news agencies wherever it chose. Reuters would likewise have the same rights in all territories, including the United States.

I said there could be no money differential paid by either party. This meant the elimination of all question of the payment that Sir Roderick had demanded as the price for continuing relations.

What I feared would be an insurmountable obstacle and what almost proved to be so was my insistence that whatever benefits The Associated Press obtained in the contract its ally, the Canadian Press, should have the same. Sir Roderick agreed to consider over the week end every point that I outlined, but said he felt that, Canada being a part of the British Empire, the Canadian Press should apply directly to Reuters for a contract to take care of its needs and not expect to deal with Reuters through The Associated Press for Reuters service.

I explained that the contractual commitments The Associated Press had made with the Canadian Press barred that procedure. I told him that the Canadian Press link with The Associated Press was indissoluble, and that for the purposes of any negotiations with Reuters or any other agency the Canadian Press and The Associated Press would have to be considered as one and the same thing. He hesitated some little time, but finally said:

"All right, I agree to that."

On Monday, February 12, Sir Roderick told me he was ready to sign the contract with the terms as I had specified them. Thus the day of liberty for The Associated Press had arrived. But it was also the day of liberty for Reuters, DNB and Havas, since as a result of this contract two-party agreements between all agencies originally in the four-party contract were later signed, each in harmony with the new contract.

It was something to be a signatory of the contract on that day. Many less important treaties in history have been signed with pompous ceremony. In this case it was simply in the day's work between the executive heads of two great news agencies. How important it really was is expressed in my conviction that if these contracts could have become operative simultaneously with the signing of the Versailles Treaty, the second World War surely would not have occurred so soon, if at all. As it was, the seeds of discontent and jealousy were planted through the form that the international news agency relationship took at the end of the first World War. Fifteen years later too much mischief had already been done for the new relationship represented by this new form of agency contract to overcome.

Reuters acceptance of the policy of freedom of international news exchange which The Associated Press had long desired and which it devoutly wished to bring about was far more important than the mere availability to The Associated Press of Reuters news. I have said any deficiency in that respect could be made up by The Associated Press.

But Reuters acceptance of the practical idealism

which had charted The Associated Press course meant that the two greatest news agencies in the world were in accord, not on a nineteenth century basis of activity but on a really modern twentieth century basis. And operating under the new contract for seven years before Sir Roderick retired from Reuters, I found him always sincerely adhering to the ideas we put into our contract that twelfth day of February, 1934.

There has always been a sentiment in The Associated Press about Reuters in spite of what were felt to be great and deeply grounded faults of that news agency. No wonder, then, that in the eight years since 1934 that sentiment has increased. No one knows how long the relationship will continue, but I know that if it ends something will be mutually lost without anything to take its place.

Deference to Reuters retarded The Associated Press development abroad. But sparring partners for twenty-five years come to have some sort of sentimental attachment for each other regardless of the mauling in which they engage. And, after all, Reuters was and still is the agency that the English people have proclaimed as their own. It was, then, sentiment, not the efficiency of Reuters, that often quieted my impatience over the fact that in deferring to Reuters, The Associated Press was losing precious time in putting its plans into execution. That being true, I hope too much was not lost in waiting almost twenty years for what happened on that February 12.

If the importance of news to its daily life could be brought home to laymen, as well as realization of the importance of the disseminator of the news being trustworthy, a drama could be written around this story that would be "good theater." And the moment of the signature of the Reuters-Associated Press contract in 1934 would be the crisis of that drama.

After Sir Roderick and I parted that day, my mind went back to the time twenty years before when I saw the cable from *La Nación* of Buenos Aires, which I remembered so well as having been transmitted from Buenos Aires to New York via London. New York is nearer to Buenos Aires than is London, but in the mind of Argentines at that time communications had to go to New York via London—the center of all cable traffic in spite of the fact that there was a direct New York cable from Buenos Aires with very little business.

I thought, too, of the gratification that Mr. Stone would have felt had he been alive to see that The Associated Press was getting what he knew I felt it ought to have from Reuters and that the two agencies would still remain side by side in what I hoped would be an unending relationship. And I shall not forget the satisfaction of Mr. Noyes with the conclusions that I had reached with Sir Roderick as to terms. Indeed, satisfactory conclusions might not have been reached except for the preliminary discussions between Mr. Noyes and Sir Roderick. Mr. Noyes very much wanted the matter amicably settled. If Reuters accepted the principle for which The Associated Press stood in contractual matters, I felt it would be a still greater Reuters.

Earlier, as Sir Roderick sat beside my desk and we looked each other straight in the eye, I could not remember having felt that there was any time when he was almost cruelly unreceptive to my ideas. I remembered my presumptuous suggestion of fifteen years earlier that perhaps he and I might help in the mutual progress of our institutions, each organization absorbing from the other the best that experience had developed and facing the world in a broad-minded spirit as two news agencies of Anglo-Saxon origin could well do. I felt no supreme moment of victory and somehow or other I felt that I myself had done nothing to bring about the conclusion that was then put into written form and signed by us.

Those were my thoughts at that moment. In retrospect I feel how very unimportant any one individual is in the life of a great institution that has labored on-ward and upward for nearly one hundred years; how many minds and how many hands, indeed how many lives, have been devoted to bringing The Associated Press, for example, to the position it has attained; how the twenty years that I spent intensely interested in the subject that came to a conclusion that day were such a long part of my own life, but how very little twenty years amounted to in the unending life of The Asso-ciated Press.

In retrospect I have wondered whether Sir Roderick felt the same way about it. Reuters had done, was doing and will continue to do a great work in carrying the news of the world to its four corners in spite of the fact that as this is being written in 1942 Sir Roderick has not been the managing director of Reuters for over a year. Institutions find means to go on with their work and to endure if there is a reason for their being. Mis-takes of new and old managements can cripple but can-not kill an institution that ministers perpetually and constantly to the public good. An honest news agency does just that.

So I was glad that I was present at the dawn of a new era not only in the relations between Reuters and The Associated Press but of all news agencies. For breaking Reuters control produced wide changes in the dissemination of news and its acceptance by the press of many lands.

Before the first World War news went to the world east, west, south and north from London. New York was merely a distribution point for the American continent and no American agency was sending news elsewhere.

The search of *La Nación* of Buenos Aires for news, which the great agency monopoly denied it, started a chain of circumstances that had in a few years made New York a distributor of news to the world and started a flow from American news agencies that was reciprocal to what they received from everywhere—thus setting up here a real international news exchange exceeding in wordage that of London.

Outward bound from America goes the news of the world told in a new way—not new to America but new to much of the rest of the world—news told truthfully, without bias and without a tinge of propaganda.

It is not sent out by the American news agencies to extend American influence abroad and to increase American prestige in a commercial world, as had been the avowed intention of the Old World agencies on behalf of their countries. It is the news as such, wholly unbiased and without intent to influence. In the case of The Associated Press it is sponsored by American newspapers to let the world know what the world is doing.

XXX

Russia Opens Its Doors

THE new contract had not long been signed before I sailed to Europe on a trip that took me as far east as Moscow.

I went because it seemed necessary to restore contractual relations between Havas and DNB which, under the four-party contract, would otherwise have terminated on March 31, 1934. There was also the thought that in courtesy to these two agencies there should be personal explanations that would clear any doubt as to the purpose of The Associated Press.

Knowing that it might take some time to complete the business in Moscow and Berlin, I took Lloyd Stratton, now assistant general manager of The Associated Press, with me. Aboard ship I dictated a letter to my friend Charles Houssaye, which Mr. Stratton took to Paris and began negotiations for a treaty between The Associated Press and Havas exactly similar to the one between The Associated Press and Reuters. Non-exclusivity was emphasized.

There were some heartburnings on the part of Havas in connection with the new form of contract. When Mr. Stratton told me of this I regretted it greatly because it was Mr. Houssaye's refusal to sustain Reuters in its demands upon The Associated Press that had brought Sir Roderick to America posthaste.

Mr. Houssaye gave Mr. Stratton to understand that he had told Sir Roderick that if a break came between Reuters and The Associated Press Havas would continue with The Associated Press by preference. Having made this as his contribution toward The Associated Press side as against Reuters he was naturally disappointed over the contract offered Havas. He felt that Havas deserved some preference. Then, too, Havas had been going through bad times and Mr. Houssaye never wanted anything that affected Havas to change unless it changed for the better. Improvement to him meant tighter bonds of monopoly and no reduction in income. Making the best of it, however, Havas signed. Later, so did DNB.

The trip to Moscow was one of the landmarks in carrying out The Associated Press policy for non-exclusivity. The United Press desired a contract with Tass, the official Russian news agency.

Karl Bickel had been to Moscow often and he was constantly a suitor for the hand of Tass. Mr. J. G. Doletzky, managing director of Tass, liked Mr. Bickel personally but he could not make Tass service available because of the exclusive contract The Associated Press had with Tass and, as I found out later, because he had a contract with Reuters and Havas that also prevented him from making a contract with the United Press.

Mr. Doletzky was cordial to me, and I did not doubt his loyalty to The Associated Press and his admiration for it. I had a long talk with him. One point brought out was that Mr. Doletzky heartily approved of the two-party contract idea, the first of which had been written between Reuters and The Associated Press a month before. At the time Tass had a three-party contract: Reuters and Havas, the parties of the first part, and Tass, the party of the second part. He told me that his admiration for The Associated Press had increased because we had extended the right to Tass to make his news available to others. He said it would solve a great many of his troubles with the Foreign Office, which could not understand why, when The Associated Press did not serve all the newspapers in the United States, the news of Tass could not be available to those newspapers served by the United Press.

This point is emphasized because it was equal availability at the source of all news that I had insisted upon from the first. I believed that no news agency should have the exclusive right to the news of another agency in a foreign country. My reason for advocating this was that the government news of any country should be freely available to all, lest one having it exclusively would be considered in its home country as being the official mouthpiece for the government of a foreign country.

As a matter of fact I never got any satisfaction out of The Associated Press being the only news agency authorized to have exclusive access for the United States to the official propaganda statements of any foreign government. I felt they should be free to all and that enterprise in transmitting them from their source and the manner in which they were presented for publication with explanatory background material should give the lead to the one showing the greater enterprise and the best editing.

In a letter to Mr. Noyes from Moscow I said:

"Mr. Doletzky is happy The Associated Press has been generous. He said, however, that before he can make a contract with the United Press he will have to adjust his contract with Reuters and Havas, which he is determined to do so that it will be in non-exclusive form. The United Press will in due course receive the Tass service."

This was nothing more than The Associated Press keeping faith with the United Press. It took until the succeeding November for Tass to make arrangements with Reuters and Havas in the matter of serving the United Press.

The final step as respects contractual realignments was the receipt from Sir Roderick of the contract between the Press Association of England and The Associated Press. My feelings about this contract were expressed in a letter to Mr. Noyes which I wrote on my way back to New York:

"I have left England with enthusiastic hopes as to our relations with the Press Association, and in reporting my visit to Sir Roderick Jones it will gratify you to know that Sir Roderick really humbly expressed his regrets for what he termed 'this Japanese incident in which I am now completely convinced I was led to act upon matters that were reported to me as facts which I am now convinced were an error.' He showed emotion and added:

" 'I earnestly hope you will believe me that I regret it and that I deeply recognize that our mutual personal friendship has endured and will always endure. You and I have to work things out in the future, and I hope to find your goodwill as genuine as mine.'

"I tried to give him adequate assurances that there was no personal feeling, and also tried to leave matters so that at no distant date I could get his goodwill, and at least his benevolent non-cooperation toward a closer alliance on our part with the Press Association.

"Our talk began with the statement by me of my visits with DNB, Havas and Tass. I told Sir Roderick that I had told Tass that so far as The Associated Press is concerned it would be all right for Tass to make its news available to the United Press, but that Tass replied that it would do this after the first of the year, but before it could do so it would have to adjust its contract with Reuters and Havas.

"It was quite evident from the conversation that Sir Roderick had heard nothing of the contract we have with the United Press. He said the United Press had been sitting on his doorstep twenty years; that Bickel had called upon him just before he left New York after signing the contract with me and discussed a contract with Reuters.

"'I gave him no encouragement whatever,' said Jones.

"I next discussed with him our talks with Havas and told him that Havas objected strenuously to the non-exclusivity idea, whereupon I had told them that so far as we are concerned we ask nothing exclusive, that they could serve whom they chose anywhere.

"'You mean they could serve newspapers, not that they could serve a news agency in the United States competitive with you,' Jones said.

"I told him it would be quite all right with The Associated Press if they did, but I do not believe Havas would solicit a connection with another agency.

" 'Do you mean that the new contract permits Reuters, for instance, to make a contract with the United Press?' Jones asked.

"I said, 'certainly it would, just as it permitted us to make a contract with the Exchange Telegraph Company of London.' I said we could put the Exchange far ahead of its present standing if we turned all of our news over to the Exchange, but that we were not likely to do this unless Reuters were dealing directly with one of our competitors.

" 'I don't want to see The Associated Press make its news available to the Exchange,' he said with emphasis, 'and therefore I have no idea of approaching the United Press.'

"I told him I wanted him to understand exactly what the contract meant so far as we were concerned—that we insist on nothing exclusive and want no contracts with anyone that restrain us in any way.

"All of this, I said, he must have recognized when he talked with Mejer, and when he, Havas and DNB signed their new contract which makes all territory outside of Europe free territory to Reuters, Havas and DNB, except the Dominions, mandates and protectorates of one of the three. In other words, the three of them made North and South America, China, Russia, etc., open to any one of them. This seems to have occurred as a strategic retreat from the world at large, with a confinement of future exclusive agency activities to the European continent alone.

"Sir Roderick said that things are changing rapidly, and that today Havas alone deplores the fact that the tight grasp Reuters and Havas have had on the entire world is finally being loosened, and so far as Reuters is concerned, it is entirely removed both actually and as a matter of policy outside of British territory.

"I did not say so, but I am convinced that the so-called Japanese experience of Sir Roderick brought him to the conclusion that Reuters could no longer consistently nor effectively claim to own the news rights of a nation foreign to Britain. This, of course, represented one of the chief principles I have stood for.

"Reuters has its five year contract with Rengo, and even if it did not have it, it does not feel Havas or DNB would have any attraction to Rengo in a contractual way. On the other hand, by releasing its grasp on China, Reuters gains a free hand in all of Latin America, which in the previous contract (with the exception of Mexico and Central America) was entirely the property of Havas.

"This development is the culmination of what I have often repeated to Sir Roderick in our talks during the last seven years, namely, that an agency of one country must not own the rights in a country foreign to it, but must let the agency in that foreign country reach its own decisions as to the connections it makes. This I got from you. I think you used the words that Rengo, for instance, should be able to decide with which foreign agency it desires its prime connection.

"I am sketching these facts·here to show the real influence The Associated Press has had in what I call a refinement of the European agency practices which always heretofore have encompassed pure selfishness.

"Of course I do not overlook the fact that our friend Mussolini, through Mr. Morgagni, President and Director General of the Stefani Agency, was looking for Italy's place in the sun, and Stefani was the first European agency to break away. Since the first of January Italian news agency activities have in no sense been the property of Havas. [Prior to this Italy was regarded as Havas' property and Stefani was not a free agent.] Stefani decides for itself.

"When Mejer demanded the same for DNB and when we had made our entry into Japan, the old theory of ownership of foreign territory collapsed. All of which exposes the fact that history is being made in the news agency situation, and I am proud that The Associated Press has had a part in that history—indeed a very prominent part.

"Sir Roderick in our talk fully recognized all of this, and he told me that when in Paris recently Havas undertook to blame him for the changing conditions: 'I put an end to that discussion promptly,' he said, 'by flatly declaring that I would not be a party to an inquest. I told them I made the contract that I made with you in good faith, and that I would see it through regardless as to what Havas or DNB did, and I tell you now I mean just that.' "

I saw Sir Roderick two or three times after the contract was signed and before the fateful fall of 1939 when the war began. His cordial and apparently sincere acceptance of the final result of my twenty-year effort gave me great satisfaction. If I had not been confident that sooner or later under the new agreement Reuters would begin greater activities on a more modern basis I would have felt that there would have been some disappointment over what The Associated Press gained.

XXXI

Reuters Takes New Form

THE open door for Reuters gave that institution new opportunity. It began selling news to the New York *Times* and other American newspapers, radio stations in the United States, and it even sold its service to the American news agencies that are competitive with The Associated Press.

But, with less than one hundred and fifty British newspapers left to support Reuters in Britain and war cutting off all revenue from the continent of Europe, to say nothing of war troubles in the empire creating disadvantages for Reuters, the latter obviously needed this new revenue. The contractual stand taken by The Associated Press permitted it to get it even in The Associated Press home territory. Reuters entered South America, too, where it vied with The Associated Press, the United Press and what was left of the Havas organization on that continent. I have no idea how much money was afforded Reuters because of its acceptance of the non-exclusive policy of The Associated Press which opened up new fields to Reuters, but I hope it is a great deal.

Even though news services competitive with The Associated Press had the news of Reuters, The Associated Press did not suffer. Naturally, I am glad it did not as I think of the long years of discussion by the Board of Directors which had been led to fear the loss of Reuters to the opposition—or even sharing Reuters with the opposition. Gratification that the results have improved the services of The Associated Press is lessened only by contemplation of how much better it all could have been for all concerned if what happened between Sir Roderick and myself in my office on February 12, 1934, could have taken place fifteen years earlier!

In February, 1941, Sir Roderick laid down the burdens of administering the affairs of Reuters, and the Press Association acquired the shares he still held. The management of Reuters was then taken up by the provincial newspaper co-operative, which elected Samuel Storey chairman of the board. Mr. Storey was also a member of Parliament and a publisher of newspapers. This arrangement lasted only a few months, however.

The war and negotiations that resulted because of the stand taken by The Associated Press had divested the old British institution of practically its last exclusive contract. Reuters had slipped from the throne that had given it hegemony over the news of the world. But then came the rainbow with promise of better things, for in losing that domination—perhaps because of losing it— Reuters acquired a new status.

On October 28, 1941, there was announced in London the creation of a trust agreement which placed ownership of Reuters in the hands of the entire British press. The announcement carried with it the statement that the move "guaranteed preservation of the agency's integrity, independence and freedom from bias at all times." The announcement further said that the Press Association which owned all the shares of Reuters had sold one-half to the Newspaper Proprietors' Association of London.

The desirability of this transformation was something that Mr. Noyes had impressed upon Sir Roderick originally in 1920 and was emphasized by Mr. Noyes to Sir Roderick every time the two met thereafter. The Associated Press of America wanted to see Great Britain, with its free press assured, enter the full brotherhood of co-operative news agencies. With the London papers having no share of the ownership of Reuters, and control of it resting only in the Press Association, there could be no solidarity in England in a co-operative way. With all British newspapers owning Reuters much became possible.

Under this unusual arrangement both parties agreed that the new ownership was to be "regarded as in the nature of a trust rather than as an investment" and that the news agency should "at no time pass into the hands of any one group or faction."

The trust thus established is irrevocable for a minimum of twenty-one years, and thereafter is not to be changed or dissolved without approval of the Lord Chief Justice. This arrangement was made with the approval of the government and Reuters made the following announcement:

> After discussion with the Chancellor of the Exchequer and the Minister of Information, the following arrangements are announced:

Press Association, who were the sole holders of the shares of Reuters, Limited, have decided in co-operation with The Newspaper Proprietors' Association to enter into a common and equal partnership in Reuters and set up a Reuters Trust.

To this end The Newspaper Proprietors' Association has purchased from Press Association one-half of the capital of Reuters. The effect of this is that Reuters is now owned by the British press as a whole.

A declaration of trust has been signed by both parties, setting forth principles which are to be maintained under the new ownership, which is regarded as in the nature of a trust rather than as an investment. In particular, the parties have undertaken to use their best endeavors to ensure:

A. That Reuters shall at no time pass into the hands of any one interest, group or faction.

B. That its integrity, independence and freedom from bias shall at all times be fully preserved.

C. That its business shall be so administered that it shall supply an unbiased and reliable news service to British Dominion, Colonial, foreign and other overseas newspapers and agencies with which it has or may hereafter have contracts.

D. That it shall pay due regard to the many interests which it serves in addition to those of the press, and

E. That no effort shall be spared to expand, develop and adapt the business of Reuters in order to maintain in every event its position as a leading world news agency.

An equal number of trustees are being appointed by Press Association and The Newspaper Proprietors' Association to carry out the above undertakings. An independent Chairman of Trustees is to be

appointed by The Lord Chief Justice. The First
Trustees of the Reuters Trust are:

Lord Rothermere (Publisher of the London
Daily Mail and Associated Newspapers), Lord Camrose (Editor-in-Chief of the London Daily Telegraph and Morning Post), Lord Kemsley (Chairman
of Allied Newspapers, Ltd. and Editor-in-Chief of
the London Sunday Times), Lord Southwood
(Chairman and Managing Director of the Oldham
Press Limited), Mr. J. R. Scott (Chairman and
Managing Director of the Manchester Guardian
and Evening News, Ltd.), Mr. Allan Jeans (Managing Director and Managing Editor of the Liverpool Daily Post and Echo), Honorable Rupert
Beckett (Chairman of Yorkshire Post), and Mr. W.
T. Bailey (President of the Newspaper Society,
which represents the Provincial Press).

The management of the company will be a Board
of Six Directors representing Press Association and
The Newspaper Proprietors' Association. The Directors of the new Board are:

Raymond Derwent (Westminster Press and Pro-
vincial Newspapers, Ltd.), Ralph Deakin (London
Times), A. McLean Ewing (Glasgow Herald), W. J.
Haley (Manchester Guardian and Evening News,
Ltd.), H. M. Heywood (Allied Newspapers, Ltd.),
and Robert J. Pew (London Daily Mail).

Provision has been made that the Trust shall be
irrevocable for a minimum period of 21 years and
that thereafter it shall not be amended or dissolved
unless the matter has been submitted to The Lord
Chief Justice, and it shall not be dissolved unless he
is satisfied that by reason of the circumstances then
existing it is impracticable to secure the objects of
the Trust as set out above by continuing its operation in its present or any amended form.

Prior to this announcement the question of the proposed deal was raised in the House of Commons and precipitated a considerable debate. At that time Brendan Bracken, Minister of Information, himself a former newspaper editor, rejected a proposal which he characterized as tantamount to nationalization of Reuters.

"The position of the government in this matter is very simple," he said. "The Chancellor of the Exchequer and I are actually negotiating with the parties concerned. It is quite open to the government to bring in a bill to nationalize Reuters, but would that help from the point of view of Reuters? Certainly not.

"If a news agency were regarded throughout the world as being the property of the British government, its news value would be very small."

The Minister of Information at another point in the debate paid a tribute to The Associated Press. He did this in addressing a remark to Samuel Storey, Conservative member of Commons and chairman of Reuters, who had joined the opposition to the sale and had proposed that control be placed in "a genuine trust, which would be truly representative of the national interest."

"I want to put this on record," said Minister Bracken. "If my honorable friend, the Member for Sunderland [Mr. Storey], who is Chairman of Reuters, thinks that in the past ten or twelve years Reuters' position as a world news agency has been equal to that of, say, The Associated Press of America, he is greatly mistaken. Reuters, to my mind, have lost ground. We have got to face up to that; they have lost ground in a most remarkable way.

"I think my honorable friend under his administration has been doing his best to improve it, but nevertheless we must face up to the facts that it is not a Canterbury Cathedral or an ancient British institution which is at stake. It is a commercial business and a competitive commercial business."

At this point another member interjected:

"With an early English name."

"Well," retorted Bracken, "we are proud of the old school tie and the old English name. We have to remember that if the government nationalizes Reuters we shall have a difficult job to manage that business."

With that Sir Roderick Jones, who had retired from the chairmanship of Reuters early in the year, took a hand in the argument. Through a letter to the London *Times* he replied stoutly to the critics of the plan to admit London newspapers into the joint ownership with provincial newspapers. Said the former head of Reuters:

"Sir,—My admiration for Mr. Bracken's gallant stand yesterday against a House in arms is slightly chilled by his opinion that, in comparison with The Associated Press of America, Reuters as a world news agency has lost ground in a most remarkable way in the last ten or twelve years.

"If that were true it would scarcely be surprising. All the other foreign agencies with whom Reuters has had to do constant battle either have been financially munitioned by their Governments (e.g., Berlin, Paris, Rome) or, as in the case of The Associated Press, have had money poured copiously into them by a Press many times more numerous than that of the British Isles.

"But I cannot allow Mr. Bracken's statement to pass unchallenged. Throughout the 25 years of my chairman-

ship and managerial control of Reuters, the Agency's
record was one of continued and vigorous expansion,
thanks to the enthusiasm and devotion of the band of
men at home and abroad whom I had the privilege of
leading. And the recent decision of the London newspapers to secure a half share in the ownership of Reuters, the other half to remain in the hands of the provincial newspapers, had nothing to do with commercial
consideration, good or bad. It was inspired by high public motives."

As Sir Roderick's letter continued he once more gave
evidence of the influence of the ideals President Noyes
had outlined to him some twenty years before when the
chairman of Reuters first met Mr. Noyes in New York.
At that time Mr. Noyes completely sold Sir Roderick on
mutualizing Reuters and placing it in control of the
British press just as The Associated Press is owned by
American newspapers. From the time he left Mr. Noyes
in New York in 1920, Sir Roderick began to crystallize
in his mind the sale of Reuters to the British newspapers. While he did not mention Mr. Noyes in his letter to the London *Times* he dated his contact with Mr.
Noyes in his letter as he continued:

"For 20 years or more I have striven to bring about
that which is now on the eve of being accomplished—the
complete ownership of Reuters by the British Press. In
the year 1925, as principal proprietor and sole controller
of Reuters, I offered this ownership to the newspapers.
I felt strongly that the future of so important a national
and international organization should not be dependent
upon the life of one man, myself, and be open at my
death to the danger that threatened it during the last

War. I could have allowed the Agency, with its solid corpus and its world-wide reputation, to be floated very advantageously as a public company. But that would have revived the danger: a free market in the shares would have exposed Reuters to the menace of undesirable influence and perhaps control.

"No such risk could spring from ownership by the newspapers as a body, representative as they are of every shade of political, social, and economic thought, and penetrated as they always have been, whatever their internal business rivalries, often acute, by a healthy patriotism and robust independence. Consequently I offered the ownership 50/50 to the Newspaper Proprietors' Association, representing the London papers, and to the Press Association, representing the provincial papers. The Press Association were willing to accept the offer; the Newspaper Proprietors' Association not.

"I was extremely disappointed. But London friends whose advice I valued urged me to go ahead with the Press Association alone (which I did). They were indulgent enough to express the belief that, so long as I remained Head, Reuters would retain the London papers' confidence, and that these papers would one day join with the provincials in Reuters.

"When I resigned last February the Newspaper Proprietors' Association decided that that day had come, and they acted at once. Their action, and the wise response of the Press Association, were entirely public spirited, and the members of Parliament who yesterday, with a vigilance and a sense of duty that can only be commended, expressed misgivings about this transaction, did so without having been placed in possession of all the facts. As Mr. Bracken correctly said, only one side of the case had been heard.

"The very sound under-structure of a great news agency, ownership by the Press of its country, the fruit of which in the shape of The Associated Press of America is so much admired by Mr. Bracken, has been my dream and my labour for 20 years, and I can only regret that it has now been presented so unfortunately and so damagingly to the House of Commons. Nevertheless, I am optimistic enough to believe that the dream will be fulfilled.

"I have the honour to be, Sir, your obedient servant.
"Roderick Jones."

To me this final paragraph of Sir Roderick's letter was a salutation of respect and admiration for Mr. Noyes, who, in 1920, as I have pointed out, so clearly showed the then chairman of Reuters the sound sense and practical idealism of "the very sound under-structure of a great news agency, ownership by the Press of its country, the fruit of which in the shape of The Associated Press of America is so much admired . . ."

Time will show how strong Reuters can become under its ownership by the entire British press. If the new plan of ownership had been a real co-operative like The Associated Press; if it had embraced all its owners into one membership company; if, thereupon, the one company would have taken over the domestic activities of the Press Association as well as the foreign activities of Reuters and if the name for the one great membership company had been the "Press Association," my confidence in its future success would have been unbounded.

As a real co-operative it would have obtained news for its members and would have been the unit representing Great Britain that would exchange news with similar co-operative units in the British Commonwealth of Nations, as well as with co-operative associations in foreign countries, such as The Associated Press of America.

Although Reuters is owned and directed by the entire British press, such unity has not given Reuters the very important function of collecting the domestic news of Great Britain. All the other great agencies like The Associated Press, the Canadian Press, the Australian Associated Press, the United Press and International News Service fulfill the requirements of their newspapers for both domestic and foreign news. Already it has been claimed by a somewhat doubting dominion press that Parliament gave its benediction to the new Reuters for just one reason: because the agency will aspire to be the means not only of keeping the empire together but of maintaining England, the mother country, as the center of the empire. If that must be one of its missions, it will be a disappointment to its well-wishers.

While England's hour of greatest danger as a European power, if not of its existence, awakened Britain to the fact that a profit-making and dividend-paying news service is not the instrument that will effect solidarity in empire affairs, the press of the dominions questions whether a unified effort of the entire British press under the Reuter name can carry out the political mission of keeping the empire together. A real non-profit-seeking co-operative embracing a complete news agency activity in Great Britain could do it, but a real co-operative begets a philosophy of true equality and brotherhood.

Many publishers of the dominions would like to see evidence that the British press in the form of a real cooperative concedes equality and brotherhood to the press of the rest of the empire. They say that overlordship by Reuters—regardless of whether or not Reuters is owned by the entire British press—is no longer going to be accepted by the press of Australia, Canada, India, or even South Africa. Perhaps the new ownership of Reuters has not yet had time to develop the new character that Reuters will come to have. The press of the empire has not heard a public announcement that Reuters will not operate with the profit motive. Yet a prerequisite of confidence that the newspapers of the rest of the empire discuss is that Reuters not seek to profit financially in its arrangements with them. Prior to its reorganization Reuters profited by the sale of news to the dominions. With the barriers down by which the organized press of each great unit of the empire can choose its foreign connections, matters are quite different.

The real preference of the empire press, as it has been explained to me, is that the Press Association of Great Britain accept the London newspapers as members and then that the Press Association would be to Great Britain what the Canadian Press is to Canada and what the Australian Associated Press is to Australia; that the Press Association even then be given no greater prestige or facilities from the British Government than the Australian Associated Press and the Canadian Press receive.

Naturally the uncertainties and stress of a great war do not make a good setting for the accomplishment of permanent plans of reconstruction. There must be done only what will meet the urgent needs during war.

Nevertheless, empire newspapermen today think consideration could well enough be given to more permanent plans. Perhaps the Canadian Press and the Australian Associated Press ultimately will have sufficient persuasiveness with the British press really to bring matters to a conclusion entirely acceptable to all.

I have a conviction that such an adjustment will take place because, as I shall tell, the new management of Reuters already has made a new approach to The Associated Press. As a result, relations between these two agencies are today more harmonious and more equitable than they have ever been.

XXXII

Truth — The Best Propaganda

ENGLAND had been in the throes of conflict two years before the British press closed ranks and co-operatively took charge of its principal news service in 1941. In a newer country—America—the press had demonstrated for nearly one hundred years that a sound journalism and sound national welfare demand ownership of its news agency by the press of the country—not by a capitalist or a group of capitalists, nor by the government (which in the United States may heaven ever forbid!). In this matter a young country showed an old country the way.

Yet even as England's press was trying to get its house in order so that it could own and manage the world news service that delivered it news, there were those who would have had the British Government take control. Talked of in the House of Commons, the government wisely declined to avail itself of the opportunity offered. Its declination as disclosed in Parliament was on the ground that only ownership by the press of Great Britain afforded a sound solution. The American way had shown the method and the standing and success of The Associated Press the proof.

Nothing in the long history of the British press can be as satisfying. At the turn of the century, under similar circumstances, the government would have taken over. That it did not do so at a time when England was in a life-and-death struggle may have been due to a number of things; perhaps one was that the English press and people had really come to know The Associated Press. Having gained freedom to serve England's newspapers, it had for two years been delivering its news to practically all the British newspapers.

During the long years that Reuters banned The Associated Press service from England, The Associated Press was known by distant observation only. With the ban lifted, The Associated Press service was first examined, then accepted, and finally embraced by all of Britain.

The British government did not take over Reuters. Instead, the new ownership gained its independence with government benediction. More than that, with its great news service controlled by the press of England, I am told that the British government for the first time in any war has placed no demand on Reuters that it serve the government through any form of foreign propaganda. Instead, the government is carrying on its own propaganda as are all the warring nations. One can hope that this means the British government has acquired a better understanding of the desirability of leaving untouched the regular news channels.

Nevertheless, it is, of course, axiomatic that the purer the stream of news the more eagerly do government interests and self-seekers generally want to use it. The purer the stream the easier can it be tainted "a little" without the public taking notice.

Since America in 1942 is at war, America has a story to tell the world. The question is, how can that story best be told? In the first World War the American news services were provincial. The United Press and International News Service had made modest beginnings in foreign news dissemination—The Associated Press only in Mexico, Cuba and Canada. In the second World War the news of the American press services was being read throughout the world when the United States went to the support of those who were fighting the Axis.

In the first World War, through its "Committee on Public Information," the United States ambitiously undertook to spread news of the ideals of President Wilson to the four corners of the world. In the second Great War the world is being similarly bombarded by the United States Government with news which the government wants printed everywhere. What goes to the Axis countries is aimed to destroy the morale of the people in those countries. What goes to the United Nations is aimed to restore the morale of the people of the United Nations. What goes to the neutral countries is aimed to gain the admiration for the heroic role America is playing.

There is no means by which the success of these governmental propaganda measures can be weighed. In the effort to get its news printed or its broadcasts heard, the government has engaged a small army of newspapermen. Some of them are novices at foreign news dissemination. Others are experienced. I mention one who carried a large responsibility even in the prewar defense administration who is not a newspaperman but was responsive to and understanding of a presentation of the moralities of the business. He was not slow in comprehending that the best way to get facts to the people is to place them where they will be read with reliance upon their truth. That place is in the newspapers. And the way to get them into the newspapers of foreign lands, as well as at home, is to preserve the function of the press associations in their work of news dissemination.

The well-advised individual to whom I refer is Nelson Rockefeller. When, in 1941, before Pearl Harbor, President Roosevelt decided to further the defense effort by placing Mr. Rockefeller in charge as Co-ordinator of Inter-American Affairs, Mr. Rockefeller asked me to release to him some men who had long been trained by The Associated Press in its Latin-American service. He wrote me:

"I know the temporary loss of any one would represent a sacrifice to The Associated Press, but I feel that this is a contribution to the defense effort which The Associated Press may desire to make."

To this request I replied:

New York, November 12, 1941.

Dear Nelson:

Your letter of October 31 was not received here until November 5. It presented a great problem for The Associated Press—practically one as to whether or not The Associated Press would withdraw from Latin America, a step that might be necessary if several of the key men upon whom the organization must rely should take up other work.

I fully recognize the grand work you are undertaking and I wish you as fully recognized the importance of what The Associated Press is doing.

Because I feel you should know this, I am briefly stating some facts.

For twenty-five years I have been endeavoring to get The Associated Press into the foreign fields to deliver the news of the Americas throughout the world. In order to do this we had to completely revamp the contracts that we had with the foreign news agencies so that we could have a free hand. It was a long and difficult struggle because these contracts had been in existence in some form from the beginning. Under them The Associated Press had no rights to operate outside the United States and Canada.

The long story of the development is too much to impose upon you. Suffice it to say that through the efforts of a quarter of a century and at considerable financial loss, The Associated Press today is a basic service for the newspapers of Great Britain, Australia, Canada, Japan and all of the Latin American countries. We have not the trained personnel to spare from the Latin American effort to fulfill your request, much as it hurts to be put in the position of denying you. I do not, however, think you should judge The Associated Press as not being willing to help in the matter of national defense. Since you put your appeal on that basis, however, I have to beg of you not to feel that way about it.

I could with truth and modesty assert that the work that The Associated Press is doing in Latin America is far more valuable than anything that your Committee could undertake to do, regardless of the amount of money which is available to it which is not available to The Associated Press. I first placed The Associated Press service in South America to displace a German propaganda service and creditably to establish the ethics of the press of the United States in the hearts of Latin American journalists. We said there would be no propaganda in The Associated Press service, not even from the United States. We have carried through on that basis for all of these years. My belief is that there is so much of merit in the United States' point of view that the truth serves as the best possible propaganda.

Finally, I have been worried that all of this is not understood by the powers that be in the national defense effort. If The Associated Press' effectiveness in Latin America is reduced, it will disappear and after the national defense effort has been successful because of its great resources, I do not believe it will be possible to re-establish The Associated Press in the position which it has through struggles obtained.

Men, Nelson, are all The Associated Press has. It has nothing else but the work and devotion of its men. It has no sources for money other than the papers it serves and far from making a profit it has endured a loss in Latin America. The financial part of it can be made up by the more prosperous journals. The loss of its trained men cannot be made up.

There are scores of men on American newspapers who, while they have not had experience in Latin America, could quickly accommodate themselves to the work you have in mind. In that field there are ten to one of men available compared to The Associated Press. I do hope that you will seek them in that field.

Regretting that I cannot acquiesce in your suggestion for the reasons I have stated but with assurances of my earnest good wishes for you, I am

Sincerely yours,

(Signed) KC

His reply was:

Washington, November 22, 1941.

Dear Kent:

Thank you for your letter of November twelfth. Although I was sorry to learn of your decision about granting leaves of absence to one or two of your men to work with us, I understand your reasons perfectly as I am well aware of the fine record that press associations have made in the field of the other American republics.

We agree with you entirely as to the importance of truth in news. I have stressed many times that as democracies we cannot combat untruths and misinformation by false representations equally vicious, and I have found that this point of view is shared by all members of the government with whom I have worked in this particular field.

I appreciate greatly the careful consideration you have given to our request and will follow your suggestion of looking into the field of American newspapermen, for this particular work.

Sincerely,

(Signed) Nelson
Nelson A. Rockefeller
Coordinator

The exchange of letters took place before the United States was at war. The letters referred to proposals that, if adopted, would have weakened The Associated Press in its Latin-American service. The extreme necessity that comes with a country at war had not arisen. When it did, Associated Press men far and wide went to the colors. They went with enthusiasm and with the benediction of their employer. Moreover, on the battlefronts its correspondents, by their courage and enterprise under fire, have risked their lives to write the biggest stories of the war. Many of the dispatches from these correspondents have been acclaimed as exemplary. Widely quoted and reprinted, they were inspirational to the morale of the United Nations.

The Associated Press at all times has operated consistently with the public interest and at no time in its history has this fact been more self-evident than it is today. At the request of the United States Government in 1942, it, as well as all the other American news services, makes its news available free to various propaganda branches of the government. The news of these government agencies is broadcast throughout the world for use without charge. Though the American news services are thus finding some departments of the government in competition with them, the news disseminated by the American news agencies is giving to the world the best picture of a substantial, earnest and determined America. It goes out from them because it is true. America is earnest, it is honest and it is determined in the part it plays in the titanic struggle. The news agency picture of America is not sent abroad as propaganda. And coming from them it is believed. If government-backed news dissemination displaces the American news agencies abroad, a loss to the American war effort and to the American way will have occurred.

While the government has thousands of dollars to spend for its propaganda dissemination to each dollar made available to The Associated Press by foreign newspapers, for example, I believe that The Associated Press news, not being sent as propaganda, returns better results than all the elaborate and expensive efforts of the government.

Foreign newspapers are not unlike individuals anywhere in one respect. They value what they have to pay for. And they all have to pay the expense of getting news from the American news agencies. The fact that at least until July of 1942, when this is written, the United States Government has placed no hand of authority on The Associated Press nor interfered in any way with its high mission, would indicate that the status of its news dissemination is understood and its effectiveness appreciated. For the sake of my country I hope this will always be true.

XXXIII

A Different Approach

ONE day in May, 1942, W. J. Haley, one of the directors of Reuters, arrived in New York. Mr. Haley came to acquaint me personally with the changes that had taken place and to suggest the desirability of a new contract that would better represent the intentions and personality of the new Reuters. I was deeply interested in his exposition of the unusual and even dramatic changes that had taken place: new personalities were in Reuters; the great British institution was looking out upon the world with new eyes.

Before Mr. Haley reached New York, or before I even knew he was coming, I had bowed Reuters out of this story with the following paragraphs:

"A hopeful augury of great promise of what may be expected of Britain in properly establishing freedom of news exchange after this second World War may be found as a result of what has been happening in the control and management of Reuters to which I have referred.

"The Press Association of England, which is a co-operative, composed of the newspapers published outside of London, actually acquired stock control of Reuters in 1925 but left the management of it to Sir Roderick Jones, who had taken over when Baron Herbert de Reuter tragically ended his life in 1915.

"For reasons which were not publicly announced Sir Roderick retired from the management of Reuters in 1941. Newspaper members of the Press Association then took active control of Reuters and six months later the Press Association shared equal control of Reuters with the London newspapers by a trust agreement that was explained in Parliament and which was acceptable to the British government. The trust agreement will be quoted later. Suffice it to say now that the principal news activity in Britain at this writing is wholly in charge of the newspapers, as it is in the United States, and no single autocrat, such as Julius Reuter, Herbert Reuter or Sir Roderick Jones holds management control in 1942.

"All of this may indeed mean that the British press may ultimately accept the principles which The Associated Press first declared and to which it adheres in the matter of unrestricted international news exchange conducted without special privilege to any news agency.

"If the British press can be brought to view the exchange of world news as The Associated Press has brought itself to see it, a world free press after this war is assured. In that case, the world should find in the acceptance of this view the means of accomplishment of a prolonged peace instead of the temporary peace that was gained after the first World War. When this peace is written the American news agencies and their British contemporaries should be available to counsel specifications that may be included in the peace treaty respecting freedom of the press and implement that free press through the principle of free and direct news intercourse between all nations."

While Mr. Haley and I had several talks that led up to the signing of a new contract, it took only the first of the talks to show me that this part of the story could end on a more definite note. For Mr. Haley, of the Manchester *Guardian,* a director of the Press Association as well as a director of Reuters, became a friend. We found that we looked to the future operations of our respective institutions upon the same principles. He pointed out that he is only one of the six directors of Reuters, but expressed the opinion that his fellow directors would be in accord with the basis of our discussions. The idea of six directors operating an institution was new to me and I spoke of this fact.

"Well," said Mr. Haley, "Reuters has been operated by two barons, a knight, a member of Parliament, all in succession over a period of eighty-four years, and now six honest-to-God newspapermen are going to see what they can do with it."

I liked that. Except for the short chairmanship of Mr. Storey, who is a publisher as well as a member of Parliament, Reuters had never been operated by men trained on newspapers as has been invariably the case with the American news agencies. There is conviction in America that in order to serve newspapers well news agency men should first have newspaper experience. In other words, a news writer should at least learn how to write for one newspaper before he undertakes to apply his abilities to write satisfactorily for as many as 1,400 newspapers.

It seemed to me essential that before framing a new

contract, for which Mr. Haley was asking and I was not, I should put in writing for him my thoughts respecting an ideal relationship between the two agencies. So I wrote him:

"In your absence this week, I have been giving thought to your proposal of a new contract. You will understand that the references I make herein are as to the Reuters I have known in the past—not the Reuters that may be in the future. Indeed it is what the Reuters of the future will be that so greatly concerns me.

"Not knowing your future plans for Reuters and without any stipulations that all the agency relationships will not revert to what they were before this war, I can say personally that without some understanding as to the future, I would not favor continuance.

"However, I have not discussed Reuters with our Board of Directors for eight years and in that time there have been a large number of changes in the personnel of our Board, which is now composed of eighteen members. You have come to me directly from a Board composed of only six members, apparently with definite plans for the future concerning which I know nothing and upon which you and the other members of your Board have been working through the winter. I am therefore disadvantaged in speaking authoritatively for The Associated Press as compared to the authority that you bring freshly from the consideration that your Board has given to this subject.

"Whether or not The Associated Press and Reuters formulate a new agreement, it seems important to me that I state for your benefit what I shall state to The Associated Press Board as to my convictions. They may be summed up as follows:

"1. It is desirable that Reuters and The Associated Press continue relations, if they can be made one hundred per cent mutual and harmonious as respects individual ideals and aspirations of both concerns.

"2. Between 1919 and 1934, when the last contract was signed, The Associated Press went through a very unhappy struggle to obtain from Reuters what The Associated Press earnestly desired and which it felt it should have in the matter of world relations as the designated trustee of the entire press of North America with the exception of only a very few newspapers. You should bear in mind that although The Associated Press has competition in North America, the owners of that competition both are members of The Associated Press and are thoroughly in accord with the principles of the delivery of a truthful, unbiased news report without any propaganda whatsoever, government inspired or otherwise inspired. I have not the slightest doubt but that the owners of both competing agencies will stand foursquare for the maintenance of those principles by The Associated Press, in which each has a large interest, as well as by the agencies that they own. Thus I am convinced that the entire press of this continent is opposed to selfish special rights for any agency anywhere when granted by any government, whether through preferential traffic in news or by subvention. Remember I am speaking from past experience and in ignorance of what is planned for the future.

"3. In time of war, I feel there must be a responsiveness by the news agencies to whatever their national governments indicate may be necessary as respects news that comes into possession of the agencies, but that the responsiveness shall not include acceptance of any dictum that the presentation of news be only in such form as would please government. There is acceptance of the right of government to have us withold news for the common good, but no acceptance of any right of government to say how we shall word what we do transmit, if any government anywhere undertakes to impose specifications. In time of peace, government should impose no control upon the agencies as to any attitude respecting the news they transmit.

"4. I am devoutly interested in extension of the principles of freedom of the press, freedom of international news exchange and that all news everywhere shall be equally available at the source to all without delay or hindrance and I do not want to see any agency given any exclusiveness or any advantage in the matter of availability of government news. Truthful and unbiased news only can be guaranteed the public when there is equal availability at the source and no favoritism in its transmission.

"5. I feel that each agency should prosper upon its own enterprise in getting news and transmitting it and that its success should be upon the character, personality and efficiency with which it is made available.

"6. I feel that if The Associated Press and Reuters make a contract in harmony with these basic principles, neither should make contracts with agencies which do not find themselves in harmony with these principles. More than that, I think the view of all allied agencies should be a militant one upon maintaining the principles outlined.

"7. In what I have said I have had to speak personally because I have not recently discussed these matters with my Board, but I feel, and I hope you and your Board may feel, that there is a tremendous pent-up force and determination in the press that we represent that the principles that I have outlined shall control in the destiny to which we direct our separate institutions. For example, once more the world is at war and again there will be a peace. It is unthinkable that that peace will not be dictated by America and Britain and that there should not be included in its terms the principles affecting the press as I have outlined them and upon which you probably can make improvements, which would be welcome. I do not claim to be a Messiah in the matter.

"8. When the last peace treaty was being framed, I tried to have included in it a direct declaration as to the freedom of the press and freedom of international news exchange without government favoritism or hindrance. Backed only by my own voice, I got nowhere. It was Reuters (under its then management) backed by Havas that dictated what would be the agency arrangements for Continental Europe after the war. The dire results of those arrangements were evident in the ensuing twenty years and played no small part in the rupture of international amity in the fall of 1939.

"9. In another peace treaty in which our nations shall play leading roles, I would hope that The Associated Press and Reuters, representing the respective press of their two countries, would see to it not only that there is consideration of freedom of the press everywhere as well

as freedom of international news exchange, but that
their inclusion would be in as positive terms as any other
items of the peace treaty. I do with all my heart wish
that since Reuters now has proclaimed its ownership by
the entire English press, a sponsorship that approximates
that of The Associated Press, the avenue will be found
on which The Associated Press and Reuters, dominant
and representative of the press of their two countries,
can march down arm in arm toward a greater press freedom and international exchange of news arrangements
that will have none of the mischievousness and selfishness of the arrangements the last time they were made.

"10. This, then, as to a new contract should not be
merely a matter of making another traffic arrangement as
respects the mutual news availability from our two agencies, for that will be of little importance if it is not
founded upon complete mutual understanding of what
our two institutions are going to stand for in the future.

"11. If Reuters feels it must maintain broadly what
The Associated Press found objectionable under the
Reuters management that ended last year, and if Reuters wishes to go it alone upon the great adventure of
the future when this war shall have concluded, well and
good. If so, it will mean that The Associated Press, after
bringing to its standard those who would accept what
will be the principles that I hope The Associated Press
will stand for (which I have necessarily stated as my
own), will face this great adventure when peace comes
resolute in the determination that the welfare if not the
peace of the world will best be served by freedom of the
press and freedom of international news exchange. That
would mean the eradication of favoritism, special priv-

ilege and government support in the matter of news availability and news transmission. With all of these we have had experience in the past. If there is to be a new contract, there should be an understanding that The Associated Press and Reuters shall do what they can to build new standards of action and that what one has shall be open to the other on the same terms. If there is to be no contract, you at least know what my attitude is."

To this Mr. Haley replied:

"It is very good of you to have put your thoughts so clearly on paper and I am grateful to you for having epitomised a good deal of the larger aspects of our discussions.

"I agree with you that we are facing not only the possibility of a new Contract but also a new phase in the relationship between The Associated Press and Reuters. It was with the hope that this might be achieved that the Boards of Reuters and of the Press Association determined to send one of their number across the Atlantic. I and, I am sure, my Boards welcome the basic principle of the unfettered exchange of truthful, unbiased news upon which you propose we build.

"Reuters is now owned 100% by the British Press and I do not think that in the matter of freedom of expression, liberty of printing, and what C. P. Scott once called 'the sacredness of news' the British Press has ever been anywhere but in the forefront of the fight. By its striving came many of the rights which are now our common heritage. For centuries, from the time of Milton, of

Wilkes, and of Prynne, it has led the vanguard. It will do so until the battle is finally won throughout the world.

"It realises its great responsibilities and, so far as Reuters is concerned, it has clearly expressed them in a Trust Deed. Some of its wording is almost that of your letter. Among other things, it says:

" 'The British Press, which owns REUTERS, regards its holding in the nature of a trust rather than as an investment.

" 'In particular it has undertaken to use its best endeavours to ensure

(a) That REUTERS shall at no time pass into the hands of any one interest, group or faction.

(b) That its integrity, independence, and freedom from bias shall at all times be fully preserved.

(c) That its business shall be so administered that it shall supply an unbiased and reliable news service to British, Dominion, Colonial, Foreign and other overseas newspapers and agencies with which it has or may hereafter have contracts.

(d) That it shall have due regard to the many interests which it serves in addition to those of the press.

(e) That no effort shall be spared to expand, develop and adapt the business of REUTERS in order to maintain in every event its position as a leading world news agency.'

"If there are any who believe Reuters news is any way influenced by any government they are under a misapprehension. It is not. There have been times, quite frankly, when it has been necessary for Reuters (and

the Press Association) to protest sharply at some bureau-
cratic infringement on the freedom of news. I have no
doubt you have had the same wartime troubles over
here. But at every stage such attempts have been successfully resisted and I myself had the honour to preside
over a recent Board meeting at which it was clearly re-
stated, once for all, that Reuters control over all its news
is absolute, that editorial decision is final and uninflu-
enced, and that except for the censorship—to which we
all have to submit—Reuters is the only arbiter of what
shall or shall not go into its services.

"The hopes you express for the part our two Agencies
can play in establishing world peace on a sounder basis
than it has rested in the past are those of my Board also.
The history of Nazi Germany is a terrible enough example of what can happen when news is either polluted
or stifled. I have already given you our assent to the idea
underlying Clause 12 of the Draft Agreement, and I am
sure my Board will concur with the aim we are thereby
trying to achieve. Reuters has no secret undertakings or
understandings with anyone about relationships after
the war.

"As you say, the Reuters Board has been looking to
the future. It, too, is deeply conscious of the tremendous
tasks which lie ahead. They will be even greater when
peace has been declared than they are now. And nothing
has made my whole journey so worth-while as the fact
that in our talks together we found so much common
ground. Provided we can build between us a mutually
satisfactory and enduring foundation I believe our
Agencies will have it in their joint power to do a great
deal for the future not only of our peoples but of those

of the whole world. In facing that duty you will find the ideals of the Reuters Board not one whit less than those of The Associated Press.

"You ask me for suggestions or improvements upon your ideas that there shall be included in the Peace Treaties some safeguarding of the principles of international news exchange. I cannot, at the moment, think of any myself, and you will realise you have raised many questions upon which I have had no opportunity to consult my fellow Directors. But, provided we can come to an agreement, I propose, with your permission, to carry your letter home with me to England and to table it at the first available meeting of the Reuters Board. There could then be upon every aspect of it a full and frank discussion and my Board could in due course communicate to yours its considered views upon the various points you raise. In this way there would come about that clarification of principles and establishment of common aims which we both desire.

"I whole-heartedly agree with you that 'it is desirable that Reuters and The Associated Press shall continue relations' because, from all you have said, I know we shall be travelling the same road. That being so, it is surely to the common good we shall travel it together. Free, independent, unreservedly owned by the Presses of their two nations The Associated Press and Reuters now have the opportunity to seal an understanding based on equality, on friendship, on trust, and on mutual respect. Let us but accomplish this and we can confidently go side by side into the future to achieve our high mission."

With such an exchange a forward-looking contract was promptly written and approved by the Boards of Directors of both institutions. The first paragraph thereof strikes the new note in international news agency relationships, upon which I place profound hope:

"Associated and Reuters, recognizing the desirability of world-wide acceptance of the principle of a free press and international exchange of truthful, unbiased news between the press and the instrumentalities of the press of all nations solely on the basis of the actual cost for its collection and dissemination, and Associated and Reuters desiring to put this principle into effect in a practical, mutual and reciprocal manner as affecting themselves by each making its news available to the other without charge, except for the expense incurred in the delivery thereof, the parties hereto hereby mutually agree as follows."

The contract with Reuters is the third such contract made by The Associated Press in the last few years. The other two were with the Canadian Press and the United Press. In the case of the United Press contract, previously quoted, there is no mutual availability of news as there is in the contracts which The Associated Press has made with the Canadian Press and Reuters. The United Press naturally did not agree to operate on a basis of actual cost since it is a profit-making company. But the statement of ethics is the same, although differently worded.

It is not usual for competitors to contract with each other. The United Press, being an American news agency, is, of course, a much more direct competitor of The Associated Press than is Reuters. Still Reuters and

The Associated Press are in competition throughout the world, their approach to newspapers being upon the personality and character of their news reports. While a contract as a basis for competitive effort is an experiment, it nevertheless seems to be an experiment that is well worth while.

In these turbulent times it is not possible to say how enduring may be the business relationships of The Associated Press with Reuters. But something has been attained if both institutions, even without a contract, operate on the same ethical principles. Personally I have hopes that it will bring closer than ever before the entire press of the United States to the entire press of the British Empire. And having expressed my own hopes I can be forgiven for quoting a final salutation from Mr. Haley for Reuters—the last reference in this story to this great British institution.

At a luncheon of the Board of Directors of The Associated Press on June 12, 1942, Mr. Haley was a guest. He referred to his impending return to England, the trials through which the world is passing, the hopes of a permanent Reuters-Associated Press alliance and, most generously as to me, added:

"Whatever may come, I want to acknowledge my debt to Mr. Kent Cooper. The discussions I have had with him since I came here have made a profound impression upon me which I shall carry with me always.

"Reuters's aims and plans for the future have been laid largely on the same basis as the principles and ideals and practices of The Associated Press. Reuters will go forward with the same objectives of service rather than of dividends, of unbiased reporting of the world's news in a co-operative endeavor."

To this I responded appreciatively and with assurance of full reciprocation.

XXXIV

Retrospect

THE urge within each of us that furnishes the impetus to act in the sphere of human relations arises from something we have observed, something we have heard or something we have read.

In retrospect as to the activities recorded in this story I believe I went onward after the disappointment over there being nothing in the Versailles Treaty about a world-wide free press because of something I observed in Paris shortly after the treaty was signed. There they told me there was going to be a parade of the Allied troops through the streets of Paris on Bastille Day. But I had no idea of the profound impression that parade would make upon me.

I had an excellent vantage point from which to view it all, from a window overlooking the Arch of Triumph built by Napoleon and under which Napoleon had decreed none but conquerors ever should pass. Built over a hundred years ago no French troops, until that day, had earned the right to march under it. It was the Prussians who were victors in the Franco-Prussian War. It was the Prussians' turn then. But it was the French and Allied forces on July 14, 1919.

The French are nothing if not dramatic and perhaps the spectacle of that day may never again be equaled. First through the Arch were the French wounded. Carried on cots, rolled in wheel chairs those pitiful fragments of bodies were borne through, many of them clasping hands in prayer as they passed. Others tried to shout or sing as they heroically attempted to lift their pain-racked bodies.

Heroes indeed, for I was told that several had died during and immediately after the parade. All had pleaded to be allowed to lead that procession; they would willingly die if given that one chance for glory in life. So from the hospitals they were brought, even as life ebbed out of them.

They were followed by the commander in chief of the Allied forces, Marshal Foch. Then came the marching hosts.

First, the Americans, for the detachments representing each country proceeded in alphabetical order. Pershing led them, a picked body of men apparently exactly the same height and weight, with shining helmets and new uniforms, marching briskly to the music of the band.

Next came the Belgians, their uniforms and equipment quite drab in comparison with the Americans. Then the British, Italians, and so on through the list of Allies until as a courtesy to all the rest at last came the French.

The procession already had taken hours to pass and yet the packed mass of spectators waited expectantly. The day had been cloudy but as the French officers rode through the Arch the sun came out to shine upon their sabers as they gave the salute. The crowds who had waited became hysterical with their cheers when the French infantry followed, not in new uniforms and shining helmets but in blue, bespeckled with mud, just as one might expect to see them emerge from trench warfare.

When the day was done I had witnessed an aggregation representative of the greatest war strength ever gathered to meet a common enemy. And as I watched I thought that the soldiers of most any one of the nations might seem to have fitted into the ranks of any other nation by the mere change of uniform.

The same thought struck me when I went over to Germany and saw discharged German soldiers still wearing their trench clothing. But language, environment, and something else had driven them to war. The type of civilization that each had known was the same in its broad aspects and yet there was something that compelled them to occupy from one to four years of their lives in trying to kill each other.

The only time that millions of them had ever been near to the other millions was when they were at death grips. They had come from all corners of the world for one purpose, and that was to kill!

And yet these men as children had played much the same the world over. They had grown into manhood under the care of mothers who were all of the same instinct. And those who had survived and shortly were returning to those waiting would take up a workaday life much the same regardless of nationality.

Few of them had ever studied that war's causes. They only believed they had reason to hate. When they read of what was going on in other countries before the war their prejudices were stirred. Each of them had but one source of foreign news in their newspapers back home to read before they went off to war. That source was the news agency that brought the news of foreign affairs to their newspapers.

Some of that news may have been intentionally directed to create prejudice. Many governments had engaged in propaganda long before that war, well aware that the decision as a result of their propaganda ultimately would rest on the number of dead on the field of battle.

Prejudice, once aroused, is indeed a consuming passion. It can be fed easily and people become slaves to it. They want confirmation of their prejudices in what they read rather than to have them justly questioned. They eagerly seek news that agrees with their views rather than read that which opposes them. This fact gives status and circumstance to sources of biased propaganda. Prejudice takes on the color of hate. So it must have been with what all those millions who fought in that war read in their newspapers; either they or those back home who sent them. So it must be as to those who bring on any war.

The parade of the Allied powers on Bastille Day, 1919, was the impetus for me to disregard discouragements and to do what I could to rid international news exchange of controls that intentionally feed men's prejudices. That was the only effort that I could make personally to erase one of the causes of war.

Looking backward, it comforts me to know that where the obstacles were not too great some progress was made that brought saner international relations. For instance, the ever-increasing exchange of unbiased news with

South America for a quarter of a century has contributed a great deal to the establishment of the present more friendly international relations between the Americas.

Whether equal progress could have been made in Europe and thus operated to postpone another war will never be known because, as I have said, exchange of news developments like those in the Americas could not early enough or thoroughly enough get under way in Europe with the same freedom of action. Nor with Japan.

Every layman should be monitor of the sources of information open to him. He should note "who said so," and thus he can learn to know what source he can trust. And the place to apply the test is on the printed page which he can read and reread if necessary—things he cannot do in noting words flashed and gone on the air or pictures flashed and gone on the screen.

If newspaper readers would monitor the news they could take the prop out of propaganda, and only unbiased news sources could prevail. Moreover, the press would profit by more critical observation. And the right to this critical observation is one of the proofs that a free press is after all a heritage of the people themselves.

Thus far America has had a distinct advantage over the peoples of most foreign countries because it has had a free press. I say "thus far" because I do not know of the morrow. If there is a curb by any power in any country that now has a free press, it will be the people who will lose.

Convinced of this, it must be the people who shall secure the guarantee of a free press. And any country that comes out of this war with power to impose the terms of peace should insist upon not only a free press but freedom of international news exchange. I come to this conclusion because, having had no freedom of the press on the European continent and no means of international exchange of unbiased news, this war that now is had to be.

If, therefore, some great authority that will dictate the terms of peace would ask me what points should be included respecting the press I could only say now, as I replied in 1919, that there should be five such points as follows:

First, guarantee freedom of the press throughout the world as we know it;

Second, guarantee that at least one news agency in each country be owned and controlled mutually by the newspapers it serves;

Third, guarantee that each agency may make such international news exchange arrangements as it chooses;

Fourth, guarantee equality to all in the matter of availability of all official news and transmission facilities, and

Fifth, prohibit the intentional covert inclusion in any news service of biased international propaganda.

If these constituted the basis of international news exchange and if they were implemented by the conviction of all free men that they shall always endure, a happier day for the world would ensue. International intercourse would rise to heights of perfection with the barriers down as to news exchange.

❦

And as for me—I believe I have already said that I'm glad I found that little cable message which had been filed away unanswered in September, 1914!

Index

Agence Télégraphique Belge, 17

Agence Télégraphique Bulgars, 17

Agence Télégraphique Esthonienne, 17

Agence Télégraphique Hongroise, 17

Agence Télégraphique Lettone, 17

Agence Télégraphique Lithuanienne, 17

Agence Télégraphique Polonaise, 17

Agence Télégraphique Suisse, 17

Albert, King, 102

Albertini, Luigi, 103, etc.

All America Cable Company, 44, etc.

Allied Newspapers, Ltd., 282

Amtliche Nachrichtenstelle, 16

Anotolie, 17

Antofagasta El Mercurio, 81

Associated Newspapers, Ltd., 282

Associated Press, The, 3, etc.

Associated Press of Australia, The, 152, etc.

Associated Press of Germany, The, 189, etc.

Associated Press of Great Britain, Ltd., 189, etc.

Associated Press of India, The, 152, etc.

Athena, 17

Australian Associated Press, The (see Associated Press of Australia, The)

Avola, 17

Bailey, W. T., 282

Baillie, Hugh, 260

Beckett, Hon. Rupert, 282

Bickel, Karl A., 164, etc.

Boston Globe, 40

Bracken, Brendan, 283, etc.

British United Press, 254, etc.

Buenos Aires Herald, 81

Buenos Aires La Nacion, 4, etc.

Buenos Aires La Prensa, 44, etc.

Buenos Aires La Razon, 76, etc.

Buenos Aires Patria degli Italiano, 81

Buenos Aires Standard, 81

Bureau de Presse Czechoslovakia, 17

Camrose, Lord, 282

Canadian Press, 178, etc.

Cervera, 13
Chamberlain, Sir Austen, 155
Chancellor, Christopher, 211
Chicago Daily News, 40
Chicago Tribune, 180
Christian Science Monitor, 3
Clark, H. B., 243
Continental Telegrafen Bureau, 173
Cowles, W. H., 134
Creel, George, 47

Davies, W. W., 85
Davis, Elmer, 47
Davis, John W., 252
Deakin, Ralph, 282
Derwent, Raymond, 282
Deutsches Nachrichtenbüro, 18, etc.
D.N.B. (see Deutsches Nachrichtenbüro)
Doletzky, J. G., 270, etc.
Domei, 149, etc.

Edwards papers, 82
Edwards, Agustin, 83
Ewing, A. McLean, 282
Exchange Telegraph Company of London, 274

Fabra Agency, 17, etc.
Field, Cyrus, 11
Finska Notisbyran, 17
Foch, Marshal Ferdinand, 316

Gandhi, Mahatma K., 153
Gannett Newspapers, Frank E., 3
Glasgow Herald, 282
Greece, King of, 202
Guayaquil El Telegrafo, 81
Guayaquil Ilustrado, 81

Haley, W. J., 282, etc.
Havas Agence, 6, etc.
Hawkins, W. W., 243, etc.
Hearst Newspapers, 3, etc.
Hearst, William Randolph, 179, etc.
Heywood, H. M., 282
House, Col. Edward M., 89
Houssaye, Charles, 66, etc.
Houssaye, Henri, 21, etc.
Howard, Roy W., 56, etc.

Indian News Bureau, 152, etc.
Institute of Journalists, 29
International News Service, 4, etc.
Iwanaga, Yukichi, 129, etc.

Jeans, Allan, 282
Johnson, Lorin, 242, etc.
Jones, Sir Roderick, 28, etc.
Journal of the Institute of Journalists, 29

Kabayama, Count Aisuke, 129, etc.
Kaiser, German, 64
Kansas City Star, 40
Kemsley, Lord, 282
Kennedy, J. Russell, 147, etc.
Koenigsberg, Moses, 165
Kokusai, 17, etc.

Lawson, Victor, 40
Lee, Clayton D., 243
Lima El Comercio, 81
Lima El Tiempo, 82
Lima La Cronica, 82
Lima La Prensa, 82

Liverpool Daily Post and Echo, 282
Livesay, J. F. B., 234, etc.
Lochner, Louis P., 249
London Chronicle, 26
London Daily Mail, 282
London Daily Telegraph, 282
London Morning Advertiser, 24, etc.
London Morning Herald, 26
London News Agency, 95
London News of the World, 159
London Post, 26, etc.
London Standard, 26
London Star, 26
London Sunday Times, 282
London Telegraph, 26
London Times, 24, etc.

McClatchy, V. S., 36, etc.
McCormick, Col. Robert R., 180, etc.
McLean, W. L., 40
Manchester Guardian and Evening News, Ltd., 282, etc.
Mantler, Dr. Heinrich, 105, etc.
Martin, Henry, 236
Mejer, Otto, 235
Merrill, John L., 80
Meynot, A., 155, etc.
Milan Corriere Della Sera, 103
Miller, James I., 73
Mitre, Bartolome, 54
Mitre, Jorge, 54, etc.
Mitre, Luis, 114
Mitsunaga, Hoshio, 148, etc.
Morgagni, Manlio, 276
Murray, William L., 242
Mussolini, Benito, 276

Nederlandsch Telegraaf Agentschap, 17, etc.
Nelson, W. R., 40
Newspaper Proprietors Association of London, 159, etc.
Newspaper Society, 282
New York Evening Post, 51
New York Staats-Zeitung, 40
New York Times, 37, etc.
New York World-Telegram, 71
Nippon Dempo, 148, etc.
Nippon Shimbun Rengo, 149, etc.
Norsk Telegram-bureau, 17
Noyes, Frank B., 37, etc.

Ochs, Adolph S., 37, etc.
Oldham Press, Ltd., 282
Osaka Mainichi, 150

Panama El Diario, 81
Panama Star & Herald, 81
Paz, Ezequel, 73, etc.
Pew, Robert J., 282
Philadelphia Bulletin, 40
Prensa Asociada, 74, etc.
Press Association of Great Britain, 93, etc.
Price, Byron, 229
Providence Journal, 67
Provincial Newspapers, Ltd., 282
Publishers Press, 152

Rador, 17
Rathom, John R., 67, etc.
Rengo (see Nippon Shimbun Rengo)
Reuter, Baron Herbert de, 21, etc.
Reuter, Paul Julius, 7, etc.

Reuters, 6, etc.
Riddell, Lord, 159, etc.
Ridder, Herman, 40
Rio de Janeiro Correio de Manha, 81
Rio de Janeiro Jornal do Brazil, 81
Rio de Janeiro O Imparcial, 81
Ritzaus Bureau, 17
Robbins, H. C., 236, etc.
Roberts, Elmer, 35, etc.
Rockefeller, Nelson A., 294, etc.
Ronconi, Romeo, 84
Roosevelt, President Franklin D., 294
Rosta, 17
Rothermere, Lord, 282
Rothschilds, the, 21
Roy, K. C., 152
Russia, Czar of, 64

Sacramento Bee, 36
Saito, Hiroshi, 148, etc.
Santiago El Mercurio, 81
Santiago La Nacion, 81
Santiago Ultimas Noticias, 81
Scott, C. P., 308
Scott, J. R., 282
Scripps, Robert P., 244
Scripps-Howard Newspapers, 3, etc.
Scripps-McRae League, 71
Scripps-McRae Press Association, 152
Scripps News Association, 152
Sidlo, Thomas, 252

Sola, Vildo, 83
Southwood, Lord, 282
St. James Gazette, 27
Stefani, 17, etc.
Stockmar, Baron, 30
Stone, Melville E., 4, etc.
Storey, Samuel, 279, etc.
Stratton, Lloyd, 269, etc.

Tass, 192, etc.
Taylor, Charles H., 40
Telegrafen Union, 194
Teleradio, 17
Tidningarnas Telegrambyra, 17

United Press Associations, 4, etc.
United Press Deutschland, 254, etc.

Valparaiso El Mercurio, 81
Vandercook, John W., 243
Victoria, Queen, 21
Villard, Oswald Garrison, 51, etc.

Washington Star, 37
Westminster Press, 282
Wilhelm II, Emperor, 21
Wilson, Admiral Henry B., 72
Wilson, President Woodrow, 47, etc.
Wolff Agency, 6, etc.

Yorkshire Post, 282